Feed My Sheep
Feed My Lambs

Caring for and Nurturing the Soul

Harold R. Dewberry PhD, MREd

New Wine Press

New Wine Press
PO Box 17
Chichester
West Sussex PO20 6YB
England

First published 1985
Dewberry Ministries

Second Edition 1991
Third Edition 1995

Scripture taken from the King James Version of the Bible except
where noted as AMP – The Amplified Bible, NIV – New
International Version, LB – The Living Bible, or NAS – New
American Standard.

ISBN: 1 874367 39 6

Cover image by Ken Duncan Panographs, Sydney, Australia
Typeset by CRB Associates, Lenwade, Norwich
Printed in England by Clays Ltd, St. Ives plc

Dedication

I dedicate *Feed My Sheep, Feed My Lambs* to my lovely wife Sandy, who has been faithful to fulfil my full potential in God. Also to our sons Kerry, Paul and Anthony, and daughter Lisbeth; daughters-in-law Lannie and Bonita, and our grandchildren Tommy, Nicky, Cassie, Tina ... and the youngest addition to our family, Ross. All have faithfully sacrificed to give me the freedom to minister world-wide.

Acknowledgements

Many, many thanks to all who have worked so tirelessly on the manuscripts: Gayle Woodward, Doug and Noela Neil, Sandy Dewberry, Peter Besley, Kate Clayden, Ann Harding, Meuros Dobson, and our friend Ken Duncan for contributing the magnificent cover photograph.

Contents

Foreword

by Bill Subritzky

Bill Subritzky – International Evangelist writes . . .

Harold Dewberry has few equals in expressing life-giving principles from the Word of God. His own personal steadfastness, integrity and strength of purpose in his walk with the Lord are reflected in his writings and teachings.

The anointing of the Holy Spirit is manifestly present as he expresses God-given wisdom. His writings and teachings have been an inspiration to the Body of Christ.

It is a privilege for me to recommend this book.

Bill Subritzky has an interdenominational world-wide ministry of evangelism and teaching. He has authored several books and produced numerous teaching videos and other material.

Foreword

by Dr Kevin Dyson

'Having known Harold Dewberry for some sixteen years, I have had the opportunity to not only hear the teaching, but to witness the long term beneficial effects on those to whom he has ministered in Jesus' Name. The fruit speaks volumes for the unique giftedness that the Lord of the Church has bestowed upon His servant.

It is not surprising therefore that when Harold has committed some of these truths to written form, that the readers are instantly challenged to re-evalute some of the traditional understandings that have pervaded Christendom in fuzzy thinking over this subject.

Harold is not writing from a position of a theoretician, but rather from that of a practitioner who has "tried the doctrines, to see if they be true".

Feed My Sheep, Feed My Lambs will provoke you to re-examine the Scriptures and to study carefully the wisdom and practical insight that are contained in the Word. It has been said that the battleground of this decade is the mind, and this book is a timely contribution to show how God our Heavenly Father wants us to know His healing and sustaining power through the renewing and restoring of our minds, so that we will have "the mind of Christ".'

Dr Kevin Dyson, Principal and Founder of the New Covenant International Bible College, maintains oversight of the growing network of schools, colleges and seminaries that embrace some forty seven learning centres in twenty nine nations, utilising twelve languages. The Dysons relocated their international office from New Zealand to the United States in January 1995.

January 1995

Introduction

Over the last several decades, we have seen the Holy Spirit restore to the Body of Christ the charismatic giftings. In early Pentecost, tongues and interpretation of tongues were the predominant manifestation of the Holy Spirit. The gift of prophecy was exercised by a few; but, on the whole, prophecy – particularly directional prophecy – was generally viewed with suspicion.

As the concepts of meditation and renewing of the mind came forth in teaching, we began to see more manifestations of the word of knowledge, the word of wisdom and the discerning of spirits.

As the Lord began to pour out His Spirit in a greater measure, many believers from the traditional denominations began to receive the Baptism of the Holy Spirit (they were called neo- or new Pentecostal). A hunger for a more spontaneous and liberal form of worship then came.

Those who participated in this new found freedom of worship, and especially the free exercise of all the gifts of the Holy Spirit, became known as Charismatics.

With the renewed focus and seeking after the Holy Spirit and His functions, there came a restoration of the ministry gifts. Great emphasis was placed on the teacher, the evangelist and, in this last decade, on the ministry of the prophet.

As we enter into this next decade, we will see the restoration of the apostolic ministry. As the early church was founded on the ministry of the apostle, the prophet and the teacher to fulfil divine order (of the first being last and the last being first), so shall we see the restoration of the ministry of the apostle (who will establish divine order within the church).

When the five-fold ministries harmonize together in proper and functional order, the gospel, which has been weakened by the intrusion of vain traditions and worldly philosophies, will bring a fresh and more powerful and dynamic anointing of the Holy Spirit upon our congregations. Signs, wonders, divine miracles will then draw the unsaved into our midst, as the Lord adds to the church, daily, as many as should be saved.

As the believers' lives express 'truth in all things' (speaking truly, dealing truly, living truly) and are exhibiting love, each member of the church, being bonded together and empowered by the Holy Spirit, will grow to full maturity (Ephesians 4:15–16).

If we study world missions from a New Testament perspective, we see that evangelists and missionaries were sent out from the local church setting.

In his book, *Sharpening the Focus of the Church*,[1] Gene A. Getz writes:

> 'The church, therefore, exists to carry out two functions – Evangelism (to make disciples) and edification (to teach them). These two functions, in turn, answer two questions: First, "Why does the Church exist in the world?" and the second, "Why does the Church exist as a gathered community?"'

The major emphasis was then placed on the nurturing and growth in character of these young converts. They could, then, attain unity of mind and soul through the development of Agape love, in order to impact their local communities with the gospel.

Jesus referred to this concept when He said:

> *'By this shall all men know that you are my disciples, if you love one another – if you keep on showing love among yourselves.'* (John 13:35 AMP)

In summarizing their spirituality, the Scripture concludes:

> *'And with great power gave the Apostles witness of the resurrection of the Lord Jesus: and great grace was upon them all. Neither was there amongst them that lacked.'* (Acts 4:33–34a)

> *'And the believers were the more added to the Lord, multitudes both of men and women.'* (Acts 5:14)

Both Jew and Gentile entered the family of God after the Church expanded its outreach and its impact into the world. As a result, we see, as the Apostles and Evangelists made disciples, local churches came into existence.

People who lived in various communities came together in a new order of relationship. The family became a part of a larger family. These we know as local churches.

Great emphasis is placed, by the writers of the epistles, on corporate responsibility. As the individual believers brought their lives under the government of God, a new dynamic was established in the local community. The local Church, made up of individual believers, became a **light** (a model) for the world to gaze upon and to be drawn towards.

As the new believers took Godly principles and practice into the market place and the highways and byways of life, they became **salt** to the earth.

Community evangelism was to be preceded by a corporate example of love (Agape) amongst the believers. This then is a fulfilment of Jesus' command as He approached the hour of His humiliation:

> *'A new commandment I give to you, that you love one another.'*   (John 13:34)

The objective of this love is seen in the next few words:

> *'By this all men will know that you are My disciples, if you love one another.'*   (John 13:35)

We see the full manifestation of this principle as we behold the power of the early church in Jerusalem when the multitude of them that believed were of one heart and one soul! They walked in humility of mind toward one another, so that:

> *'neither said any of them that aught of the things which he possessed was his own; but they had all things in common.'*   (Acts 4:32)

All that I have just stated is to put a correct emphasis on the order that is established in the New Testament, for the function of the local church in its global setting. It is also to re-emphasize the importance of the ministry that I feel has been so sadly neglected: the ministry of the shepherd of the flock – the Pastor.

I am convinced that, although the previously mentioned ministry gifts are vital and important to the completeness and wholeness of the body, these ministries, while in the local setting, must function with the pastoral ministries.

The ministry of the Apostle, Evangelist and Prophet may seem to be more spectacular. They are definitely vital and important to the completeness and to the wholeness of the Body of Christ. However, while these ministries are localized in a local church setting, they must function as part of pastoral ministry.

This concept is emphasized by the Apostle Peter when he wrote his epistle to the strangers scattered throughout Pontus, Galatia, Cappadocia, Asia and Bithynia. To these elect, he said:

> *'The elders which are among you, I exhort, who am also an elder and a witness of the sufferings of Christ, and also a partaker of the glory that shall be revealed. Feed the flock of God.'*
>
> (1 Peter 5:1–2)

The word 'feed', *'poimaino'*, means to shepherd, tend (involves much more than to feed). It implies the whole office of the shepherd, guiding, guarding, feeding of the flock as well as leading it to nourishment (Zodhiates' *Lexical Aids to the New Testament*).[2]

We also see the importance placed on the Pastor or Shepherd of the flock as we study the designations of the names of Jesus in His office as the **Bishop of our Souls**.

He is called in John 10:11, the Good Shepherd: *'the Good Shepherd that giveth His life for the sheep.'*

The writer of Hebrews calls Him the Great Shepherd:

> *'Now the God of peace, that brought again from the dead, our Lord Jesus, that great Shepherd of the sheep, through the blood the everlasting covenant.'*
>
> (Hebrews 13:20–21)

As the Great Shepherd, He is our sanctifier to make us complete in Himself.

The Apostle Peter reveals Him as the Chief shepherd.

> *'And [then] when the Chief Shepherd is revealed you will win the conqueror's crown of glory.'*
>
> (1 Peter 5:4 AMP)

References

1. Getz, G.A. (1984). *Sharpening the Focus of the Church*. Illinois: Scripture Press
2. Zodhiates' *Lexical Aids to the New Testament*

SECTION A:

Priestly Ministry of Christ

Chapter 1

The Shepherd's Role in Nurturing the Flock

In Ezekiel 34, the Lord brings a strong prophetic word through the Prophet Ezekiel against the shepherds of Israel:

> *'Thus saith the Lord God unto the shepherds: Woe be to the shepherds of Israel that do feed themselves! Should not the shepherds feed the flocks?'*   (Ezekiel 34:2b)

> *'Ye eat the fat and ye clothe you with the wool, ye kill them that are fed, but ye feed not the flock. The diseased ye have not strengthened, neither have ye healed that which was sick, neither have ye bound up that which was broken, neither have ye brought again that which was driven away, neither have ye sought that which was lost, but with force and with cruelty have ye ruled them.'*   (Ezekiel 34:3–4)

When the pastors of God's flock are dysfunctional or they are misusing their office and position of authority, the flock will be sick, fragmented and also dysfunctional.

Because the sheep were scattered by the shepherds, many had strayed into the mountains and high hills – turning to idolatry and idol worship, looking to other gods, as the focus of their faith and as a supplier of their needs.

We see from Ezekiel 34 the result of the shepherds of Israel being harsh and demanding instead of nurturing the flock: the sheep are wounded and scattered.

Instead of true healing, religious platitudes are given:

> *'You say, said God, Peace! Peace! where there is no peace. And you have not healed my people.'*
>
> (Jeremiah 8:11)

If the basic character of the pastors is not consistent with the nature and character of Christ or if they are immature in character and misuse their office, Satan will take advantage of the sheep.

In the Book of 1 Samuel, we see such a condition of heart in the sons of Eli, the priests who served in the tabernacle. The Scripture said that they were *'Sons of Belial'* and that they were base, worthless, unteachable and rebellious. They misused their office and caused the people to despise the offering of the Lord (1 Samuel 2:12, 17).

The strength of the Lord went into captivity and His glory was given over to his enemies. That is, the word spoken was no longer a creative word, a word that brought change and freedom and conviction to the hearers. The work of the Lord had become a reproach to the world (Psalm 78:61; 1 Samuel 4:10).

Adam Clarke says of Ezekiel 34:

> 'The shepherds include, first the priests and the Levites; secondly, the kings, princes and magistrates. The fat and the wool means the tithes and the offering, the taxes and the imports.'
>
> (*Clarke's Commentary*)[1]

He further comments:

> 'The reprehensible feeding and clothing with these, as to the priests and Levites, the using of the tithes and

offerings, not to enable them the better to fulfil the work of the ministry, but to pamper their own bodies and to support them in an idle, voluptuous life.'

It was because of the lack of caring and nurturing for the flock by the shepherds of Israel that God sent forth His own shepherd, the Lord Jesus Christ for His sheep.

The ascended Christ gave gifts to men. One gift to the Church was to put a special anointing on specially chosen and prepared vessels to continue His shepherding responsibility to the flock (Ephesians 4:8–11).

The Lord made a promise to the flock of God through the prophet Ezekiel. He said that He would search for His sheep (Ezekiel 34:11, 13–16). This promise finds fulfilment in Jesus' own words:

> *'For the Son of man is come to save that which was lost.'*
> (Matthew 18:11)

He would gather them from the country, and feed them in good pastures, and cause them to lie down (John 10:9, 16; Psalm 23). He also promised to seek the lost and bind up that which was broken and strengthen (heal) that which was sick (Luke 4:18).

This promise is fulfilled in the New Testament as the Lord is revealed as:

1. **The Good Shepherd**:

> *'I am, He said, the Good Shepherd, the Good Shepherd gives His life for the sheep.'* (John 10:11)

2. In Hebrews 13:20, He is revealed as **The Great Shepherd**:

> *'Now the God of peace, that brought again from the dead our Lord Jesus, that great Shepherd of the sheep, through the blood of the everlasting covenant.'*
> (Hebrews 13:20 KJV)

He is the great shepherd by virtue of having died a substitutionary death for us and having risen from the dead for our justification. We will therefore be glorified together with Him – raised up to a heavenly dignity and condition (or state of being) (John 10:11; Romans 5:8; 2 Corinthians 5:21; 1 Peter 2:24; Ephesians 2:14–16; Romans 8:30 AMP).

The word 'glorified', *'doxazo'* (dox-ad-zo), is from the root word *'doxa'* (dox'ah) and it means to give recognition to, to esteem, to acknowledge, to set in a position of honour.

We see the Heavenly Father giving such acknowledgment to the Lord Jesus Christ.

As He came up out of the waters of baptism, the voice of the Father spoke from heaven saying: *'This is My Beloved Son, in whom I am well pleased.'* On another occasion, the Father again spoke from heaven, although some said it thundered: *'This is My Son, hear you Him.'*

When Jesus was raised from the dead, the Father again gave His Son affirmation: *'Thou art My Son, this day have I begotten Thee.'* Although the Scripture does not share to whom it was spoken, the Scripture gives record of it for us.

To receive this kind of appreciation, we have to be sanctified or set apart for the Lord. The writer of the epistle to the Hebrews states:

> *'For both He who sanctifies [making men holy] and those who are sanctified all have one [Father]. For this reason He is not ashamed to call them brethren.'*
>
> (Hebrews 2:11 AMP)

It is through the blood of the everlasting covenant that He is able to sanctify us and bring us into a place of honour.

It is through His resurrection that we have become His inheritance, His generation. Because we are His seed and inheritance, we receive acknowledgment from our Heavenly Father that we are His children.

As we separate ourselves from being bonded and united to the cosmos, (away from our love for the world) and become separated unto God, (by our new found love that He has for us), He receives us kindly and treats us with favour. He says:

> *'I will be a Father to you and you shall be My sons and daughters.'* (2 Corinthians 6:18)

The Amplified version renders Hebrews 13:20–23 from which the revelation of Jesus as the Great Shepherd is taken as:

> *'And make you what you ought to be and equip you with everything good that you may carry out His will; [while He Himself] works in you and accomplishes that which is pleasing in His sight, through Jesus Christ the Messiah.'*

Not only is He the Good Shepherd, who has given His life for the sheep and the Great Shepherd, who through His resurrection has made His inheritance and His seed; but He is also the Chief Shepherd.

The Chief Shepherd, says Peter,

> *'And [then] when the Chief Shepherd is revealed you will win the conqueror's crown of glory.'*

It is a *'conqueror's crown of glory'*, so translates the Amplified version of 1 Peter 5:4.

Let us now study how this Great Bishop of our soul expedites His ministry to His flock and for what purpose.

And He Gave Gifts Unto Men

Let us read Ephesians, chapter 4, verses 8 and 11 (AMP):

> *'Therefore it is said, when He ascended on high, He led captivity captive – He led a train of vanquished foes – and He bestowed gifts on men.'* (verse 8)

'And His gifts were [varied; He Himself appointed and gave men to us,] some to be apostles (special messengers), some prophets (inspired preachers and expounders), some evangelists (preachers of the gospel, travelling missionaries), some pastors (shepherds of His flock) and teachers.' (verse 11)

In these specific verses, we see how He carries out His ministry as the Shepherd of His Sheep. He, Himself, was anointed by His Heavenly Father to function in all of these roles. He is the great Apostle, Prophet, Teacher, Evangelist and Pastor.

When He ascended to the Father, He shed forth this special anointing upon chosen and prepared vessels in order for them to carry out His work.

The next question is for what purpose did He give these gifts unto men?

The next verse (Ephesians 4:12) states:

'For the perfecting of the saints, for the working of the ministry, for the edifying of the body of Christ.'
(cf. Hebrews 13:22-23 KJV)

Ephesians 4:13, 14a (from the Amplified Version) states:

'[That it might develop] until we all attain oneness in the faith, and in the comprehension of the full and accurate knowledge of the Son of God, that (we might) arrive at really mature manhood – the completeness of personality which is nothing less than the standard height of Christ's own perfection – the measure of the stature of the fullness of the Christ and the completeness found in Him. So then we may be no longer children.'

The King James version quotes verse 13 as:

'Till we all come in the unity of faith, and of the knowledge of the Son of God unto a perfect man.'

Zodhiates' *Lexical Aid to the New Testament*[2] defines

'teleios' as attaining to a goal and a purpose. To be full grown, as opposed to a little child. In its application in 1 Corinthians 2:6; 14:20; Philippians 3:12, 15; Ephesians 4:13 and Hebrews 5:14 it means to be fully grown.

'Teleios' is not to be confused with *'anamartetos'* (an-am-ar'-tay-tos) which means without sin.

It would be beneficial for us to emphasize (*selah*) the importance of reaching completeness of personality and maturity of character.

Remember: To have a deep inner desire to reach maturity of character is something that we follow and pursue after.

Paul, expressing His intense desire to obtain the moral freedom as of one resurrected from the dead says:

> *'It is not as though we have already attained to this goal, but it is something to apprehend, that is, to siege or lay hold of. For in doing so, Christ, in turn, apprehends or lays hold on us and in doing so reveals His Word to us.'*

This revealed knowledge brings us into a state of grace and peace. The Amplified Bible defines grace and peace as:

> *'perfect well being, all necessary good, all spiritual prosperity and freedom from fears, agitating passions and moral conflicts.'* (2 Peter 1:2 AMP)

Paul in his Epistle to the Philippians testifies and attests to having reached the desired goal with the helping hand of Christ. He finds a place of godliness with contentment.

In its rendering of Philippians 4:11–13, the Amplified Version states:

> *'I am not implying,* said Paul, *That I was in any personal want, for I have learned how to be content (satisfied to a point where I am not disturbed or disquieted) in whatsoever state that I am in* (see also 1 Timothy 6:6; 2 Peter 1:4–10).
>
> *I know how to be abased and live humbly in straitened circumstances, and I know also how to enjoy plenty and*

*live in abundance. I have learned in any and all circum-
stances, the secret of facing every situation, whether
well-fed or going hungry, having a sufficiency and to
spare or going without, and being in want.'*

(Philippians 4:12 AMP)

*'I have strength for all things in Christ Who empowers
me – I am ready for anything and equal to anything
through Him Who infuses inner strength into me (that
is, I am self-sufficient in Christ's sufficiency).'*

(Philippians 4:13 AMP)

Paul, here, is expressing the freedom of soul that comes
through reaching perfection or maturity of character.

We can gain further insight from Peter's Epistles (Ephesians 4:12–13 AMP). He exhorts us to add to our faith
several virtues of character. When we arrive at perfect
love, we will never lack or be destitute of the knowledge of
Christ. To fail to desire maturity of character will cause us
to be near sighted and be oblivious to the fact that we are
emotionally and psychologically free from the repercussions of past sin.

We who are parents would be dismayed and recoil in
shock at the thought that our children would remain infantile.

So it is with our heavenly Father, being perfect in His
love towards us. Through His foreknowledge He arranges
circumstances of life (reproofs) to bring us to maturity. Our
love and faith are, thereby, perfected.

As we respond correctly to the reproofs of life, we
progressively become like Him in nature and character;
therefore, we obtain freedom.

By developing perfection of character, we build a platform for our faith to be operative and functional.

Paul said to the Corinthian Church community: *'To have
faith without love is to be a noisy gong or a clanging cymbal.'*
He further states:

> *'When I was a child, I talked as a child, I thought like a child, I reasoned like a child; now that I have become a man, I am done with childish ways and have put them aside.'*　　　　　　(1 Corinthians 13:11 AMP)

The word 'child' that Paul uses in this text is *'nepios'* and it means to be weak in faith, to be immature in character, one who is not able to yet speak plainly. This same word is used in Ephesians 4:14 and also in Galatians 4:1–3.

In Paul's epistle to the Galatians, he says:

> *'Now, I say, That an heir (*kleronomos, steward*) as long as he is a child (*nepios*) differeth nothing from a servant, though he be head of all.'*

The heir, the Lord of all, when a child, is like a servant, or one who is under the domination or will of another. He is also under bondage to the world.

Although there is a 'common grace' in which God supplies the needs of His children and even though it is through faith that we have access to God's grace and favour, total achievement and attainment and full freedom will be only experienced by those who allow the Lord to bring them into maturity (Galatians 4:1–3; Matthew 5:4–5; James 1:1–8; 2 Peter 1:4; Romans 5:3–4).

Let us examine from Scripture, how God accomplishes, achieves and develops our personality, and brings us into a state of manhood.

For the Perfecting of the Saints, for the Work of the Ministry to the Edifying of the Body of Christ

Although there are three phrases in this one text, we will pay particular attention to the first phrase: *'For the perfecting of the saints.'*

The word 'perfecting' is the Greek word *'katartismas'* and it is used five times in the New Testament in this form.

The good definition would be to adjust, to bring back into order or to realign.

It could aptly describe the work of a chiropractor who, through manipulation, readjusts or brings the spine into correct alignment.

The work of the ministry gifts is to make functional the body of Christ by bringing individual believers into perfection or maturity of love (Ephesians 4:15–16).

If we study the word *'katartizo'* as used in Hebrews 11:3, we will understand how and by what means God can accomplish this. *'Through faith, we understand that the worlds were framed'* (*katartizo*) by the Word of God.

To understand the magnitude of this achievement, we need to picture the primal world in its chaos; and *'the earth was without form and void and darkness was upon the face of the deep'*. There was no demarcation between night and day, heaven and earth, sea and dry land. Then as the Spirit of the Lord began to move, God spake and the world realigned itself into proper order: formed (*katartizo*), brought back into order, re-adjusted and aligned.

It is through the Word of God that we, who are out of alignment or in disorder, are brought back into harmony with God and His precepts, in order to be blessed.

If our individual lives are dysfunctional or our families fragmented and dysfunctional and, in a broader sense, our church, then it is the gift ministries role to bring order through the word of God. (Genesis 1:2; Luke 11:28)

To summarize and to define what a blessed man is, we need to look at a simple, yet very profound, statement that was made by Jesus. He said: *'Blessed is he that hears My word and does it.'*

Restoration and Redemption

As a part of the ministry of bringing into perfection, there is another usage of the word *'katartizo'*. It is found in Galatians 6:1. Paul writes:

'Brethren, if a man be overtaken in a fault, ye which are spiritual restore such an one in the spirit of meekness.'

The word 'restore' is the word *'katarizo'*. We are to restore the one who has been taken in a fault. The word 'fault' has a two-fold application. Firstly, it means to be defiled or spotted by false doctrine.

Peter, in his Epistle, warns us about false teachers and prophets. These false teachers will bring in erroneous teaching in a very subtle way. He calls this kind of error 'damnable heresy'. The word 'damnable' means rottenness, corruption, defilement. In the progressive meaning of the root word 'heresy', it meant to be strongly opinionated to such a degree as to cause division. In Peter's Epistle it meant that there was so much distortion that it had no foundation from the Word of God.

Secondly, the word 'fault' has a connotation of someone taken in a moral fault.

Possibly our first thought would be of someone who has been involved in immorality, yet we need to broaden our concept on what is immoral.

Lot is a good example of a righteous man who is taken in a fault. He pitched his tent toward Sodom. Then he is dwelling in the city. There are two words that express the cause of his inner conflict. He was vexed with the filthy conversation of the people of Sodom. The word 'filthy' means sensuous bodily movement, the unchaste handling of male and female, the wantonness of women. The word 'vexed' as used in 2 Peter 2:7 means a wearing down, a breaking down of resistance.

Lot allowed that which he saw to become a part of his imagination; and, in verse 8, his righteous soul was vexed from day to day. This word 'vexed' means to be anxious, tormented in mind.

It was through the intervention of Abraham's intercession that Lot was delivered from the overthrow of Sodom.

Another area of moral spotting is that which is revealed to us in the Book of Jude. Jude wrote:

> *'Woe unto them, that have gone the way of Cain, and ran greedily after the error of Balaam for reward, and perished with the gainsaying of Core. These are spots in your feasts of charity.'* (Jude 11–12)

The word 'spot' here, has a root meaning of being a hidden reef. Alexander and Hymenaeus had shipwrecked their faith because they had defiled their conscience.

If we link Jude's exhortation to Paul's comment about Alexander and Hymenaeus, we can get a clearer picture of a very subtle form of moral fault. So, 'go the way of Cain' means to hold hatred, jealousy and bitterness in an unforgiving heart toward our brethren.

'The error of Balaam' is to prostitute the gospel for money through unresolved covetousness of heart.

Thirdly, the 'gainsaying of Core' is to despise God's appointed leadership, holding them in disrespect. These things cause defilement of conscience and will contaminate others (1 Timothy 1:18–20).

As we who are spiritual go to our brethren taken in a fault (in a spirit of meekness) and admonish them, their obedience to the word will bring purity to their souls and bring them back into right relationship with God and their brothers and sisters in Christ.

How Wounding Comes Through Those Who have been Called to Nurture Us

As we study the Word of God, we see that God has given a special designation to those who He has called to nurture and guide our souls through the course of life.

The pastors or shepherds have a special anointing to feed, strengthen, restore, bind up, to lead and to rule the people of God. But unfortunately those who have this calling can sometimes be the very instruments that can wound the souls of those whom God has entrusted to them.

Parents, particularly fathers, can be responsible for much wounding of their children. To rule harshly or to be too demanding of the children, can cause the children to be morose, depressed and develop inferiority. The wounding of the spirit by the parents is the major root cause of a communication breakdown between parents and children and may cause the child to develop moral problems and/or go into rebellion (Colossians 2:21 AMP; Ephesians 6:4).

Husbands have been entrusted by God to nurture the emotions of their wives. A failure to do so will cause a breakdown within the marriage relationship. Great emotional stress is then placed on both partners of the relationship.

In the book, *Happiness is a Choice*[3] (Minirth and Meier), the authors list three conditions that are the major cause of deep emotional pain:
1. a sense of being rejected by God;
2. loneliness;
3. a feeling of not being needed.

Although these conditions that they list hold great merit in understanding the cause of emotional pain, especially depression, the Word of God reveals a deeper repercussion that takes place in our soul when those who have been called to nurture us fail in their responsibilities.

Let us study together this concept of wounding as we look at the story of the Shulamite maiden's quest to find inner tranquillity and peace through the development of an intimate relationship with her Shepherd–King.

This story is found in the Song of Solomon. The Shulamite maiden's outward desire was to develop an intimate relationship with the King (a type of the reigning Christ). Her innate quest was to find peace of heart.

As she is drawn into deeper communion with the King, she realizes that in her natural or outward personality there are shadows and spots that in some way have a tendency to isolate and separate her from her beloved (Song of Solomon 1:6; 2:9; 3:1; 4:6; 5:2, 5).

Her response to her own inward scrutiny:

> *'Look not upon me, she cries; Because I am black, because the sun hath looked upon me: my mother's children were angry with me; they made me the keeper of the vineyard, but mine own vineyard have I not kept.'*
>
> (Song of Solomon 1:6)

As she is drawn into deeper communion with the one who is the centre of her affections, she realizes that in her natural outward personality there are spots and shadows that in some way have marred her character. These shadows and spots cause her to feel an isolation and separation from her beloved.

In this sense, we see those negative situations that cause the deepest wounding, crippling and deforming of the soul. Let us look more closely at these areas that she mentions, for they expand our understanding of the wounding which can take place by those who have authority over us or have been chosen by God to nurture us.

As we take a more penetrating look at her cry, we see three negative conditions that she has experienced in her socialization that have caused her deep wounding of spirit, and the retarding, crippling and deformity of her social personality.

'Because the sun hath looked upon me.' The sun shining upon me can only be interpreted as my allowing the Holy Spirit to enlighten and teach me. This expression can only be rightly divided and interpreted as we allow the Holy Spirit to illuminate and teach us.

We see a similar expression used by Jesus in the Parable of the Sower. The seeds that fell on the stony ground and were withered by the sun are those, Jesus said, that receive the Word joyfully. But when tribulation and trial come, because of the Word, they only endure for a short season. That is the testing and trying of our faith, as being tried by fire, so that the stony condition of the heart can be cleansed so that the Word can be engrafted within.

These, said Jesus, have no root within themselves. that is because of lack of maturity of character, they do not have the persistence to wait patiently for the promise to be fulfilled.

The sun then looking upon us, in the broader sense, are the reproofs of life, the chastening of the Lord. These are allowed by God to bring forth a depth of character and to bring us into inner transformation of soul, conforming us to His image (James1:1–4; Hebrews 12:5–11; Romans 5:1–6; Romans 8:28–29).

Because of our lack of knowledge into the ways of God, most of us have responded to these reproofs of life incorrectly and have crippled or deformed our personalities.

The measure of our deformities of personality will be governed by the severity of the reproofs. If our response to the reproof has been negative then trauma can result. The intensity of our personality projections (anger, fear, bitterness, etc.) will depend upon the depth of trauma that we have experienced.

Let me illustrate this concept from the testimony of a young woman who had been medically diagnosed as schizophrenic. As a child she had been traumatized by her abusive parents. She had watched them physically abuse her younger brother by holding his naked little bottom over an open gas burner.

Her reaction to this trauma was to become schizoid to escape the reality of the pain from her own personal rejections and emotional pain. She created within herself an imaginary personality of a little boy she called Mickey.

Mickey, or the projection of this imaginary personality that she had created, was her escape from the pain of rejection. When faced with personal conflict, she would retreat into a catatonic condition, and lose all contact with reality. As she rocked back and forth, beating her head upon the floor, she would be muttering, Mickey! Mickey!

Although this may seem to be an extreme example of a response to a negative situation of life, it portrays, in some measure, what our response is when we face trauma. We either withdraw or we become aggressive when we cannot accept the pain, rejection and trauma – especially the pain and rejection from those who are called to watch over and guard our emotions and sensibilities.

The second reason given by the Shulamite is extremely interesting and informative.

The maiden's next expression is extremely interesting, for instead of my father's children, she says, my mother's children: *'My mother's children were angry with me.'*

My Mother's Children Were Angry at Me

The expression 'mother's children' means those who have been called to nurture us but they are, themselves, immature in character, therefore, they wound because they speak without knowledge. They contend more for objective truth than inward affections; they are more concerned for idle defence of doctrine rather than expressing forgiveness and mercy.

Watchman Nee, in his book, *Song of Songs* (1965), when giving his exposition on this phrase, says,

> '"Mother", here denotes the principle of promise which is founded upon God's grace, as in Galatians 4:26–28. But Jerusalem, which is above is free, which is the mother of us all ... Now we brethren, as Isaac was, are the children of promise.'

The phrase 'my mother's children' refers, therefore, to all those who become God's children through the principle and promise of grace (all we are saved by grace).

The expression 'mother's children' could also include all those who have been called by God to nurture us, but are, themselves, immature in character. They wound us when they misunderstand or misinterpret our motives or wrongfully judge and criticize us.

The maiden of our story is deeply wounded by the watchmen. She said,

> 'The watchmen that went about the city found me, they smote me, they wounded me; the keepers of the walls took away my veil from me.'   (Song of Solomon 5:7)

These watchmen, the keepers of her soul, the ones who had been called to guide her through her conflicts and trials of life were, because of their own lack of knowledge of the purposes of God, actually causing her great pain and wounding.

Instead of receiving comfort and consolation from them, she received nothing but rebuke. Mrs Penn-Lewis (cited in Nee, 1965) in connection with this verse quotes Psalm 69:26:

> 'For they persecute Him whom Thou has smitten, and they talk to the grief of those whom Thou hast wounded.'   (KJV)

Watchman Nee writes,

> 'Presuming that a scolding would help, they berated her with words like sharp piercing weapons. At this moment she could really cry out the words of Psalm 69:20: "Reproach hath broken my heart, and I am full of heaviness: and I looked for some to take pity, but there were none; and for comfort, but I found none."'

Not only did these watchmen wound her by words, but they caused great grief and shame to her because instead of covering her, they put her to open shame.

I well remember counselling a middle-aged woman who very reluctantly came to me for ministry. She had been sexually and emotionally abused by her father and a close relative. These 'keepers of the wall', the ones entrusted to guard over her emotions and mind, deeply wounded her by betraying this sacred trust. Fear, shame, bitterness and hatred for men became her shield to protect her from further abuse and humiliation.

As a young woman, she had sought counsel from a priest and, much to her amazement and horror, he took sexual liberties with her. From this encounter, she developed homosexual tendencies.

After a commitment of her life to Christ, she sought Christian counselling to overcome her homosexual tendency. Her marriage had become dysfunctional, her children were turning toward rebellion.

Her counsellor promised confidentiality, but reported her sexual preference (she had not been involved in any homosexual relationships since conversion) to the pastor of her church. He, instead of allowing love to cover a multitude of sins, publicly denounced her from the pulpit. He condemned her, but he had no answer for her deep cry for deliverance. You can well imagine the humiliation and shame this lovely but needy woman of God experienced.

It is these kinds of shepherds that take a strong stand on doctrinal issues. They are more concerned for the denomination than restoration, redemption, forgiveness and mercy. The soul of the person is sacrificed to protect the reputation of the good name of the church.

In a broader sense, the expression 'mother's children were angry at me' also embraces and includes all those who have a position of authority over us and abuse this authority.

Much wounding and emotional scarring can be caused by parents who provoke their children to anger.

In Ephesians 6:4, Paul says:

> 'Now a word to you parents. Don't keep on scolding and nagging your children, making them angry and resentful. Rather, bring them up with loving discipline, the Lord Himself, approves, with suggestions and Godly advice.' (LB)

The King James Version says:

> *'Fathers provoke not your children to wrath, but bring them up in the nurture and admonition of the Lord.'*

The Wounding of the Spirit has Far-reaching Ramifications

A merry heart doeth good like medicine, says the writer of Proverbs. But, he said, a broken spirit drieth the bones. The word 'drieth' comes from the Hebrew *'yabesh'* and means to become dry, to be parched, to wither, to be dried up.

In Ezekiel 37:11, it portrays Israel who has grieved through loss of expectation and has become spiritually destitute and barren.

In our ministry of healing, we have seen a correlation between those who have been disciplined in anger, when they were children, and spinal infirmities.

> *'The spirit of a man will sustain his infirmity; but a wounded spirit who can bear.'*   (Proverbs 18:14)

I believe our bodies in some way bear the 'image' of our spirit. That which touches or grieves our spirit will manifest outwardly in physical problems.

Let me give you an illustration of this principle from a personal testimony. (Most of the illustrations used in the following pages are from those who testified, having received healing from the Lord in our seminars.)

A young lady had a deformity in the spine which much previous prayer and surgery had not corrected. She lived in perpetual pain.

The Holy Spirit granted me a vision of a wounding that had taken place when she was a child. One day, as she was playing with her doll, she angered her grandmother. In her anger, the grandmother snatched the doll out of the little girl's arms and broke its back. From that time forward, she (the little girl) began to suffer spinal pain and as she grew older, her spine became deformed.

As we ministered healing to her wounded spirit, she was instantly healed.

The third cause of wounding in the Shulamite maiden came in relation to those who are in authority over us demanding 'performance orientation' from us. She was forced to labour in a vineyard which was not her own.

Children are socialized by many people in society and this can be a very complex process. The more complex the society, the more children have to learn in order to be socialized.

According to David Elkind, not only are adults affected by the frustrations, insecurities and tensions that are produced because of our ever changing moralities, advanced education and technology, but children are also affected. Elkind sees today's parents as being very concerned with the intellectual abilities of their children.

As a consequence of this parental emphasis upon nourishing the intellect, Roberta M. Benns (1985)[4] says,

> 'Children are under pressure to become intellectually independent at an early age.'

She further states that children are under pressure to gain more knowledge than their parents which causes tension in the child–parent relationship.

Unfortunately, most parents are too busy working in order to maintain their 'executive' lifestyles to emotionally socialize with their children.

As a result, when the parents put high expectations of performance upon the child (without taking into account the child's emotional maturity to cope with their intellectual capacity), wounding occurs. This is one of the major causes of depression in adolescents today. Because of the wounding of the spirit, the child alienates himself away from parental authority and, many times, drops out of school.

May we offer the same admonition given by the Apostle Paul to the Colossian father:

> *'Fathers, do not provoke or irritate or fret your children (do not be hard on them or harass them), lest they become discouraged and sullen and morose and feel inferior and frustrated (Do not break their spirit).'*
>
> (Colossians 3:21 AMP)

Wounding that takes place when the Husband fails to Nurture his Wife Emotionally

To understand the wounding that comes because of a failure of the husband to nurture his wife emotionally, we need to understand the concept of family dynamics and system thinking.

Family Dynamics

This kind of family concept is much like what has been psychologically defined as the Family System Concept (Friedman, 1985).[5] 'The family approach', said Friedman, 'is called systems thinking.' Each person is interdependent rather than independent. Each component, therefore, rather than having its own distinct identity or input, operates as part of a large whole.

The sick or dysfunctional person is not viewed as the 'sick one' but rather as the one in whom the family's stress or pathology has surfaced.

In a child it could take the form of bed-wetting, hyperactivity, rebellion, etc. In the spouse, it could manifest as defensiveness or some form of psychosomatic condition.

We saw this concept very clearly in the case of a wife and mother in her early mid-life. She was suffering from a chronic spinal condition which would respond to prayer for a short season and then reappear. Several surgeries did not correct this painful condition either.

As we began to understand the Systems Thinking concept and apply it to our Pastoral Care and Counselling, we began to see that Jane (not her real name) was a victim of a deep problem that existed in the family. Jane had a teenage daughter by a previous marriage and there was periodic conflict between this daughter and her stepfather. Jane was the person in whom the tension between her daughter and husband surfaced. As this conflict was resolved, Jane's spine was permanently healed.

Systems Thinking can even be applied to genetics, where recent evidence from microbiology has shown that the same gene can function differently depending on its relationship to other genes.

Man is not an island unto himself. We see the result of one man's sin (Adam) and the repercussions it had upon his individual life and the effect it had upon his family, tribe and nation.

An individual is affected by his relationship both from within the family and by those he is in some form of socialization.

As we can see from the diagram on the next page, socialization is a very complex process.

The effects upon the children of dysfunctional parents are devastating and many carry the scarring into their adult lives.

Let me illustrate this concept by sharing a testimony that came from a counselling encounter.

A middle-aged woman came for counselling. She had been many years under psychological counselling and care and was being treated for severe anxiety and depression. In the course of our conversation, I asked her if she felt that her husband had a hate/love relationship with her. She began to weep and said that she had tried to tell her husband that this is what she felt, but he had denied such feelings.

I then asked the husband to share with me about his relationship between himself and his parents. His father

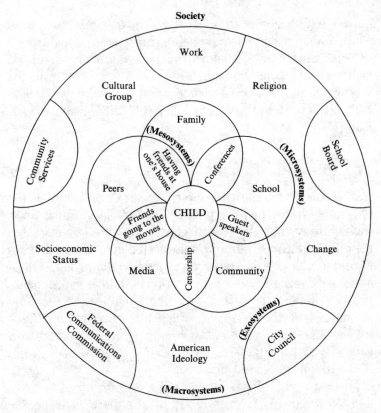

An ecological model of human development.
Adapted from Urie Brofenbrenner,[6]
The Ecology of Human Development.

had abused the family emotionally as well as physically. He interjected, at this time, and reassured me that he had already forgiven his father. I pressed the point, saying that this was good, but had he ever cleansed his heart from the attitudes and feelings that he had experienced from his father's abuse. He had not done this – for his father had caused him to feel insecurity, shame, etc.

Then I asked him to examine his feelings when his mother had failed to protect him from his father's abuse. Well, he said, I felt anger and hatred toward her. The hatred had become an idol in his heart and the hatred toward his mother was now being transferred to his wife.

This committed Christian brother was a victim of his father's and mother's abuse. This is what the Bible calls the sins of the parents being visited upon the children (Ezekiel 14; Matthew 15:8; Ephesians 2:2; 1 John 5:21; Exodus 34:7; Psalms 78:1–8; 103:17).

The Sins of the Parents

In the late 1960s, the Holy Spirit began to reveal to us the effects of the sins of the parents being visited down upon the children unto the fourth generation. We began to see the effects of these iniquities manifested not only pathogen-etically (i.e. a product of or pertaining to the production of a disease from a previous generation) but also psychogene-tically – (where the origin was inherited through the state or actions of the mind) as well as pneuma-genetically – (pneuma is spirit, the wind or breath of life combined with genetic which pertains to the inherited generational origin of the manifested condition).

At that time, we were ministering to a group of Austra-lian Aborigines. It was joyous to see these dear people come to the Lord and be filled with the Holy Spirit, but we were frustrated in our endeavours to see them 'stand for the Lord'. Although we daily nurtured these baby Chris-tians, it was almost impossible to keep them from backslid-ing and returning to their old ways and habits.

In that same community, there were second generation Christians who were evangelically traditional but were not believers in the Baptism of the Holy Spirit (were actually opposed). Yet these second generation Christians seemed to have a far greater maturity of character and endurance than our first generation converts. I began to see that with these second generation Christians, the sins of the parents (spiritualism, in this case) had lost most, if not all, of its power.

A personal experience in our family gave us deeper insight into this concept of iniquities.

My former wife was a beautiful charismatic Christian endowed with many natural and spiritual gifts. Yet there was a shadow over her life that cast a negative reflection upon her Christian witness. She exhibited a syndrome of contention, confusion, fear, anxiety and depression. These negative characteristics would often surface and destroy her Christian testimony.

In prayer one night, the Holy Spirit caused me to prophesy in prayer. I found myself, in a very authoritative way, commanding the curse of witchcraft to be broken over her life in the name of Jesus. As I persisted in prayer, she experienced a catharsis in which she saw in a vision herself as a young child in a crib. She saw her mother entering into the room and taking a ribbon from her hair. The mother then took the ribbon to a medium for psychic reading.

I need to mention that Lorraine had no personal experience in any way with the psychic or occultism; but that evening as we took authority over the curse, she was released and the negative emotional syndrome vanished out of her life.

We enquired of her sister (her mother had been dead a long time) whether her mother had been involved in occultic practices. She affirmed that this was so. The mother and father, after the death of their first born child had, through their grief and fear of loss, tried through the powers of necromancy to establish communication with the dead child. This had opened the doorway for psychic intrusion and the related curse to come down upon their children.

John and Paula Sandford, in their book *Healing the Wounded Spirit*, (1985)[7] state:

> 'Generational sin and its effects come to us in three ways. First, we inherit our propensities to sin through our genes. The second way sin descends is by example and the third way sin and its effects descends is

perhaps the most cogent, if not in the long run, the most influential: the law of sowing and reaping.'

The effect of one person's sin can be far-reaching and devastating.

Nicholas Zell, a psychologist and executive director of Child Trends Inc. (a Washington based organization that studies social changes affecting children), recently released a report for the National Center for Health Statistics. This report stated:

'Emotional and behavioural problems have become the new morbidity of childhood that affects 10 million children in the USA. It is more prevalent than asthma, dermatitis, heart murmurs, bronchitis, bone disorders and other chronic childhood maladies.'

He goes on to state:

'There are two factors in contemporary society that are contributing to the increase in childhood psycho-logical disorders which are profoundly affecting family functions and children's life changes. The most important involves family dynamics.

The increased number of children who experience their parents' divorce, are born outside of marriage or are raised in conflict-filled families or low income, low education or single parent households.'

He further states:

'Children are affected by environmental pollutants and more babies are being born to mothers addicted to drugs, especially crack or cocaine. Millions of our children today are being affected by the sins of the parents.'

Family Dynamics based on Iniquities of the Fathers

It seems, as we study the covenants that are given by God to families, that they are in a three dimensional cycle. A covenant promise was given to Abraham, Isaac and Jacob.

We see that Abraham (in one period of his life) abused Sarah spiritually by depending upon her for protection and guidance. He encouraged Sarah to lie about their relationship because of his fear of being killed by the Pharaoh when he saw the beauty of Sarah.

Later, God speaks to Abraham and says: *'Fear not Abraham, for I am your shield and exceeding great reward.'*

As a result of Abraham's failure to protect and cover Sarah, Abraham became a victim of deception, through his wife's advice. As the result of this deception, a son of the flesh was born. That son of bondage became an enemy of the child of the Promise.

Later, the Scripture reveals that Sarah obeyed Abraham, following his guidance and acknowledged his leadership over her by calling him Lord, master, leader, authority.

When Abraham took his rightful position over Sarah, we see Isaac, the seed of the Promise, subject to his father's authority.

In the second generation, we see that Isaac's weakness was soulish. He lacked masculinity. We see Isaac worshipping masculinity and he favoured Esau, the red man of the earth, the hunter, over Jacob who was his mother's favourite child.

It is strange that Isaac would favour Esau seeing that God had foretold that Jacob would rule over his brother Esau.

Not only did Isaac worship masculinity, a sign of his own lack of manhood, but he turned to his wife Rebecca for mothering and nurturing. The Scripture says when he married Rebecca that he took her into his mother's tent and was comforted.

Here we see a very subtle form of transformation of roles. Instead of nurturing Rebecca, as Scripture implies is the man's responsibility, we see, through his passivity, a need to be mothered emotionally.

He abused his wife, Rebecca, by asking her to nourish and nurture him. In turn, he abused Jacob by not accepting him as he was, and by showing favouritism toward Esau.

The repercussions of this violation of God's order was that Isaac forced Rebecca into independence and he then became a victim of her independency. The house was divided and fragmentation took place.

When we see the father in passivity and the mother acting independently, the children will either despise spiritual values (birthright) or become more subject to the mother's influence than the father's. This is the root cause of double-mindedness and the manic-depressive condition.

In the third generation, we see that Jacob's weakness is sexual and he chooses a wife based on sexual preference. He abuses his wife by valuing her in terms of how she pleased him physically.

Jacob abuses his children by showing favouritism on sexual preference – sons of his favoured wife.

The greatest wounding that a woman receives is possibly from being abused emotionally and/or sexually by her father (for he is the one entrusted to protect and nurture her) or from the husband who forces her into a wrong position in their relationship.

If there has been wrong socialization because of the sins of the parents, then we need to understand how to break these. The spiritual principles that link us to our father's sins must be dealt with in order to heal the personality. The wounds must be healed and the negative character traits that have been projected must be released in order for change to take place – releasing the new nature within.

Principle of Iniquities

Iniquities are the results of transgressions (which are violations of God's commandments). The punishment of these sins is called the iniquities of our forefathers (Field, 1990).[8]

Under the law, only as the person confessed his own iniquity and the iniquity of the father, would release be given. He had to acknowledge that what he was suffering, or the curse that was upon him, was the punishment for his father's sin.

Under Law

The punishment of sin was upon children.

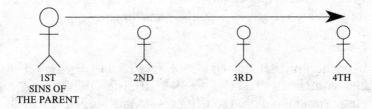

1ST
SINS OF
THE PARENT

2ND

3RD

4TH

'But if they confess their own and their fathers' iniquity in their treachery which they committed against Me, and also that because they walked contrary to Me, I also walked contrary to them and brought them into the land of their enemies; if then their uncircumcised heart is humbled, and they then accept the punishment for their iniquity, Then will I [earnestly] remember My covenant with Jacob, My covenant with Isaac, and My covenant with Abraham, and [earnestly] remember the land. But the land shall be left behind them, and shall enjoy its sabbaths, while it lies desolate without them; and they shall accept the punishment for their sins and make amends, because they despised and rejected My ordinances and their soul scorned and rejected My statutes.'

(Leviticus 26:40–43 AMP)

If the person accepted his condition as being a punishment for his father's sin and confessed it as such he would be released.

Under the dispensation of grace, the principle of iniquities is the same but the application for release is different. The punishment for the iniquity was taken by Christ on His cross.

> '*He was wounded for our transgressions, he was bruised for our iniquities. All we like sheep have gone astray; we have turned every one to his own way; and the Lord hath laid on Him the iniquity of us all.*'   (Isaiah 53:1–10)

As we take accountability for the sins of our forefathers, we transfer the punishment from us to the cross of Christ, thus freeing ourselves from the punishment.

Under Grace

If we accept that our condition is a result of parental sin and confess it as such, we then transfer punishment of ourselves and children to Christ, who has borne the punishment for us already.

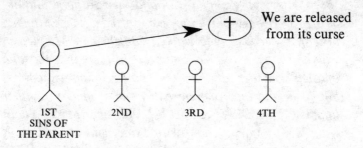

We are released from its curse

1ST
SINS OF
THE PARENT

2ND   3RD   4TH

Punishment is borne by Christ (Isaiah 53:1–10).

Summary

I have tried, briefly, to show the importance of the pastoral ministry, its strengths and its weaknesses. But above all, I have attempted to demonstrate the need for the ministry of nurturing, whether it be by pastor, husband, father or the person who is in the position of authority over us.

If we have been wounded, it is only through the anointing of God and His Word that real, lasting, complete healing can come.

The Gospel of Christ is the only Gospel that gives us an opportunity to re-discover lost opportunity and to redeem the past. It is the power of God unto *'sozo'* (wholeness, maturity) unto all who will accept and believe it (Luke 4:18; James 1:21; 1 Peter 1:22; James 1:22–25; Romans 1:16; Isaiah 61:1–4).

References

1. Clarke, A. *Clarke's Commentary*. Abingdon Press
2. Zodhiates' *Lexical Aids to the New Testament*
3. Minirth, F. & Meier, P. (1989). *Happiness is a Choice* (44th edn). Michigan: Baker Bookhouse
4. Benns, R.M. (1985). *Child, Family, Community*. CBS College Publishing
5. Friedman, E.H. (1985). *Generation to Generation*. Guildford Press
6. Brofenbrenner, U. (1979). *The Ecology of Human Development*. Cambridge, Massachusetts: Harvard University Press
7. Sandford, J. & Sandford, P. (1989). *Healing the Wounded Spirit*. Bridge Publishing Inc.
8. Field, C. (1990). *Family Dynamics based on Iniquities of the Fathers*

Chapter 2

Introduction to Pastoral Care and Counselling

There is a great need to re-evaluate the pastoral ministry, making it contemporary to this generation in light of the Church's basic need for outreach into the local community.

Pastoral care and counselling goes beyond preaching, teaching, the administering of sacraments and administrative leadership, into the sphere of guidance and healing. On either a congregational or a one to one basis, we go deeply into interpersonal, moral and spiritual areas.

The whole work of the ministry of a pastor has been defined as *'Cura Animarum'*, 'the care of the souls'. Our specialized ministry, therefore, is the care of the inner life, the mending and nurturing of a person's personality.

Pastoral care and counselling deals with the care of the inner life of the person and seeks to address the internal wellspring of personal decision.

To be given care of the soul means to be accountable as a minister for admonishing and shepherding the person through their times of crisis, emotional conflict and interpersonal pain. Through gentle, but firm, confrontation, one learns to take personal responsibility for the past as well as present, actions of sin and negative responses to victimization.

In the New Testament the care of the soul is not confined to that of the Pastor, but also to those who are abounding in the highest goodness and are richly supplied with perfect knowledge.

> *'And I, myself, also am persuaded of you, my brethren, that ye also are full of goodness, filled with all knowledge, able also to admonish one another.'*
>
> (Romans 15:14)

Paul admonishes the Church at Colossae to let the Word of Christ dwell richly in them, with all wisdom: teaching and admonishing one another in psalms, hymns and spiritual songs, singing with grace in their hearts to the Lord.

> *'Let the Word of Christ richly dwell within you with all wisdom teaching and admonishing one another with psalms and hymns and spiritual songs, singing with thankfulness in your hearts to God.'*
>
> (Colossians 3:16 NAS)

The word 'admonish' is *'noutheses'*, in the Greek, which is translated by some of the newer versions as 'having counsel'. A literal translation of this word would be to confront in love in order to change not only the direction but the personality of the person.

Through continued personal interaction under the direction and anointing of the Holy Spirit, we endeavour to bring healing to the damaged emotions and to the painful, delusive or re-awakened mind and consciousness. The inner personality, or the soul, would then be restored.

> *'He restoreth my soul: He leadeth me in the paths of righteousness for His name's sake.'* (Psalm 23:3)

The pastoral care and counselling ministry is to ultimately lead the Christian who is oppressed or in bondage into victory and the establishment of inner tranquillity and peace.

What medical science terms *'persona'* or personality, the

Scripture defines as *'nephes'* or *'psuche'*, the soul. Soul is translated from the Greek word *'psyche'*, which is rendered in Latin, *'anima'*. Both terms were used to translate the Hebrew word, *'nephes'*. The primary meaning in Hebrew is possessing life, or that which lives. When God breathed into Adam the breath of life, he, Adam, became a living soul.

> *'And the Lord God formed man of the dust of the ground and breathed into his nostrils the breath of life and man became a living soul.'* (Genesis 2:7)

'Nephes' is that which moves and animates a body whether human or animal and distinguishes a living from a dead being. *'Nephes'* is also considered the seat of physical appetite, the source of emotions and the seat of longings.

The soul is closely intertwined with the will and moral actions. The soul is capable of stumbling and falling, of abusing freedom and of being led into captivity.

The role of pastoral ministry is holistic in concept, not merely ministering to the spirit of man, but also to the soul and body in the context of seeing a person's life in relationship to eternity.

> *'And the very God of peace sanctify you wholly; and I pray God your whole spirit and soul and body be preserved blameless unto the coming of our Lord Jesus Christ.'* (1 Thessalonians 5:23)

> *'Beloved, I wish above all things that thou mayest prosper and be in health, even as thy soul prospereth.'* (3 John 2)

Pastoral ministry offers a bond of kinship more than any other profession.

The pastor, by tradition, has an unwritten invitation to be intimately present with the individuals and families amid critical situations of birth, marriage, sickness, trauma and death.

'*And in those days Peter stood up in the midst of the disciples and said . . . "Men and brethren . . . "*'

(Acts 1:14–16)

'*See that none render evil for evil unto any man; but ever follow that which is good, both among yourselves and to all men.*'   (1 Thessalonians 5:15)

'*Till we all come in the unity of the faith, and of the knowledge of the Son of God, unto a perfect man, unto the measure of the stature of the fullness of Christ.*'

(Ephesians 4:13)

'*Whom we preach, warning every man and teaching every man in all wisdom; that we may present every man perfect in Christ Jesus.*'   (Colossians 1:28)

The pastoral ministry leads the Christian community, the church, into a covenant relationship, bonded not by race or blood or natural kinship but by a covenant with God and a spiritual relationship with Jesus Christ and one another through the Holy Spirit.

In the Book of Judges we see the young man Gideon in mental defeat and spiritual confusion because he could not reconcile in his mind that God's presence could be with Israel when she was so oppressed by the hand of the enemy.

'*And Gideon said unto Him, O my Lord, if the Lord be with us, why then is all this befallen us? And where be all His miracles which our fathers told us of, saying, Did not the Lord bring us up from Egypt? But now the Lord hath forsaken us, and delivered us into the hands of the Midianites.*'   (Judges 6:13)

Let us consider the spiritual types as we briefly study this incident. Gideon was of the half tribe of Manasseh which had entered into Canaan to possess their inheritance.

*'And the rest of Gilead, and all Bashan, being the king-
dom of Og gave I unto the half tribe of Manasseh.'*
(Deuteronomy 3:13)

When Manasseh, along with the rest of the nation Israel,
entered into the land, they found it a land flowing with milk
and honey. But it was also full of giants, great walled cities
and a militant enemy which had to be overpowered and
conquered.

To enter into Canaan (which is life in the Holy Spirit)
demands that we rightly divide the Word of God, not judging according to appearance but judging righteously. To
judge righteously is to consider the facts and base our decisions on the Word of God by viewing the situation from a
Godly perspective.

To understand this principle, let us consider the story
from the Scripture of the twelve spies who had been sent
into Canaan to determine the conditions of the land and the
strength of the inhabitants who they were commanded to
destroy.

Ten of the spies returned from Canaan with a negative
report sowing fear and discouragement into the hearts of
the people and causing them to turn back into the wilderness. These ten spies made a negative mental decision based
solely on what was seen rather than on what God had
promised. This is the foundation of rational, human faith.

Caleb and Joshua, who were of the right spirit, reported
that they too had seen the giants in the land, the great
walled cities and the militant enemy, but proceeded to base
their decisions on what God had said about the negative
situation.

This is rightly dividing the Word of Truth.

*'Study to show thyself approved unto God, a workman
that needeth not to be ashamed, rightly dividing the
Word of Truth.'* (2 Timothy 2:15)

Our faith, inspired by the Word of God, is based on truth rather than facts.

To enter into our Canaan, the life in the Holy Spirit, demands that we rightly divide the Word of God and not judge according to appearances, but judge righteously.

Let us return to the story of Gideon. Here we see this young man fearful and intimidated by the circumstances, threshing wheat behind the winepress to hide from the Midianites.

The threshing of the wheat is the separation of the husks from the wheat, and speaks spiritually of studying to show yourself approved by God by rightly dividing the Word of Truth.

The meaning of the word 'Gethsemane' is 'winepress' and portrays the agony of the soul in conflict. It is written of Christ that while in Gethsemane, His soul was exceeding sorrowful, even unto death.

> *'Then saith He unto them, My soul is exceeding sorrowful, even unto death: tarry ye here and watch with Me.'*
> (Matthew 26:38)

The Book of Hebrews gives us a more graphic description of the suffering Christ than is portrayed in the Gospels, for it says of Him:

> *'Who in the days of His flesh, when He had offered up prayers and supplication with strong crying and tears unto Him, that was able to save Him from death, and was heard in that He feared; though He were a Son, yet learned he obedience by the things which He suffered.'*
> (Hebrews 5:7–8)

Jesus trod the winepress alone and suffered the same human emotions of those in soul darkness and conflict, feeling forsaken by God, the Father, the rejection of self, *'I am a worm and no man'*; and the pangs of helplessness and isolation, *'there is no man to help.'*

'But I am a worm, and no man; a reproach of men, and despised of the people.' (Psalm 22:6)

Jesus now can sympathetically offer us comfort, encouragement and condolence as we, too, face the temptations of life.

The angelic pronouncement to Gideon, which led him to the revelation of Jehovah-Shalom, the Lord is my peace, was simple:

'The Lord is with you, you mighty man of valour.'
(Judges 6:12–24)

To go in the strength of this revelation is to gain victory over those circumstances of life that cause us emotional and psychological stress.

'And the angel of the Lord appeared unto him, and said unto him, The Lord is with thee, thou mighty man of valour. And Gideon said unto him, Oh my Lord, if the Lord be with us, why then is all this befallen us? and where be all His miracles which our fathers told us of, saying, Did not the Lord bring us up from Egypt? But now the Lord hath forsaken us, and delivered us into the hands of the Midianites. And the Lord looked upon him, and said, Go in this thy might, and thou shalt save Israel from the hand of the Midianites: have not I sent thee?

And he said unto Him, O my Lord, wherewith shall I save Israel? Behold, my family is poor in Manasseh, and I am the least in my father's house. And the Lord said unto him, Surely I will be with thee, and thou shalt smite the Midianites as one man. And he said unto Him, if now I have found grace in Thy sight, then show me a sign that Thou talkest with me. Depart not hence, I pray Thee, until I come unto Thee, and bring forth my present, and set it before Thee. And He said, I will tarry until thou come again. And Gideon went in, and made ready a kid, and unleavened cakes of an ephah of flour: the flesh he put in a basket, and he put the broth in a pot,

*and brought it out unto Him under the oak, and
presented it. And the angel of God said unto him, Take
the flesh and the unleavened cakes, and lay them upon
this rock, and pour out the broth. And he did so. Then
the angel of God put forth the end of the staff that was in
His hand, and touched the flesh and the unleavened
cakes; and there rose up fire out of the rock and
consumed the flesh and the unleavened cakes. Then the
angel of the Lord departed out of his sight. And when
Gideon perceived that He was an angel of the Lord,
Gideon said, Alas, O Lord God! for because I have seen
an angel of the Lord face to face. And the Lord said unto
him, Peace be unto thee; fear not: thou shalt not die.
Then Gideon built an altar there unto the Lord, and
called it Jehovah-Shalom: unto this day it is yet in
Ophrah of the Abiezrites.'* (Judges 6:12–24)

This knowledge of the Lord's presence being with us,
even in the midst of the most severe and negative circumstances of life, creates peace which passes all understanding.

*'And the peace of God, which passeth all understanding,
shall keep your hearts and minds through Christ Jesus.'*
(Philippians 4:7)

David also learned this concept when he was afraid for
his life. When his enemies threatened him, his natural
human response was to be afraid.

*'Mine enemies would daily swallow me up: for they be
many that fight against me, O Thou Most High. What
time I am afraid, I will trust in Thee. In God I will praise
His Word, in God I have put my trust; I will not fear
what flesh can do unto me.'* (Psalm 56:2–4)

A question to ask is, 'Can faith and fear be in the human
heart at the same time?'

David shows us a principle applicable to all negative

emotional responses. He did not deny the existence of fear he was experiencing, but rather used it to stimulate, motivate and strengthen his faith in God in order to conquer the things he was afraid of.

> *'In God I will praise His word, in God I have put my trust: I will not fear what flesh can do unto me. In God will I praise His word: In the Lord will I praise His word.'* (Psalm 56:4, 10)

To repress negative emotions will deny us the motivation to praise the Word of the Lord, which is the source of empowerment to our faith. By strengthening his faith, by praising the Word of the Lord, David conquered that which was causing his fear.

> *'He staggered not at the promise of God through unbelief, but was strong in faith, giving glory to God.'* (Romans 4:20)

Basic Concepts for Maturity and Growth

Over the years the Holy Spirit has been establishing Christ's gifts to the church. In the introduction of his book, *Pastoral Theology – Essentials of Ministry*, Thomas C. Oden states,

> 'Pastoral theology as a unifying discipline was flourishing a century ago and remained robust until the beginning of this century, yet it has largely faded into such hazy memory that none of its best representatives are still in print.'

The danger that we, who have dedicated ourselves to follow the 'cloud of the Spirit', face, is to embrace only the new move without retaining the best and workable and necessary principles from the old. Old traditions should be the foundational springboard for us to move into the new.

The ministry gifts need to be re-awakened by a renewal

of the charisma bestowed upon us by the Holy Spirit. Paul exhorts Timothy, *'That is why I now remind you to stir into flame the gift of God, which is within you through the laying on of my hands.'*

> *'Wherefore I put thee in remembrance, that thou stir up the gift of God, which is in thee by the putting on of my hands.'*
> (2 Timothy 1:6)

The pastoral ministry will always be the heart of Christian growth and maturity, for the good shepherd leads his sheep to green pastures and still waters.

> *'The Lord is my shepherd; I shall not want. He maketh me to lie down in green pastures: He leadeth me beside the still waters. He restoreth my soul: He leadeth me in the paths of righteousness for His name's sake. Yea, though I walk through the valley of the shadow of death, I will fear no evil: for Thou art with me; Thy rod and Thy staff they comfort me. Thou preparest a table before me in the presence of mine enemies: Thou anointest my head with oil, my cup runneth over. Surely goodness and mercy shall follow me all the days of my life: and I will dwell in the house of the Lord forever.'*
> (Psalm 23)

Because there has been a blurring of pastoral identity, confusion exists today in the minds of many who have a deep burden to care for the souls of people as to what is the office and ministry of pastoral care and counselling.

For those who have been called to pastor or counsel, we must be aware that heart preparation is critical; a prophet can rise and deliver his message and disappear into obscurity, but pastoral relationships must be developed and maintained with care, and the training process for a pastor can be tedious and painful. Moses was forty years in the wilderness school of the Holy Spirit. David's deep personal conflicts of depression and anxiety were preparatory to establishing a shepherd's heart within.

We need to make a distinction between that which is prophetic and that which is mediatorial and priestly. The critical difference is that the prophet speaks for God to the people, while the priest speaks for the people to God.

Christ Himself provides our example of the development of the priestly ministry. Seeing Jesus came to represent us who are partakers of flesh and blood, it was necessary for Him also to become flesh and blood in order to be capable of dying in our place; and by this act, destroy Satan and annul his power of death over mankind. This is the manifestation of Christ's redemptive love toward us.

> *'Forasmuch then as the children are partakers of flesh and blood, He also Himself likewise took part of the same; that through death He might destroy him that had the power of death, that is the devil; and deliver them, who through fear of death were all their lifetime subject to bondage. For verily He took not on Him the nature of angels; but He took on Him the seed of Abraham. Wherefore in all things it behooved Him to be made like unto His brethren, that He might be a merciful and faithful High Priest in things pertaining to God; to make reconciliation for the sins of the people. For in that He Himself hath suffered being tempted, He is able to succour them that are tempted.'*
>
> (Hebrews 2:14–18)

The secondary work of His abounding love is that through the things He personally suffered, He became sensitive to our needs, our faithful high Priest with the ability to succour and show mercy to us when we are being tempted.

Heart preparation can be best understood in defining the nature of pastoral counselling. The Greek word *'nouthesia'* is usually translated as admonition, counsel, warning or instruction. It involves correction when things go wrong and may require confrontation. It is not a coercive act that manipulates change but a respectful, firm dialogue providing the possibility for voluntary redirection of behaviour.

Admonition can only take place in the context of love and humility, for it requires the admonisher to first of all remove the log in his own eye in order to take out the splinter in another's.

> *'But let every man prove his own work, and then shall he have rejoicing in himself alone and not in another.'*
>
> (Galatians 6:4)

> *'Agree with thine adversary quickly, while thou art in the way with him, lest at any time the adversary deliver thee to the judge, and the judge deliver thee to the officer and thou be cast into prison.'*   (Matthew 5:25)

Redemptive love seeks to restore and not condemn. Humility then becomes the foundation of all true heavenly wisdom.

Chapter 3

Pastoral Care and Counselling

After being tempted in the wilderness, Jesus returned in the power of the Spirit into Galilee and announced His public ministry in the synagogue of Nazareth.

He was handed the book of the Prophet Isaiah and He began to read:

> 'The Spirit of the Lord is upon Me, because He hath anointed Me to preach the gospel to the poor; He hath sent Me to heal the broken-hearted, to preach deliverance to the captives, and recovery of sight to the blind, to set at liberty them that are bruised...'   (Luke 4:18)

This proclamation was a fulfilment of the prophecy of Isaiah 61:1–6 and speaks of the prophetic ministry of Jesus, whose primary ministry was to call to repentance the lost sheep of Israel.

> 'The Spirit of the Lord God is upon Me; because the Lord hath anointed Me to preach good tidings unto the meek; He hath sent Me to bind up the broken hearted, to proclaim liberty to the captives and the opening of the prison to them that are bound; to proclaim the acceptable year of the Lord and the day of vengeance of our God; to comfort all that mourn; to appoint unto them that mourn in Zion, to give unto them beauty for ashes, the oil of joy for mourning, the garment of praise for the

spirit of heaviness; that they might be called the Trees of righteousness. The planting of the Lord, that He might be glorified. And they shall build the old wastes, they shall raise up the former desolations; and they shall repair the waste cities, the desolations of many generations. And strangers shall stand and feed your flocks, and the sons of the alien shall be your plowman and your vinedressers. But ye shall be named the priests of the Lord; men shall call you the ministers of our God; ye shall eat the riches of the Gentiles, and in their glory shall ye boast yourselves.' (Isaiah 61:1–6)

The coming of Jesus in the flesh was for a multiple purpose. This is expressed in Hebrews:

'Forasmuch then as the children are partakers of flesh and blood, He also Himself likewise took part of the same; that through death He might destroy him that had power of death, that is, the devil. And deliver them who through fear of death were all their lifetime subject to bondage. For verily He took not on Him the nature of angels; but He took on Him the seed of Abraham. Wherefore in all things it behooved Him to be made like unto His brethren, that He might be a merciful and faithful high Priest in things pertaining to God, to make reconciliation for the sins of the people. For in that He Himself hath suffered being tempted, He is able to succour them that are tempted.' (Hebrews 2:14–18)

It is rather interesting, as we study this passage, that Jesus came in His flesh in order that He might be a partaker, *'koinoneo'*, of our humanity. In Genesis, God created us in His image (*tselem:* resemblance, shade, image) and likeness (*dmuwth:* model, fashion, to shape).

The Gnostics taught that the human flesh, *'soma'*, was sinful, therefore, Christ did not come in human flesh but a spiritual form. John, in his Epistle, counters this heresy by a simple test: 'Has Jesus come in the flesh? Every spirit that confesses not that Jesus Christ is come in the flesh is not of God, and this is the spirit of anti-Christ.'

> *'Hereby know ye the Spirit of God: Every spirit that confesseth that Jesus Christ is come in the flesh is of God: And every spirit that confesseth not that Jesus Christ is come in the flesh is not of God: and this is that spirit of antichrist, whereof ye have heard that it should come; and even now already is it in the world.'*
>
> (1 John 4:2–3)

In the book of Ezekiel, the expression 'Son of Man' is used eighty-three times to illuminate the relationship the prophet had with the people, for he was a partaker in their captivity and suffering.

Jesus expresses Himself in a like manner. In Matthew 16:14, He asked His disciples, *'Whom do men say that I, the Son of Man, am?'* Their response was, *'Some say that thou art John the Baptist, some Elias; and others, Jeremias or one of the prophets.'* Jesus denotes Himself not as a son of man but the Son of Man, which expresses the importance of His coming in His humanity.

The purpose of Him coming in human flesh is multiple.

> *'Through death He might destroy him that had the power of death, that is, the devil. And to deliver them, who through fear of death were all their lifetime subject to bondage.'* (Hebrews 2:14)

In relation to this study, we shall look at the aspect of Him becoming the seed of Abraham that He might be a merciful (*eleemon:* compassionate by word or deed) and faithful (*pistos:* trust-worthy) High Priest in things pertaining to God to make reconciliation (*hilaskomai:* to atone for sin), or be a propitiation, for the sins of the people.

For in that He Himself has suffered (*pascho:* to experience a sensation, an impression of pain) being tempted (*peirazo:* to test, to discipline, to scrutinize). He is able to succour (*boetheo:* to aid or relieve) them that are tempted.

The maiden of the Song of Solomon, when describing her glorified lover, said,

> *'His belly is as bright ivory overlaid with sapphires.'*
> (Song of Solomon 5:14)

The word 'belly' is better understood as the seat of emotions. This verse carries the inference that the Lord Jesus, too, was a person rich with deep feelings. Ivory is a product created as a result of pain and indicates that Jesus' love is born out of His sufferings unto death.

> *'Who, being in the form of God, thought it not robbery to be equal with God: But made Himself of no reputation, and took upon Him the form of a servant, and was made in the likeness of men.'*   (Philippians 2:6–7)

Jesus' deep love for us caused Him to lay aside His heavenly prerogatives and dignity, come to earth clothed in humanity to sense and partake of our pain (yet without sin) in order to be, in His heavenly ministry, our Mediator and Great High Priest.

> *'Wherefore in all things it behooved Him to be made like unto His brethren, that He might be a merciful and faithful High Priest in things pertaining to God, to make reconciliation for the sins of the people.'*
> (Hebrews 2:17 KJV)

Isaiah adds to our picture of the purpose of His humanity, *'For He shall grow up before Him as a tender plant, and as a root out of dry ground'*. This is a horticultural term. When a seed is planted, it is placed in moist, soft mulch so that the germinated seed is not damaged by forcing its way up through the hard soil.

> *'For He shall grow up before Him as a tender plant, and as a root out of dry ground; He hath no form nor comeliness; and when we shall see Him, there is no beauty that we should desire Him.'*   (Isaiah 53:2)

Jesus, on the other hand, grew up in dry ground, branded as being born in fornication, despised and rejected. Thus He became a man of sorrows (*makobah:* anguish, affliction, grievance, pain, sorrow) acquainted with grief (*cholly:* anxiety, calamity, disease, grief and sickness). He had no form nor comeliness, (*hadar:* magnificence, splendour, honour). There was no beauty (*mareh*: countenance, fair, favoured) that we should desire Him.

When Jesus read from the book of Isaiah, He gave proclamation to His earthly ministry as the prophet who was to come, as had been foretold by Moses.

> *'The Lord thy God will raise up unto thee a Prophet from the midst of thee of thy brethren, like unto Me; unto Him ye shall hearken.'* (Deuteronomy 18:15)

> *'This is that Moses, which said unto the children of Israel, a prophet shall the Lord your God raise up unto you of your brethren, like unto Me; Him shall ye hear.'* (Acts 7:37)

The ministry of the prophet is to speak on behalf of God to the people.

> *'God, who at sundry times and in divers manners spake in time past unto the fathers by the prophets, hath in these last days spoken unto us by His son, who He hath appointed heir of all things, by whom also He made the worlds.'* (Hebrews 1:1–2)

On the other hand, the priestly ministry is to mediate between man and God and speak on behalf of man to God by supplication and intercession.

No man can take upon himself the honour of being called a High Priest. Even so, Jesus did not exalt Himself to be made a High Priest.

> *'And no man taketh this honour unto himself, but he that is called of God, as was Aaron. So also Christ glorified*

not Himself to be made a High Priest; but He that said unto Him Thou art My Son, today have I begotten Thee. As He saith also in another place, Thou art a priest for ever after the order of Melchisedec.'

(Hebrews 5:4–6)

He now has entered into the role of High Priest and is able to 'appoint'* (*erets:* to be firm, the earth at large, field or ground) *'unto them that mourn in Zion, to give them beauty for ashes, the oil of joy for mourning, the garment of praise for the spirit of heaviness; that they might be called trees of righteousness, the planting of the Lord, that He might be glorified'* (Isaiah 61:3).

The pastoral ministry is to him who is called, a ministry of:

1. Healing (*rephah:* to mend by stitch, repair thoroughly, make whole) to the sick (*chalah:* to be rubbed or worn, to be weak, sick, afflicted, to grieve or be grieved, infirmity, to fall sick, to be sorry, woman in travail, to be wounded);

2. Binding (*chabash:* wrap firmly, a compress, to rule, to bind, to gird about, to govern, healer, to bind as a turban) the broken (*shabar:* to burst, to break, broken-hearted, to bring, to build, to crush, to destroy, to hurt, to quench) hearted;

3. Reconciling those who have been:
    (a) Hurt and in withdrawal and isolation (*abad:* to wander away; to lose onself, to perish, break, destroy, fail, lose, to be void);
    (b) and those who are in indecisiveness and are at the crossroads, highway of life (*diexodod; hodos:* those we come across in our journey en route, in our daily walk).

---

* The word 'appoint' would mean spiritually to establish first the Kingdom of God and within this, in broader fulfilment, possess the new heaven and earth.

Developing Pastoral Attitudes

The prophets Jeremiah and Ezekiel speak strongly in their exhortations to those who are called to shepherd or pastor the children of God.

Ezekiel gives a stern warning against the false shepherds who feed themselves, using the flock of God for personal gain, and scattering the people rather than bringing them together.

> *'Son of Man, prophesy against the shepherds of Israel, prophesy, and say unto them, Thus saith the Lord God unto the shepherds: Woe be to the shepherds of Israel that do feed themselves! Should not the shepherds feed the flocks? And they were scattered, because there is no shepherd, and they became meat to all the beasts of the field, when they were scattered.'* (Ezekiel 34:2, 5)

A godly perspective and right attitude of heart are basic requirements for creating unity. The correct pastoral purpose is to produce fellowship and the strengthening, consoling and encouraging of relationships through deep affection and compassionate sympathy.

> *'If there be therefore any consolation in Christ, if any comfort of love, if any fellowship of the Spirit, if any bowels (affection) and mercies, fulfil ye my joy, that ye be likeminded, having the same love, being of one accord, of one mind.'* (Philippians 2:1–2)

To do this we must develop a servant's heart.

Paul, in Philippians, states that our attitude should be like that which was shown to us by Jesus Christ, who, though being essentially one with God and in the form of God, did not think that this equality was a thing to be grasped or retained. He laid aside His mighty power and became like men.

'And now, O Father, glorify Thou Me with Thine own self with the glory which I had with Thee before the world was.' (John 17:5)

'Let this mind be in you, which was also in Christ Jesus: Who, being in the form of God, thought it not robbery to be equal with God: But made Himself of no reputation and took upon Him the form of a servant, and was made in the likeness of men.' (Philippians 2:4–7)

As we study the Word of God we see a vast difference between those who seek authority for the purpose of ruling over others and those who function in authority according to the principles set out in biblical philosophy.

The twelve disciples were in continual discord while they contended for positions of leadership. Jesus' response was:

'Ye know that the princes of the Gentiles exercise dominion over them and they that are great exercise authority upon them. But it shall not be so among you: but whosoever will be great among you, let him be your minister. Even as the Son of Man came not to be ministered unto, but to minister.' (Matthew 20:24–28)

The Greek word for serve here, *'diakonos'*, emphasizes the service rendered, voluntary service as an attendant to his employer. It is service by choice.

The lowest level of slave in Israel was the slave who met the guests at the door in a linen cloth and washed their feet. Jesus set this kind of example in humility by taking a bowl of water, laying aside His garments and washing His disciples' feet and then drying them with a towel.

'He riseth from supper and laid aside His garments; and took a towel, and girded Himself. After that He poureth water into a basin, and began to wash the disciples' feet, and to wipe them with the towel wherewith He was girded.' (John 13:4–5)

He summarizes His actions by saying:

'Verily, verily I say unto you, the servant is not greater than his Lord, neither he that is sent greater than he that sent him.'   (John 13:16)

'Likewise, ye younger, submit yourselves unto the elder. Yea, all of you be subject one to another and be clothed with humility: for God resisteth the proud and giveth grace to the humble.'   (1 Peter 5:5)

His response to those who asked, *'Who shall be greatest in the Kingdom of Heaven?'* was:

'At the same time came the disciples unto Jesus, saying, Who is the greatest in the Kingdom of Heaven? And Jesus called a little child unto Him and set him in the midst of them. And said, Verily, I say unto you, except ye be converted, and become as little children, ye shall not enter into the Kingdom of Heaven. Whosoever therefore shall humble himself as this little child, the same is greatest in the Kingdom of Heaven. And whoso shall receive one such little child in My name receiveth Me.'
(Matthew 18:1–5)

The Christian Minister is not to lord it over God's heritage but, like Jesus, is to serve those unto whom he ministers and by doing so, help them reach their maximum effectiveness.

'Peter, an apostle of Jesus Christ, to the strangers scattered throughout Pontus, Galatia, Cappadocia, Asia, and Bithynia. Elect according to the foreknowledge of God the Father, through sanctification of the Spirit, unto obedience and sprinkling of the blood of Jesus Christ: Grace unto you, and peace, be multiplied. Blessed be the God and Father of our Lord Jesus Christ, which according to His abundant mercy hath begotten us again unto a lively hope by the resurrection of Jesus Christ from the dead. To an inheritance incorruptible

*and undefiled and that fadeth not away, reserved in
heaven for you.'* (1 Peter 1:1–4)

Prayer – The True Sign of Humility

Prayer is the outworking of humility of heart, for we are
stressing our own inability to meet the needs of ourselves
and others and therefore, we must seek help from God.

These principles are also to be offered to the husband
and those who manage the household.

> *'One that ruleth well his own house, having his children
> in subjection with all gravity; (for if a man know not
> how to rule his own house, how shall he take care of the
> Church of God?)'* (1 Timothy 3:4–5)

Peter exhorts,

> *'Therefore, humble (demote, lower yourselves in your
> own estimation) yourselves under the mighty hand of
> God, that in due time He may exalt you. Casting the
> whole of your care (all your anxieties, all your worries,
> all your concerns) once and for all on Him; for He cares
> for you (affectionately and cares about you watch-
> fully).'* (1 Peter 5:6–7 AMP)

> *'For I say, through the grace given unto me, to every
> man that is among you not to think of himself more
> highly than he ought to think; but to think soberly,
> according as God hath dealt to every man the measure
> of faith.'* (Romans 12:3)

To be insolent, overbearing, boastful, presumptuous,
proud and arrogant with self-seeking ambitions causes
discord and strife, emptiness and lack of fulfilment.

> *'Ye lust and have not: ye kill and desire to have and*
> *cannot obtain: ye fight and war, yet ye have not,*
> *because ye ask not.'* (James 4:2)

True humility is the proper attribute from which works true wisdom, for it is peace, peaceloving, courteous and gentle. It is willing to yield to reason and is full of compassion and good fruit. It brings about agreement and harmony between individuals, with understanding, in a peaceful mind, free from fears and agitating passions and moral conflict.

> *'Who is a wise man and endued with knowledge among*
> *you? Let him show out of a good conversation his works*
> *with meekness of wisdom.*
> *And the fruit of righteousness is sown in peace of them*
> *that make peace.'* (James 3:13, 18)

Warning

To try to change our behaviour without a change of inner attitudes (being teachable) will result in further frustration, anger, worry and fear which will in turn uncover more tension.

Consequences of Wrong Leadership

1 Kings 12 demonstrates the consequence of not following biblical ideals of leadership. After Solomon died, Rehoboam took over the Kingdom and succeeded him as King. Rehoboam went to Shechem, for all the Israelites had gone there to make him King.

Jeroboam also came from Egypt where he had fled during Solomon's reign. With the whole assembly of Israel, he went to Rehoboam and said,

> *'Your father put a heavy yoke on us, but now, lighten the*
> *harsh labour and the heavy yoke he put on us and we will*
> *serve you.'* (1 Kings 12:4 NIV)

Rehoboam answered and said,

> *'Go away for three days and then come back to me.'*
> (1 Kings 12:5)

Rehoboam consulted with the elders who had served under King Solomon and asked them how he should treat the people. They replied,

> *'If today you will be a servant to these people and serve them and give them a favourable answer, they will always be your servants.'* (1 Kings 12:7)

Rehoboam rejected their advice and consulted with the young men he had grown up with and asked them,

> *'How should we answer these people who say to me, "Lighten the yoke your father put on us?".'*
> (1 Kings 12:9)

They told him to reply thus,

> *'My little finger is thicker than my father's waist. My father laid on you a heavy yoke, I will make it even heavier. My father scourged you with whips, I will scourge you with scorpions.'* (1 Kings 12:10–11)

Rehoboam ignored the advice of the elderly statesmen and used his power and authority to manipulate, control and exploit the people.

Biblical leadership can be defined as:

> **Meeting the needs of the people as they work at accomplishing their jobs. As leadership gives itself in meeting the needs of those under authority, those under leadership will continually meet leaderships needs, eagerly and voluntarily.**

If leadership does not meet these needs, those under authority will not only rebel but, in turn, will resort to manipulation to get their own needs met.

Summary

The pastoral ministry will be only as effective as our ability to make the Great Shepherd our example and conform to Him. With his strength and anointing, great potential exists to gather in God's people and lead them to a full maturity in love.

SECTION B:

The Healing Ministry of Christ

Chapter 4

Introduction to Physical Healing

Dependency on alcohol. By the time I was 25 years old, I had reached that condition. Deep inferiority, caused by early childhood trauma and rejection, led me to become an alcoholic.

Stress increased when my first son was born with an incurable bronchial disease. As family finances were drained by medical expenses, the emotional and psychological stress level became almost intolerable. At this period of time each family member seemed to have been affected by some form of sickness.

At this critical time, the faithful witness of an elderly Baptist couple led us from a historical church background to a saving knowledge of Jesus Christ. The healing power of God was manifested in a dramatic way as each family member yielded their lives to Him. Among the miracles we experienced were my deliverance from the bondage of alcoholism and healing for my infant son.

A week after my conversion to Christ, I began to minister the Word in a small house group meeting. Two years later, I was in full time ministry, ultimately receiving pastoral ordination from the Assemblies of God, Australia.

Because of our own personal experiences of physical healing by the prayer of faith, we had a very strong emphasis in ministry in this area and saw great miracles as we ministered to those who were sick in body.

However, even though many people were healed, we experienced failures, as some did not respond to prayer and our faith in the atonement.

This led to much seeking of God through prayer and fasting. Instead of accusing the people for a lack of faith, we began to realize that healing should be ministered to the sick through a deeper understanding of the relationship between the soul and body as referred to by the Apostle John, *'I wish above all things that you may prosper and be in health even as your soul prospers'*.

It was then that the Holy Spirit began to reveal to us the scope of the healing power of Jesus.

The following Scriptures took on a new meaning as we began to apply them in ministry:

> *'The Spirit of the Lord (is) upon Me, because He has anointed Me (the Anointed One, the Messiah) to preach the good news (the gospel) to the poor; He has sent Me to announce release to the captives, and recovery of sight to the blind; to send forth delivered those who are oppressed – who are downtrodden, bruised, crushed and broken down by calamity.'*
>
> (Luke 4:18 AMP)

> *'If you will diligently harken to the voice of the Lord your God, and will do that which is right in His sight, and will listen to and obey His commandments and keep all His statutes, I will put none of the diseases upon you which I brought upon the Egyptians; for I am the Lord who heals you.'* (Exodus 15:26 AMP)

> *'He refreshes and restores my life – myself; He leads me in the paths of righteousness (uprightness and right standing with Him – not for my earning it, but) for His Name's sake.'* (Psalm 23:3 AMP)

> *'And I said, Lord be merciful and gracious to me; heal my inner self, for I have sinned against You.'*
>
> (Psalm 41:4 AMP)

I recall the first message I preached on the healing of emotions. When the altar call was given, an Anglican woman was among the many who responded. She had sought healing diligently for two years through the laying on of hands, for she had been told by her physicians that she would shortly be confined to a wheelchair.

She told us that as we were ministering the Word, the Lord had spoken to her and revealed unresolved bitterness in her heart. This had been caused by the betrayal of trust and love by her husband, who had led her into an adulterous relationship shortly after they were married.

After she followed the scriptural injunction of James 5:16,

> *'Confess to one another therefore your faults – your slips, your false steps your offenses your sins; and pray [also] for one another that you may be healed and restored – to a spiritual tone of mind and heart.'*

> (AMP)

a miracle took place, and she was instantly healed physically as her emotions were released.

From that experience, a new scope of healing was revealed to us: emotional distress often causes physical distress. When emotions are healed then physical healing can take place.

Another challenge came as the Lord called us to a deeper commitment from Isaiah 58:7,

> *'Bring the homeless poor into your house.'*   (AMP)

The first person the Lord sent to us was a paranoid schizophrenic, whom we discovered had several distinct personalities. As we lovingly ministered to him, the concept of a healing community was birthed. This would be a place where those who were in emotional, mental and physical distresses could be lovingly ministered back to health through a social, emotional and spiritual re-educational program.

I became a chaplain to the Order of St. Luke the Physician. Many doors were opened to minister to traditional, historical denominations. City wide training schools were established as people became hungry for either ministry knowledge or personal healing.

Much of what we minister today is a result of personal experiences and the vast amounts of ministry to others done in this context.

Different Styles and Areas of Healing as Revealed in the Word of God

As a foundation to our study of physical healing, let us look at Exodus 33:12–13.

> 'Moses said to the Lord, "See, You say to me, Bring up this people; but You have not let me know whom You will send with me. Yet You said, I know you by name, and You have also found favour in My sight. Now therefore, I pray You, (if I have found favour in Your sight, show me now Your way, that I may know You, progressively become more deeply and intimately acquainted with You, perceiving and recognizing and understanding more strongly and clearly) that I may find favour in Your sight. And (Lord, do) consider that this nation is Your people."' (AMP)

In the Scripture, particularly in the Old Testament, a person's name was a revelation of his character; thus Moses made confession that he did not fully understand the character of God even though he had seen many great miracles performed by Him.

The Lord's response to his request was to hide Moses in the cleft of the rock and to have His glory pass by, proclaiming the Name of the Lord. The transformation in Moses' life from this encounter with God was so great that he had to place a veil over his face so that the children of

Israel could not behold his face because of the glory of God.

It is extremely difficult to put one's trust and faith in someone if one does not know the character of that person. So it is with our faith in Christ for healing. It will be difficult for us to trust the Lord for healing if we do not see that by nature Christ is a healer, a great physician.

Let us establish this aspect of truth by reading Exodus 15:23–26 again:

> *'When they came to Marah, they could not drink its waters for they were bitter; therefore it was named Marah (bitterness). The people murmured against Moses, saying, What shall we drink?*
>
> *And he cried to the Lord, and the Lord showed him a tree, which he cast into the waters, and the waters were made sweet. There (the Lord) made for them a statute and an ordinance and there He proved them, saying, If you will diligently harken to the voice of the Lord your God, and will do what is right in His sight, and will listen to and obey His commandments and keep all His statutes, I will put none of the diseases upon you which I brought upon the Egyptians; for I am the Lord who heals you.'* (AMP)

The expression in the Hebrew text is *'Jehovah Rapha'* – I am the Lord that healeth thee. This name is a revelation of one aspect of the character and nature of our Lord. By nature, He is a healer and a great physician. He has established a healing covenant with His people.

In Numbers 15:37–39, it says:

> *'And the Lord said to Moses, Speak to the Israelites, and bid them make fringes or tassels on the corners in the borders of their garments throughout their generations, and put upon the fringe of the borders or upon the tassel of each corner a cord of blue, and it shall be to you a fringe or tassel that you may look upon and remember*

Feed My Sheep, Feed My Lambs

> *all the commandments of the Lord, and do them, that*
> *you may not spy out and follow after (the desires of)*
> *your own heart, and your own eyes, after which you*
> *used to follow and play the harlot (spiritually, if not*
> *physically).'* (AMP)

This is significant when we read of the healing of the
woman with the issue of blood as recorded in Matthew
9:20–21:

> *'And behold, a woman who had suffered from a flow of*
> *blood for twelve years came up behind Him and touched*
> *the fringe of His garment, for she kept saying to herself,*
> *if I only touch His garment, I shall be restored to*
> *health.'* (AMP)

The touching of the hem of His garment has special
insight for us. The woman's faith was expressed by the
confession of her mouth, *'If I can but touch the hem of His*
garment, I shall be healed.' The tense used in the Greek
indicates that as she spoke this from her heart, she
repeated it over and over again. *'For out of the abundance*
of the heart, the mouth speaketh.'

The blue band around the hem was a reminder of the
commands of God and that a covenant had been made
with His people. The woman's faith for healing was based
on the promise God had made to His people, the covenant
of healing given at the waters of Marah.

This was ratified by Jesus on Calvary, for

> *'He was wounded for our transgressions, He was bruised*
> *for our iniquities, the chastisement of our peace was*
> *upon Him and by His stripes, we are healed.'*

(Isaiah 53:5)

In his earthly ministry, Jesus' authority to heal and
deliver the sick is based on he revelations of His redemptive atonement on Calvary, for Matthew wrote:

> *'And when evening came, they brought to Him many who were under the power of demons, and He drove out the spirits with a word and restored to health all who were sick; and thus He fulfilled what was spoken by the prophet Isaiah, He Himself took (in order to carry away) our weaknesses and infirmities and bore away our diseases.'* (Matthew 8:16–17 AMP)

When Jesus healed the woman bowed over with the spirit of infirmity, He was criticized by the scribes and Pharisees. He justified her healing by saying,

> *'Should not this daughter of Abraham be healed?'* (Luke 13:16)

She had this right because of the faith covenant God had made with Abraham.

Ephesians 2:11–13 charges:

> *'Therefore, remember that at one time you were Gentiles (heathen) in the flesh; called Uncircumcision by those who called themselves Circumcision, (itself a mere mark) in the flesh made by human hands. Remember that you were at that time separated (living apart) from Christ excluded from all part in Him; utterly estranged and outlawed from the rights of Israel as a nation, and strangers with no share in the sacred compacts of the (Messianic) promise – with no knowledge of or right in God's agreement, His covenants. And you had no hope – no promise; you were in the world without God. But now in Christ Jesus, you who once were (so) far away, through (by, in) the blood of Christ have been brought near.'* (AMP)

Now, through the precious blood of Christ we, too, have come under the covenant of God; the wall of partition has been taken down and the commandments contained in ordinances, have been established.

Paul, in a letter to the Church of Colossae, states it this way:

> *'Having cancelled and blotted out and wiped away the handwriting of the note (or bond) with its legal decrees and demands, which was in force and stood against us – hostile to us. This (note with its regulations, decrees and demands) He set aside and cleared completely out of our way by nailing it to His cross.'*
>
> (Colossians 2:14 AMP)

Although we are no longer required to be physically circumcised to be a part of the covenant, God expects us to honour Him. Many fail to be healed because of disobedience in not honouring the Lord.

James 5:14–15 gives us implicit instructions of what to do if we are sick. He puts it in question and answer form,

> *'Is any sick among you? Let him call for the elders of the Church; and let them pray over him, anointing him with oil in the name of the Lord; and the prayer of faith shall save the sick, and the Lord shall raise him up.'*

The Lord will honour those who honour Him. In my own personal life, even when emergencies occur, we call for the elders to pray before we call for medical help. Not that we are in any way opposed to medical science; but to honour the Lord is to share in a rich life of faith.

Chapter 5

Physical Healing

In our study of the Healing Ministry of Christ, we would like to present principles which have produced more spontaneous healing and miracles in our ministry than simply teaching on the law of faith.

These principles are an understanding of the physical body's role in salvation, our relationship towards one another in the Body of Christ, and the operation of the gift of faith to men. These will all be covered as the lessons progress. This section will deal with the aspect of physical healing as shown in Christ's ministry.

Over the years the Lord has used physical healing as a means of signs and wonders, to draw many people into the Kingdom. Let us study carefully the healing of the lame man at the Gate Beautiful.

> *'Now Peter and John went up together into the temple at the hour of prayer, being the ninth hour.'* (Acts 3:1)

The stated time is significant. For example, the third hour is mentioned in Acts 2 in relationship to the outpouring of the Holy Spirit. At that time, the disciples were . . .

> *'. . . all with one accord in one place. And suddenly there came a sound from heaven as of a rushing mighty wind, and it filled all the house where they were sitting . . . And they were all filled with the Holy Ghost, and began to*

*speak with other tongues, as the Spirit gave them utter-
ance.'*   (Acts 2:1–2, 4 KJV)

'*... when this sound was heard, the multitude came
together and they were astonished and bewildered,
because each one heard them speaking in his own
(particular) dialect. And they were beside themselves
and were puzzled, saying one to another, What can this
mean? But others made a joke of it and derisively said,
They are simply drunk and full of sweet (intoxicating)
wine.*

*But Peter, standing with the eleven, raised his voice
and addressed them: ... these men, are not drunk, as
you imagine, for it is (only) the third hour (about nine
o'clock) of the day.'*   (Acts 2:6, 14)

This dynamic outpouring and infilling of the Holy Spirit
took place at the third hour, or nine o'clock in the morning. This was the moment when, religiously, the priest
would enter into the Holy place and, with his left hand,
scatter the incense as a praise offering unto the Lord.

Peter told the startled and bewildered crowd that these
men were not drunk with new wine, for it was only nine
o'clock in the morning, but this was a fulfilment of the
prophecy of Joel 2:28.

'*And it shall come to pass in the last days, saith God, I
will pour out my Spirit upon all flesh: and your sons and
daughters shall prophesy, and your young men shall see
visions, and your old men shall dream dreams.'*

(Acts 2:16)

The outpouring of the Spirit on the Day of Pentecost was
the birth or the beginning of the church as the believers
were baptized by the Spirit into one body.

The word wind is the Greek word '*noe*' meaning the
breath of life, or the breath of beginning. It is a medical
term and is used when the newborn baby takes its first
breath. At that point a chemical change takes place in the

baby's body and it is no longer umbilically dependent upon
its mother.

If we paraphrase this story, it could read something like
this: While the disciples were harmonizing (in accord)
together, at the third hour, the Holy Spirit came and
baptized them.

This is parallel to Paul's exhortation in Ephesians,

> *'And be not drunk with wine wherein is excess; but be
> filled with the Spirit, speaking to yourselves in psalms
> and hymns and spiritual songs, singing and making
> melody in your hearts unto the Lord.'*
>
> (Ephesians 5:18–19)

Let us return to Acts 3 and the miracle of the healing of
the lame man which happened at the ninth hour, or three
o'clock in the afternoon. This was the hour of prayer when
the officiating priest would go into the holy place and with
his right hand offer incense signifying God being petitioned
by the prayers of the people. The right hand speaks of the
power of God which is released by our prayers (Ephesians
3:20).

Let us choose some key words in this study to give a
deeper understanding to this miracle which was wrought
by the disciples through the Name and faith in the Name
of Jesus.

> *'... And immediately his feet and ankle bones received
> strength.'* (Acts 3:7)

This word, strength, *'stereoo'*, is the equivalent of our
English word stereotype. Kettles Exposition of New Testament words states that this term is used in relationship to
creation so that the New Testament healing of the lame
man proclaims a process of creation or new creation. This
man received a creative miracle that brought him into
harmony with God's original plan for man, that man
should be totally whole and sound spiritually, mentally and
physically.

Luke, the physician, uses this term to show us the magnitude of the healing. As Peter lifted the lame man up, a creative miracle took place which brought the unsound man back into harmony, with God's perfect will.

In Acts 3:11, *'And as the lame man which was healed...'* the word used for healing is *'therapeutic'*. Therapy is ministering remedial treatment to someone else, carrying with it the idea of being an attendant upon someone in need. Peter, through his faith in Christ, was able to minister to this man, who because of his infirmity, had never had the joy of entering into the temple to worship.

Jesus, Himself, ministered therapeutically, with a servant's heart, realizing that healing often specifically begins at one point but may continue on as therapy. How well the healing (*laomi*) of the lame man also illustrates this point. Wholeness was ministered to him, *'therapeuo'*, as an attendant ministers to his patient. As a result, the lame man was healed and thus made completely whole.

Let us look at an important truth. Jesus, as it is recorded in Philippians 2, stripped Himself of all the rights and prerogatives and privileges which made Him God. He became poor; that is, He yielded the right of ownership of all that made Him God to His Heavenly Father. He came as a servant, not to be ministered unto, but to minister and to give His life a ransom for many.

Not once can we see Jesus using His gifts or power for self or selfish purposes. After fasting for forty days *'... He was afterward ahungered.'* Satan tempted Him to use His power to turn the stones into bread in order to satisfy the tremendous natural hunger in His body. He resisted this temptation, trusting rather in God's ability to meet His need.

We, too, must resist the temptation to use our gifts for our own benefit, for to do so moves us away from being a servant.

To further understand this concept, we need to look at Eastern traditions and customs. After a meal was prepared, the host and his guests would sit and eat first, then the women and children, and last of all, the servants. The servants received all the residue of the meal, which would be more than enough to satisfy their needs.

Consider the miracle of the loaves and fishes. The disciples served the people and kept the residue, which was twelve baskets full. This is the divine principle of serving (giving) and receiving.

Later, near the end of His three year ministry, Jesus asked, *'Have you lacked anything'*, and their response was, *'Nothing, Lord.'*

Consider another example from Scripture, Luke 17:11–19:

> *'And it came to pass, as He went to Jerusalem, that He passed through the midst of Samaria and Galilee. And as He entered into a certain village, there met Him ten men that were lepers, which stood afar off: and they lifted up their voices, and said, Jesus, Master, have mercy on us.*
>
> *And when He saw them, He said unto them, Go show yourselves unto the priests. And it came to pass, that as they went, they were cleansed. And one of them, when he saw that he was healed, turned back, and with a loud voice glorified God, and fell down on his face at His feet, giving Him thanks: and he was a Samaritan.*
>
> *And Jesus answering said, Were there not ten cleansed? but where are the nine? There are not found that returned to give glory to God, save this stranger. And He said unto him, Arise, go thy way: thy faith hath made thee whole.'*

This particular man had a double disadvantage. Firstly, he was a leper and was considered to be cursed by God. Secondly, he was a Samaritan. Worshipping God, but not according to knowledge and truth, he was despised by the Jews.

Jesus' act of therapy brought this man into a saving

faith. And Jesus answering, said, *'Arise, go thy way, thy faith has made thee whole (sozo: saved, salvation).'*

Let us go back and study from Acts 3:16,

> *'And His Name, through faith in His Name, hath made this man strong, whom ye see and know: yea, the faith which is by him hath given him this perfect soundness (holokleria) in the presence of you all.'*

This particular word for soundness is again used to express physical healing.

In Acts 4:9, we find:

> *'If we this day be examined of the good deed done to the impotent man, by what means he is made whole (sozo: salvation) . . . '*

Often Christians experience difficulty in receiving healing because many in ministry have become legalistic and demand that the sick person must exercise great faith or have reached some high level of maturity in order to be healed.

Let us become servants to God and one another so that multitudes can be saved and added unto the Lord as was the response to the healing, (*therapeuo*), of the lame man.

> *'Howbeit, many of them which heard the word, believed, and the number of the men was about five thousand.'*
>
> (Acts 4:4)

Listed below are some of the methods used for physical healing set out in God's word:

Prayer of faith

> *'Is any sick among you? Let him call for the elders of the church; and let them pray over him, anointing him with oil in the name of the Lord: and the prayer of faith shall save the sick, and the Lord shall raise him up; and if he hath committed sins, they shall be forgiven him. Confess*

your faults one to another, and pray one for another, that ye may be healed. The effectual fervent prayer of a righteous man availeth much.' (James 5:14–16)

Laying on of hands

'And these signs shall follow them that believe; In My name shall they cast out devils; they shall speak with new tongues; they shall take up serpents; and if they drink any deadly thing, it shall not hurt them; they shall lay hands on the sick, and they shall recover.'

(Mark 16:17–18)

Gifts of healing

'But the manifestation of the Spirit is given to every man to profit withal. For to one is given by the Spirit the word of wisdom; to another the word of knowledge by the same Spirit; to another faith by the same Spirit; to another the gifts of healing by the same Spirit.'

(1 Corinthians 12:7–9)

Anointing of oil

'Is any sick among you? Let him call for the elders of the church and let them pray over him, anointing him with oil in the name of the Lord.' (James 5:14)

Psychosomatic healing

'For Thine arrows stick fast in me and Thy hand presseth me sore. There is no soundness in my flesh because of Thine anger; neither is there any rest in my bones because of my sin, for mine iniquities are gone over mine head: as a heavy burden they are too heavy for me. My wounds stink and are corrupt because of my foolishness. I am troubled, I am bowed down greatly; I go mourning all the day long. For my loins are filled with a loathsome disease, and there is no soundness in my flesh. I am feeble and sore broken: I have roared by reason of the disquietness of my heart. Lord, all my desire is before

Thee; and my groaning is not hid from thee. My heart panteth, my strength faileth me: as for the light of mine eyes, it also is gone from me.' (Psalm 38:2–10)

The sacrament of the Lord's table

'For he that eateth and drinketh unworthily, eateth and drinketh damnation to himself, not discerning the Lord's body. For this cause many are weak and sickly among you, and many sleep.' (1 Corinthians 11:29–30)

Confessing your faults

'Confess your faults one to another, and pray one for another, that ye may be healed. The effectual fervent prayer of a righteous man availeth much.' (James 5:16)

Deliverance from a spirit of infirmity

'There was a woman which had a spirit of infirmity eighteen years, and was bowed together, and could in no wise lift up herself. And when Jesus saw her, He called her to Him, and said unto her, Woman, thou art loosed from thine infirmity. And He laid His hands on her; and immediately she was made straight, and glorified God.' (Luke 13:11–13)

Meditation

'My son, attend to My words: incline thine ear unto My sayings, Let them not depart from thine eyes; keep them in the midst of thine heart. For they are life unto those that find them, and health to all their flesh.' (Proverbs 4:20–22)

Meditation is the key to faith and inner motivation for healing. We are aware that faith is the doorway into the grace of God, and that faith comes from hearing and hearing from the Word of God (Romans 10:17).

A number of years ago, I learned an important spiritual lesson from a young woman who was seeking healing from a common cold. I had laid hands upon her and asked for the Lord's healing to be manifested. The next night in a gentle but accusing voice she said, 'I wasn't healed last night when you prayed.'

My response was, 'Oh, did you have faith?' to which she replied, 'How would I know?'

I asked her to repeat, 'By Your stripes, Lord, I am healed.' After she repeated this a number of times, I said, 'Now what did your conscience say?' Her reply was, 'My conscience said I am lying. I am not healed.'

I said, 'Keep meditating on the Word until your conscience agrees with what you are saying with your mouth.'

After a short time, she suddenly cried out; 'I am healed! I am healed!'

Examine this incident in the light of Proverbs 4:20–22 which instructs us to give attention to the Word of God. Meditation caused the Word to be internalized into our heart so that when we confess the Word with our mouth our hearts do not condemn us.

Now read 1 John 3:20–21 from the Amplified Bible:

> *'In whatever our hearts in (tormenting) self-accusation make us feel guilty and condemn us. (For we are in God's hands) He is above and greater than our consciences (our hearts), and He knows (perceives and understands) everything (nothing is hidden from Him).*
>
> *And, beloved, if our consciences (our hearts) do not accuse us (if they do not make us feel guilty and condemn us), we have confidence (complete assurance and boldness) before God; and we receive from Him.'*

As our hearts and mouth are in agreement, we then can speak a word of faith. 'The Word (God's message in Christ) is near you, on your lips, on your heart; that is, the Word – the message, the basis and object – of faith, which we preach.'

This is then the **Word of Faith**, and gives us the authority to cast out devils and heal all manner of sickness and diseases.

> '*And Jesus went about all Galilee teaching in their syn-agogues, and preaching the gospel of the kingdom, and healing* (therapeuo) *all manner of sickness* (malakia) *and all manner of disease* (nosos) *among the people. And His fame went throughout all Syria: and they brought unto Him all sick* (kakos) *people that were taken with divers* (poikilos) *diseases* (nosos) *and torments* (basanos), *and those which were possessed with devils, and those which were lunatic* (selainiazo-mai) *and those that had the palsy* (paralytic), *and He healed* (therapeuo) *them.'*   (Matthew 4:23–24)

Our study of the following words is taken from the Thayer's *Greek–English Lexicon of the New Testament*,[1], Strong's *Exhaustive Concordance*[2] and *The Hebrew–Greek Study Bible*, Spiros Zodhiates, Editor.[3]

1. Healing (*therapeuo*): which means to heal or to serve or wait upon as an attendant.
2. Sickness (*nosos*): malady, disability, sickness, disease and infirmity. This is the most common word used for disease and sickness.
3. The verb, '*noseo*', means to be sick, implying a disease of the appetite. It is also used metaphorically of any ailment of the mind. It means to be obsessed with something as if it were a disease or to have a marked fondness for something. This would include compul-sive behaviour. Sickness (*kakos* and *kakoos*): as a noun *or* an adverb; it is used in a moral sense as wicked, base, wrong. It is used with the idea of being held in that condition of sickness. It involves that which is contrary to law, divine or human and covers all kinds of evil things. Thus, the sickness is self destructive and would imply it is a direct result of per-sonal evilness.
4. Divers (*poikilos*): many different types.

5. Diseases (*malakia*): meaning literally, softness, especially in relation to men: delicate or effeminate. It is taken from malakos, or a male who submits his body to unnatural lewdness. It is used in Paul's exhortation in 1 Corinthians 6:9:

    'Know ye not that the unrighteous shall not inherit the kingdom of God? Be not deceived; neither fornicators, nor idolaters, nor adulterers, nor effeminate nor abusers of themselves. Thus it means a weakness or a certain indisposition to receive certain kinds of sickness based on that weakness.'

6. Tormented (*basanos*): to torture or torment with acute pains. It is used to describe the kind of torment used by the tormentor using the rack, the pains of childbirth (which you cannot stop until completed), and the torments of the wicked after death. It also refers to a touchstone, basanite, used to test gold and other metals. This implies torment caused by an outside force which, when once begun, is out of control and either can never come to an end or ends only when the original stimulus has run its course.

7. Lunatic (*seleniazomi*): moonstruck, crazy.

8. Palsy (*paralytic*): to be paralysed, to be feeble.

Summary

As we develop a servant's heart and become obedient to the Word of God to heal the sick, we will see a demonstration of the power of the Lord's presence to heal.

References

1. Thayer's *Greek–English Lexicon of the New Testament*
2. Strong's *Exhaustive Concordance*
3. Zodhiates' *Lexical Aids to the New Testament*

Chapter 6

Psychosomatic Healing

Webster's Dictionary[1] defines psychosomatic as the designation of a physical disorder of the body as originating in or aggravated by a psychic or emotional process of the individual.

We, as a family, had been raised in an historically traditional church where we sought to find the reality of our faith in Christ through the Sacraments.

Sickness, disease, and the related financial stress made it difficult to maintain a relatively normal life style as each in our immediate family had some form of incurable sickness.

After coming to Christ and moving out in a new direction, we saw our captivity to sickness broken through our new found faith and knowledge in the Word of God.

A natural phenomenon had caused a young nephew to develop bronchial asthma. When David received Jesus as his personal Saviour as a teenager, his asthma disappeared. This was possibly our first experience with an emotionally related sickness, for David's coming to the Lord had released him from a trauma of fear which had taken place at the age of two.

As we became involved in full-time ministry, the Lord brought into focus a deeper understanding of the need to harmonize between the spirit, soul, and body, and, in particular, the health and restoration of the soul: mind, emotion, and will.

As we began to see the relationship between the soul and the body and deal through confession and forgiveness with negative emotional feelings, spontaneous physical healing began to take place in our altar services.

In one such meeting, a middle-aged woman responded to the altar call for prayer. She had been told by her physicians that she could not be helped medically as several surgeries had failed to correct a physical defect in the pelvic region; and ultimately, she would be confined to a wheelchair. As she confessed bitterness which had resulted from a betrayal of her husband's love, she was instantly healed.

The heart of man is the seat of his affections and interest and from it comes the issues of life. Movement creates measurable energy, and unreleased emotion causes deep inner tension and stress which, in turn, puts pressure on the 'sympathetic' part of our memory. When this stress is not released through the proper channels of expression, the physical body reacts.

Failure to harmonize our thoughts (minds), words (heart), bodily actions (will); results in discord, or disease.

Each imagination that is contrary to the Word of God has to be cast down, else it becomes a stronghold and stops the flow of power (strength) for our spirit. The imagination then becomes destructive instead of creative.

Past trauma can leave 'imprints' upon our minds. These subconscious imprints can develop strong negative emotions and cause neurotic or psychotic behavioural patterns.

A young lady in a Los Angeles meeting asked for physical healing for a condition which had not been corrected by medical treatment. As we laid hands upon her, the Holy Spirit gave revelation that her real need of healing was release from the fear of death which had gained entrance while giving birth to one of her children.

Her response was to cry out; 'Please don't make me remember! It's too painful for me to remember!' The Holy

Spirit graciously came upon her and fear was dissipated through prayer. Tranquillity and peace flooded her being as emotional and physical healing took place under the anointing of the Holy Spirit.

Restoration to a spiritual tone of heart and mind comes as we confess our faults and pray for one another.

Reference

1. *Websters New Universal Unabridged Dictionary*

Chapter 7

Many are Weak and Sickly Among You

Corinth was one of the largest cosmopolitan Greek cities in the Roman empire. It was situated about fifty miles west of Athens on a major trade route, and had a thriving economy. It was famous for its architecture and the Isthmian games were held there bi-annually.

Greeks, Romans, Jews and a mixed multitude of sailors and merchants flocked to this city which, by the end of the second century, had become one of the richest cities in the world.

Corinth was one of the most wicked cities of ancient times; degradation, immorality and heathen customs abounded. There was an abundance of various religions represented and a large temple which offered the services of a thousand sacred prostitutes. Pleasure was worshipped more than principle.

There was quite a large and established Jewish presence in Corinth when Paul began to establish a Christian witness. It was here that Paul met Aquila and his wife, Priscilla. These two had been expelled from Rome by the Emperor Claudius. The Jews of the city stood in opposition to Paul's testimony of Christ, so he shook his raiment against them and turned to the Gentiles.

Paul and his co-workers established a large congregation and laboured diligently for a period of eighteen months to establish them in the Lord. This was followed by the ministry of Apollos.

Three years later Paul received unfavourable news of division and much sin (1 Corinthians 1:14; 16:17) in the congregation. There was gross immorality, lawsuits among Christians in front of unbelievers, and many other problems relating to living the Christian life. Marriage, meat offered to idols, matters of conscience, abuses in taking the Lord's supper, disorderly conduct in congregational meetings, and confusion about women's roles in the church and heresies about the resurrection of the dead and the afterlife were problems in this church.

Yet in the midst of their carnality, they came behind in no gift (1 Corinthians 1:7). All the charismatic gifts were in evidence, the vocal and utterance gifts: prophecy, tongues, interpretation of tongues; the power gifts: working of miracles, gifts of healing, the gift of faith; the gifts of insight: discerning of spirits, a word of knowledge, and a word of wisdom.

However, it would appear that even still greater faith was in operation, for Paul stated:

> *'Though I speak with the tongues of men and of angels ... though I have the gift of prophecy, and understand all mysteries and all knowledge ... though I have all faith so that I could remove mountains.'*

(1 Corinthians 13:1–2)

Yet a great lack of love and maturity was evident.

It was to this church that Paul spoke these words:

> *'For he that eateth and drinketh unworthily, eateth and drinketh damnation to himself, not discerning the Lord's body. For this cause many are weak and sickly among you and many sleep (in death).'*

(1 Corinthians 11:29–30)

We, in early Pentecost, were taught that the reason many Christians were sick and dead prematurely was that people did not comprehend healing for the body was in the atonement.

Yet, if one truthfully examines this statement, it is obvious that just as many are sick in the body of those believing that *'with His stripes we are healed'* (Isaiah 53:5) and *'He Himself took our infirmities and bore our sicknesses'* (Matthew 8:17), as those congregations who do not teach healing in the atonement. Therefore, discerning the Lord's body must have a far deeper spiritual meaning.

Let me illustrate this by recounting an incident which took place in a series of meetings in the South Pacific Kingdom of Tonga. Each night a young lady came forward to the altar to receive the baptism of the Holy Spirit. Each night she went away disappointed until one night I noticed her weeping. She then began to speak in a beautiful, unknown language.

After the meeting, I enquired of her as to what had taken place. She shared with me this testimony.

'I was getting discouraged and disappointed, for each night when I sought the Lord I felt a wall between the Lord and myself. Tonight I asked the Lord what this wall was and He gave me a vision of Himself. I saw Him wounded and covered with blood. I cried out, "Who did this to you?" His reply was "You did." "How did I wound you, Lord?" And He answered me, "Every time you have spoken evil of your sister, you have wounded Me."'

To discern the Body of Christ may be interpreted as seeing our relationship to one another in the corporate Body of Christ. When Jesus comes in His glory and sits on His throne, He will say to those on His left hand:

'Depart from Me, ye cursed, into everlasting fire, prepared for the devil and his angels. For I was hungry, and ye gave Me no meat: I was thirsty, and ye gave Me no drink: I was a stranger and ye took Me not in: naked

and ye clothed Me not: sick and in prison and ye visited Me not. They shall also answer Him, saying, Lord when saw we Thee hungry, or athirst, or a stranger, or naked, or sick or in prison and did not minister unto Thee? Then shall He answer them, saying, Verily, I say unto ye, Inasmuch as ye did it not unto the least of these, ye did it not unto Me.' (Matthew 25:41–45)

'And Saul, yet breathing out threatenings and slaughter against the disciples of the Lord, went unto the high priest, and desired of him letters to Damascus to the synagogues, that if he found any of this way, whether they were men or women, he might bring them bound into Jerusalem.' (Acts 9:1–2)

While on the way, he was confronted by the Lord....

'And he fell to the earth, and heard a voice saying unto him: "Saul, Saul, why persecutest thou Me?" and he said, "Who art Thou, Lord?" and the Lord said, "I am Jesus, whom thou persecutest."' (Acts 9:4–5)

Saul may well have responded: *'When did I persecute You?'* When we are born again of the Spirit, we are baptized into one body. We become the joints and ligaments of His Body, flesh of His flesh, and bone of His bone.

For us to hold wrong attitudes toward one another is to hold a wrong attitude against Christ. To say we love God and hate our brother is to be in deception.

'We know that we have passed from death into life, because we love the brethren. He that loveth not his brother, abideth in death. Whosoever hateth his brother is a murderer; and ye know that no murderer hath eternal life abiding in him.' (1 John 3:14–15)

To be separated from fellowship with the Body of Christ is to be under the judgment of this world.

We then, must examine ourselves to make sure that no bitterness or wrong attitudes exist between ourselves and our brothers in Christ, lest we be chastened of the Lord and condemned (*katerkrino*; to pronounce sentence against; condemn, adjudge to punishment) with the world.

The Physical Body

In the eighth chapter of Romans, we are told that death still works in this mortal body because of sin and guilt, but the spirit is alive because of the righteousness that imputes to it.

Could it be that the spirit which raised up Jesus from the dead (Romans 8:11) which dwells in us will restore to life our short-lived mortal bodies, by the spirit, if we understand and know what God requires and expects of us in relationship to our bodies?

It is within the body (*soma*) that the natural drives (*sarkikos*) dwell and if these natural drives are not sanctified, then our bodies are not holy and acceptable to God (Romans 12:1). Therefore, the body is still prone to disease and affliction.

Even though we are indebted to look after our bodies, we are not obliged to indulge our carnal nature, to live a life ruled by the standards set up by the dictates of the flesh.

For if we live according to the dictates of the flesh, we shall surely die. But if we, through the power of the Holy Spirit, are habitually putting to death the evil deeds prompted by the body, we shall live.

Our liberty in Christ is not to be used as an incentive or excuse for selfishness, but through love we are to serve one another; for to be divisive, which causes strife, is to bite and devour one another.

We are to be careful that our liberty does not become a hindrance to cause the brother who is weak in faith to stumble, or to give them a reason to sin.

If we cause a person to perish because of our enlightenment, wounding and damaging their conscience, we have sinned against Christ.

To keep true unity of the Spirit in a bond of peace, we must learn to walk in submission, one to another in the fear of the Lord. To be submissive means to cease from being self-assertive and self-opinionated.

To be self-assertive and opinionated leads to domination. We (particularly those of us who hold delegated authority) must not lord it over God's heritage.

To truly comprehend submission, we must understand the Body of Christ and its functions. We are all like the different parts of a physical body. We who are many are a part of a whole, for *'ye are the Body of Christ, and members in particular.'*

Our physical bodies are not to be held in bondage to our physical drives. Sexual immorality and gluttony are the two areas that Paul covers in 1 Corinthians 6:

> *'our bodies have been purchased by the blood of Jesus to be sanctified and set apart for a temple of the Holy Spirit.'*   (1 Corinthians 6:19–20)

To join oneself to the Lord is to become one in spirit.

Through our spirit, we become one body in the Lord; for by one spirit we are baptized into one body. Paul then goes on to use analogy to explain this principle.

If we have intercourse with a harlot, we become one spirit with her; thus our bodies become one. For two shall become one flesh.

To use our bodies for sexual immorality is to bring judgment upon ourselves for we do not discern that we (our bodies) have become a part of the Lord's body.

To commit fornication then, is to sin against one's own body.

I witnessed the mystery of this union in a deliverance meeting in Auckland, New Zealand. I called a tall gentleman to the altar whom I perceived in the Spirit had a spirit of murder. His response was that this was true, for he had written to all the leading politicians in his country threatening them with death.

Then the Holy Spirit revealed how the spirit of murder had entered into the man. 'Son,' I said; 'I perceive that you have married a prostitute and she has never repented of her sin, and because of the sexual act you have joined yourself to her in spirit.'

The term 'prostitute' today refers to one who sells her body for money, but scriptural understanding of the prostitute is the one who has a hatred of men and through her giving of her body to the man causes the man to be joined to the dead at the portals of death. She murders the soul of the man.

The spirit of murder had entered into the man through his sexual relations with the prostitute; for to join oneself physically to a person is to become one in spirit.

The connection between moral weakness and sickness is clearly defined in the scriptures by the word *'arrhostos'*. This word was used by the Greeks to indicate moral weakness or slackness and is translated in the following passages of Scripture as sickness.

> *'And Jesus went forth and saw the great multitude, and was moved with compassion toward them, and healed their sick.'* (Matthew 14:14)

> *'And He could do there no mighty work, save that He laid hands on a few folk, and healed them.'* (Mark 6:5)

> *'They shall lay hands on the sick and they shall recover.'* (Mark 16:18)

> *'For this reason many are sickly and weak among you, and many sleep.'* (1 Corinthians 11:30)

107

Summary

As we begin to understand the relationship and interaction between spirit and body; we will gain deep insight into the mystical Body of Christ; for we being many are one bread and one body.

In submission we will develop a oneness of heart and soul that produces the manifestation of God's power. The result of this unity is demonstrated in the early church, as told in Acts 4:14–16.

Chapter 8

Healing of Demonic Oppression

In Acts 10:38, Peter, in his sermon to the household of Cornelius, summarized the ministry of Christ by saying:

> 'How God anointed Jesus of Nazareth with the Holy Ghost and with power: who went about doing good, and healing all that were oppressed of the devil; for God was with Him.'

As always, we must allow the Holy Spirit to be our teacher, for He teaches us by making comparison of spiritual things with spiritual.

To understand the meaning of the concept of oppression, we need to look at it in the light of the examples in the Old Testament where God commands His people, Israel, not to oppress the stranger, nor the poor, nor the fatherless or widow. In other words, God made strong injunction that Israel was not to take advantage over weaker people because they were in adverse circumstances. Satan will come in to oppress us by taking advantage over us when adverse circumstances exist.

An elderly Christian once shared a testimony with me that illustrates this point. In his later life, he suffered greatly with an arthritic condition in his neck. In obedience to the Word of God, he had called for the leaders of the church to anoint him with oil. Healing evangelists had laid hands upon him with no apparent result. He had sought the Lord many times in fasting and prayer, desperate for healing.

Ultimately, the Lord reminded him that as a young man he had received a whiplash injury while breaking a colt. The Lord then spoke to him and told him that Satan had taken advantage of the physical weakness which had been created by the injury and that a spirit of infirmity had entered in at that time.

In prayer, he took authority over this spirit, binding it and casting it out in the name of Jesus. As soon as the spirit of infirmity had been cast out, his neck healed.

I recall an interesting incident which took place in one of our healing services. A young woman was called out by a word of knowledge, but the prayer of faith brought no response. The Holy Spirit then instructed us to have her stand quietly to one side. Returning a little later for further ministry, we were led to cast out the spirit of infirmity. She felt a rushing sensation through her spine that then passed out through her legs and feet. As we commanded the spine to straighten, she was instantly healed.

Let us now turn to the Gospel of Luke 13:11–12 for a biblical example:

> *'And behold, there was a woman which had a spirit of infirmity eighteen years, and was bowed together, and could in no wise lift up herself. And when Jesus saw her, He called her to Him, and said unto her, "Woman, thou art loosed from thine infirmity." And He laid His hands upon her, and immediately she was made straight and glorified God.*

We see in this story that Jesus commanded the spirit of infirmity to leave and then He laid hands on the woman for healing.

It would be wrong for us to interpret that all sicknesses are a result of spirits of infirmity. The man at the Pool of Bethesda had an infirmity for thirty-eight years. Jesus said to this man:

> *'Rise, take up thy bed and walk. And immediately the man was made whole, and took up his bed and walked.'*
>
> (John 5:8–9)

Yet, there are times when a spirit of deafness, blindness, and dumbness will take advantage over a person and oppress them.

Vexed by an Unclean Spirit

In Matthew 10:1, Jesus called His disciples unto Him and:

> *'He gave them power against unclean spirits, to cast them out, and to heal all manner of sickness and all manner of disease.'*

One day I was meditating on the healing of the daughter of the woman of Canaan. This young girl was grievously vexed with a devil and I wondered why Jesus referred to bread in relationship to this incident for He had said to her mother:

> *'It is not meet to take the children's bread and cast it unto the dogs.'*   (Mark 7:27)

Understanding began to come as I realized that I had always regarded an unclean spirit as a spirit causing immoral sexual behaviour.

As I studied the words, *'vexed by an unclean spirit'*, new insight came. This word 'vexed', used to describe the young woman's condition, is *'daimonizomai'*, to be demonized or to be violently possessed.

Thayer's Greek Lexicon states that this word is used for sickness or disease.

Other usages of the word 'vex' are found in the following Scriptures:

> *'And a great multitude of people ... which came to hear Him, and to be healed of their diseases; and they*

that were vexed with unclean spirits: and they were healed.' (Luke 6:17–18)

'There came also a multitude out of the cities round about Jerusalem bringing sick folks, and them that were vexed with unclean spirits: and they were healed every one.' (Acts 5:16)

The word 'vexed' used in these two passages of Scripture is *'achleomia'*, which means to harass or to incite to riot.

'When Jesus came down from the Mount of Trans-figuration, a certain man came to Him, and kneeling down said; Lord, have mercy on my son, for he is a lunatic; and sore vexed, for oft times he falleth into the fire, and oft into the water.' (Matthew 17:14–15)

The word 'vexed' used in the context of this Scripture is *'pascao'*, and means to suffer mental and emotional torment.

Again, let us consider why bread was used in relationship to the healing of the Syrophoenician woman's daughter. Bread is something which fills, something which takes away our hunger and satisfies that need for nourishment. Jesus said in John 6:32–35:

'Verily, verily, I say unto you; Moses gave you not that bread from heaven; but My Father giveth you the true bread from heaven. For the bread of God is He which cometh down from heaven, and giveth life unto the world. Then said they unto Him: Lord, evermore give us this bread. And Jesus said unto them, I am the bread of life: he that cometh to Me shall never hunger; and he that believeth on Me shall never thirst.'

Now let us link this Scripture to Matthew 12:43–45:

'When the unclean spirit is gone out of a man, he walk-eth through dry places, seeking rest and findeth none.

*Then he saith; "I will return into my house from whence
I came out"; and when he is come, he findeth it empty,
swept, and garnished. Then goeth he, and taketh with
himself seven other spirits more wicked than himself,
and they enter in and dwell there: and the last state of
that man is worse than the first.'*

Jesus said that when the unclean spirit is gone out of a
man, it walks through dry places, seeking rest. Finding
none, it will return into the vessel which had been swept
and garnished yet remained unoccupied.

Many people have suffered from deep personal rejection.
Others, because of an inability to face conflict, have withdrawn into isolation and deep loneliness. Yet there is one
thing common in these cases ... all will feel a vacuum, an
emptiness within, a sense of isolation.

Ofttimes, we think that a person must be living an
immoral life to be vexed by an unclean spirit. But I am
convinced that unclean spirits can come in because of the
emptiness, vacuums, and unfulfilled needs within a person.
Manifestations of unclean spirits can sometimes come
through severe forms of physical sickness. Other manifestations are emotional and mental torments, while yet other
manifestations are anger, hostility and contentiousness.

As we minister to those who need healing, we must be
very discerning in order to pray effectively for release and
restoration. It is said of Mary Magdalene, Susanna, and
Joanne that Jesus cast out spirits and healed them of
infirmities (weaknesses). Satan will take advantage of our
weakness and oppress us if we do not guard carefully over
these areas of our lives.

Those Who Oppose Themselves

*'In meekness instructing those that oppose themselves; if
God peradventure will give them repentance to the
acknowledging of the truth; and that they may recover*

> *themselves out of the snare of the devil, who are taken*
> *captive by him at his will.'*　　　　　　(2 Timothy 2:25)

This wording, *'oppose themselves'*, is used twice in the New Testament. In this reference, to oppose oneself means to exalt a lie and consider it to be truth. This gives Satan the advantage of coming in and taking us captive at his will.

Recovery out of the snare and captivity of the devil will only come as God gives repentance to the acknowledging of the truth.

As a young child and teenager, I suffered a great deal of rejection and emotional conflict which ultimately led me into alcoholism. In retrospect, I have realized that the root of my rejection came from exalting a lie and believing it to be the truth.

In my younger life, I was plagued with the thought that I was an adopted child or the illegitimate son of my sister. I always referred to my mother as 'Nanna'.

At the age of twelve or thirteen, I went with my father to look at a flock of sheep in one of our back paddocks. We had an argument over some now forgotten incident. In his anger, he called me a 'bastard' and this re-enforced all that I had believed about myself. My response was to run the entire mile and a half home, take a rifle, and try to shoot myself. This incident almost totally destroyed my life.

Just recently, I was finally able to comprehend the reason why I had exalted a lie and believed it to be truth. My mother had a mental breakdown as a result of my birth and was hospitalized for a period of time. My sister had responsibility for me, taking care of me for a period of nearly two years during the time when my mother was unable to do so. A strong bonding had been established between my sister and myself. It was this strong bonding which caused me to regard her as my mother.

Through acknowledging the truth, my self-image has been healed as I have meditated upon the Word of God.

Many psychotic conditions result from believing a lie and regarding it as truth.

One dear lady who came for healing in one of our communities had years of psychiatric treatment and hospitalization. She suffered a deep guilt complex because she believed that she had been responsible for the death of her husband. As we scrutinized this incident, we discovered that this was not so; but that his death had been an accident.

To oppose oneself leads to confusion, confusion causes delusion, and delusion, if it remains untreated, can ultimately lead to insanity.

Healing, in these cases, comes through repentance of the lie, and then acknowledgment of the truth.

Forgotten Memories

Many people who are under demonic oppression have great difficulty in remembering specific events of their past or even the whole of their past.

There is a vast difference between the scriptural forgetting of that which is behind and of having mental blockages where we have no conscious recall.

Although many Christians try to deal with their problems by simply trying to erase bad or painful memories, the correct way is through the principles of renunciation and of confession.

2 Corinthians 10:4–6 gives us direction for renunciation and confession:

> *'For the weapons of our warfare are not carnal, but mighty to the pulling down of strongholds; casting down imaginations, and every high thing that exalteth itself against the knowledge of God, and bringing into captivity every thought to the obedience of Christ. And having in readiness to revenge all disobedience, when your obedience is fulfilled.'*

Not only are we to take authority over the strongholds in our minds, the lies which we believe, casting them down and bringing them into captivity; but we must also be ready to revenge all disobedience. This means to once and for all commit to God the cause of the lie, allowing Him to deal with the matter. When these things are done, we in turn can minister from a fulfilled place of obedience.

Paul, in Philippians, writes of those things in his life he had to lay aside or to count as dung: his religious, cultural, social standing; the fact that he was of the tribe of Benjamin, a Hebrew of the Hebrews, a Pharisee, and according to the standard set by the works of the law, a righteous man.

These 'fleshly' things he found in no way gave him a right standing with God. The right standing only comes from faith in Jesus Christ alone.

Paul stated:

> *'Brethren, I count not myself to have apprehended: but this one thing I do, forgetting those things which are behind, and reaching forth unto those things which are before, I press toward the mark for the prize of the high calling of God in Christ Jesus.'*   (Philippians 3:13–14)

Forgetting those things which are behind is to not regard them or give credence to these things, to press forward toward the prize of the high calling of God in Jesus Christ.

David, when his moisture had turned into the summer's drought, found release when *'he went back and confessed the past until all was told'*. His exhortation is for those *'who are Godly to pray that way'*.

I remember ministering to a young girl who was experiencing forty epileptic seizures per day. After much prayer she was partially cured and the seizures decreased to one fit per day.

I asked the mother if her daughter had experienced some trauma of such magnitude that she could have forgotten the incident. She replied that just prior to the first seizure, her father, an alcoholic, came home drunk one night and in a fit of depression took a butcher's knife out of the kitchen drawer and slashed his throat with it in front of the children.

Satan had taken advantage of the little girl's trauma and had entered in and was hiding behind the forgotten memory.

One of the most outstanding healings of this nature was experienced by a lady we will call Judy. She had been involved in occult practices prior to her coming to Christ and receiving the baptism in the Holy Spirit. Judy suffered from a twisted bowel and several surgeries had not corrected this recurring condition.

Instantly, the Lord gave the Pastor a vision of Judy as a little girl being sexually molested by an intruder coming into the family home. She had no memory of such an experience, but it was confirmed later by Judy's mother in a telephone conversation.

Judy was placed in a hospital for an operation to correct her bowel disability. While waiting for surgery, a medium, whom she had known prior to her conversion, came to visit a patient in the next bed and, upon seeing Judy, started a conversation with her.

Judy, for the first time, made a renunciation of her occultism by telling the medium that she had found Jesus Christ as Saviour and was no longer practising the art.

A shadowy form came from her body and started to converse with the medium. As Judy called upon the woman to repent and turn to Christ, the spirit disappeared and the medium fell to the floor screaming in pain. She was rushed into the emergency room and that day was operated on for a twisted bowel.

Judy's surgery was cancelled. After the surgeon re-examined her, he found no problems with her bowels. She has been free of the condition since that time.

Ministering Deliverance to the Captives

Jesus, after fasting in the wilderness for forty days, returned in the power of the spirit into Galilee. On the Sabbath day, He went into the synagogue at Nazareth and was handed the book of the Prophet Isaiah. He read the following passage:

> *'The Spirit of the Lord is upon Me, because He hath anointed Me to preach the gospel to the poor; He hath sent Me to heal the broken-hearted, to preach deliverance to the captives, and recovering of sight to the blind, to set at liberty them that are bruised.'* (Luke 4:18)

Thus, He publicly announced the type of ministry He was to have. It is through the anointing of the Holy Spirit that we, too, have the power and authority to minister healing and deliverance to the captives.

The gifts or manifestations of the Spirit are an important aid in helping us to minister effectively, for we need knowledge, wisdom and discernment.

It is important for us to realize that deliverance and physical healing are a part of our covenant right as children of God.

When Jesus loosed the woman with the spirit of infirmity and was criticized by the synagogue leader, He responded:

> *'Should not this daughter of Abraham be loosed from this infirmity whom Satan has bound, lo, these eighteen years?'* (Luke 13:16)

Once we were Gentiles separated from the covenant rights of Israel, but now we have been made righteous by the blood of Jesus and have become heirs to the promises of God.

And if we belong to Christ, then we are Abraham's offspring, heirs according to the promise.

Do not turn from the ministry of the Spirit, the same

ministry Jesus had, and which is the same calling we have. Mark 16:17–18 is our injunction:

> '*And these signs shall follow them that believe: In My name shall they cast out devils; they shall speak with new tongues; they shall take up serpents; and if they drink any deadly thing, it shall not hurt them; they shall lay hands on the sick, and they shall recover.*'

SECTION C:

Christian Maturity

Chapter 9

Introduction to Christian Maturity

The book of Job is an enigma in its portrayal of a righteous man going through severe trials and testings. Why should a righteous man suffer loss, pain and affliction?

> *'Then the Lord said to Satan, "Have you considered my servant Job? There is no one on earth like him; he is blameless and upright, a man who fears God and shuns evil." '* (Job 1:8 NIV)

Most modern preachers have accused Job, as did his friends, of breaking down God's hedge of protection.

It is true that God used this trial to convert some areas of spiritual weakness in Job's life, but God, Himself, testified that Job was a righteous man (conformed to God's will in thought, word and deed) and one who feared God. Thus, the test of Job is the test of his integrity. It was not the consequence of wrongful speech. The question was: can a man love God for who God is and not for what material benefits God may provide?

David illuminates to us the qualities of a man who fears God. His definition of this kind of man is one who keeps his lips from speaking guile and who hates evil.

> *'Then the Lord said to Satan, "Have you considered my servant Job? There is no one on earth like him; he is blameless and upright, a man who fears God and shuns*

evil. And he still maintains his integrity, though you incited me against him to ruin without any reason." '

(Job 2:3 NIV)

Satan was only allowed to test Job by God's consent and permission, for the Lord knew how much suffering Job could bear.

The silence from God, the darkness that surrounded Job's soul, brought forth deep, hidden attitudes of heart; yet, though he cursed the day he was born, he retained his faith in God. He refused to curse God. Instead he testified of the everlasting love of a Redeemer that ever liveth and one day would cause him (Job) to stand before his Maker.

'He had seven sons and three daughters, and he owned seven thousand sheep, three thousand camels, five hundred yoke of oxen, five hundred donkeys and a large number of servants. He was the greatest man among all the people of the East.'   (Job 1:2–3 NIV)

'He replied, "You are talking like a foolish woman. Shall we accept good from God, and not trouble?" In all this, Job did not sin in what he said.'   (Job 2:10 NIV)

'I know that my Redeemer lives, and that in the end He will stand upon the earth.'   (Job 19:25 NIV)

Many of God's chosen vessels have gone through the 'school of brokenness' in order to bring them into a larger capacity of service and love.

David speaks of his experience going through this same soul darkness in:

'My God, my God, why have You forsaken me? Why are You so far from helping me, and from the words of my groaning? O my God, I cry in the daytime, but You answer me not; and by night I am not silent or find no rest. But You are holy, O You Who dwell in [the holy place where] the praises of Israel [are offered]. Our

fathers trusted in You; they trusted – leaned on, relied on You, and were confident – and You delivered them.'
(Psalm 22:1–4 AMP)

In this type of testing, the deep hidden attitudes of our heart and soul are tested and subconscious feelings relating to self, others and God are brought to light.

David's cry *'I have no man to help me'* expresses his deep sense of isolation and helplessness; while his *'I am a worm and no man'* reveals the deep humiliation of the soul's rejection of self when in the fires of affliction.

> *'Do not be far from me, for trouble is near and there is no one to help.'*
> (Psalm 22:11 NIV)

> *'But I am a worm and not a man, scorned by men and despised by the people.'*
> (Psalm 22:6 NIV)

David also maintains the integrity of his lips toward God: for his cry *'Thou art Holy'* is parallel to Job's *'In all this, Job sinned not, nor charged God foolishly'*.

Most of us would have to confess that under this kind of pressure, we have not always retained the integrity of our lips: for we have said: 'If God loves me the way He says He does, then He would not allow this situation to happen.' This is attacking the character of God. Or we have said, 'If God's Word is true, this would not happen to me', thus attacking the truth of God's Word.

> *'In all this, Job did not sin by charging God with wrongdoing.'*
> (Job 1:22 NIV)

> *'Yet, You are enthroned as the Holy One; You are the praise of Israel.'*
> (Psalm 22:3 NIV)

During these times, we have responded with doubts and bitterness. David was able to overcome by enthroning God over the situation through praise and thanksgiving to God. Only as we seek God's wisdom and knowledge will we understand His purpose for suffering and affliction.

Paul's prayers for the Church of Colossae give us insight into God's ultimate goal for our lives:

> '*For this reason, we also, from the day we heard of it, have not ceased to pray and make (special) request for you, (asking) that you may be filled with the full (deep and clear) knowledge of His will in all spiritual wisdom (that is, in comprehensive insight into the ways and purposes of God) and in understanding and discernment of spiritual things; that you may walk (live and conduct yourselves) in a manner worthy of the Lord, fully pleasing to Him and desiring to please Him in all things, bearing fruit in every good work and steadily growing and increasing in (and by) the knowledge of God – with fuller, deeper and clearer insight, acquaintance and recognition.*
>
> *(We pray) that you may be invigorated and strengthened with all power according to the might of His glory, (to exercise) every kind of endurance and patience (perseverance and forbearance) with joy, giving thanks to the Father, Who has qualified and made us fit to share the portion which is the inheritance of the saints (God's holy people) in the Light.*
>
> *(The Father) has delivered and drawn us to Himself out of the control and the dominion of darkness, and has transferred us into the kingdom of the Son of His love, in Whom we have our redemption through His blood, (which means) the forgiveness of our sins. (Now) He is the exact likeness of the unseen God – the visible representation of the invisible; He is the Firstborn – of all creation.*' (Colossians 1:9–15 AMP)

Most of us have problems which are related in some measure to how we respond to God, to others, to our own personal weakness, and to the reproofs and corrections of life.

The maiden of the Song of Songs, when she was brought

into the secret place of the King, sees that her outer woman has shadows which are causing her lack of peace and rest.

'Look not upon me, because I am black...' Her initial response is that of an immature person: *'Look not on me'*. The person who responds this way fails to understand God's method of cleansing. For it is only by becoming transparent through confession of sin that we will be made without spot or wrinkle.

The desire of the maiden's heart was to find rest at noon or at the moment of greatest trial and temptation. The King's beautiful reply to her gives us deep insight into the dealings of God, causing us to be able to take pleasure in infirmities, in reproaches, in necessities, in persecutions, in disasters: for we learn that His strength is made perfect in our weakness. When we are weak, His power, resting upon us, makes us strong.

> *'But He said to me, "My grace is sufficient for you, for My power is made perfect in weakness." Therefore, I will boast all the more gladly about my weaknesses, so that Christ's power may rest on me. That is why, for Christ's sake, I delight in weaknesses, in insults, in hardships, in persecutions, in difficulties. For when I am weak, then I am strong.'* (2 Corinthians 12:9–10 NIV)

We are to follow the footsteps of the flock, that is, the way of tested faith and integrity. To sit at the 'King's table' is to learn of Him who is meek and lowly of heart.

The abundance of Solomon's table consisted of two major ingredients: bread and meat. The bread speaks of the humanity of Christ, the One who became like unto us, in order for us to become like unto Him. Meat speaks of those who have come to fullness of character (or love) and have their senses and mental faculties trained to distinguish between what is morally good and noble and what is evil and contrary either to divine or human law.

Then, we shall be nurtured, during what seemingly is separation from Him, by Him, Who will never leave us or forsake us, and Who will cause us to be comforted by our faith and trust in Him. (Romans 5:1–5).

> *'While the king was at his table, my perfume spread its fragrance.'*   (Song of Solomon 1:12 NIV)

> *'Come to me, all you who are weary and burdened, and I will give you rest. Take My yoke upon you and learn from Me, for I am gentle and humble in heart, and you will find rest for your souls. For My yoke is easy and My burden is light.'*   (Matthew 11:28–30 NIV)

> *'But made Himself nothing, taking the very nature of a servant, being made in human likeness. And being found in appearance as a man, He humbled Himself and became obedient to death – even death on a cross!'*
>   (Philippians 2:7–8 NIV)

If our reactions to negative situations and reproofs are based on our feelings or natural reasoning, it will result in conflict and negative character development.

> *'Anyone who lives on milk, being still an infant, is not acquainted with the teaching about righteousness.'*
>   (Hebrews 5:13 NIV)

If we react in a natural way, instead of being conformed to the image of Jesus, our social personality will be deformed, retarded; our emotions will be crippled and twisted. Our needs are then filled with confusion, wrong, and pain, producing distorted thought patterns which can result in neurotic or psychotic behavioural patterns.

There are three major sources of conflicts or reproofs which God uses to bring us into conformity to His character:

1. **People**: Personality traits, inconsistencies, attitudes, words and actions are a constant source of reproof.

2. **Environment**: Inconvenience and the natural world over which we have no control are a source of conflict.
3. **Ourselves**: Personal, physical defects and weaknesses and failures are a major source of reproof.

If we fail to respond correctly to God's reproofs, He will allow the same incident to confront us repeatedly, in order to conform us to the Word of God.

If we love God and are called according to His purpose, all things will work together for our good. Stumbling blocks will become stepping stones, the rock which crushes others will be the rock which sustains us.

Chapter 10

The Word of the Lord Held in Captivity

The substance of this section was born out of a painful experience our church endured several years ago, resulting from a directive prophecy given to us.

The congregation had grown from twelve adults to almost four hundred people in a space of two to three years. At this time, we had a visit from a well known minister who, under the inspiration of the Holy Spirit, prophesied that the church would double its membership within six months.

A personal word was also given; I would be able to speak creative words, calling into existence those things which be not.

Within the next six months, instead of seeing the prophetic word fulfilled, murmuring arose in a small section of the congregation. Certain brethren with self interests who were in conflict with leadership, promoted the discord. Instead of doubling our congregation, our attendance dropped to one hundred and fifty people.

I am in no way intimating that the prophetic word was in error; but the lack of its fulfilment caused us to seek the Lord for an answer to this perplexing problem of having received a *'rhema'* from the Lord and yet not seeing it fulfilled or accomplished.

The context of our study on Christian maturity is a result of that research.

The first Scripture that I would like to draw your attention to is Mark 6:41. Let us examine it in the context of Jesus feeding the multitude with a few loaves of bread and some small fishes.

'He lifted up His eyes and blessed...' This word 'bless', *'eulogeo'*, means 'to bless', or more accurately, 'to speak well of'. It originates from *'eu'* (good, well); and *'lego'* (to speak).

When God speaks, His speaking is also His action, for God's speaking and acting are one and the same thing. When God is said to bless us, eulogise us, He speaks and acts well toward us. The Scripture says, *'He has blessed us with all spiritual blessings in heavenly places in Christ'.* When we bless God, we speak well of Him, we laud or praise Him because He is worthy.

> *'Praise be to the God and Father of our Lord Jesus Christ, who has blessed us in the heavenly realms with every spiritual blessing in Christ.'* (Ephesians 1:3 NIV)

When we bless one another, we express good wishes. When we bless our food, as Christ did the loaves and fishes (when He miraculously multiplied them), it is to thank God for His benevolence. By so doing, we dedicate the object blessed as being consecrated to divine service.

Many of us say, as the disciples in our illustration: 'We do not have enough, our resources are too limited, we can't.' As we compare the magnitude of our need to the seeming lack of resources, instead of blessing, we become guilty of murmuring against God.

We are admonished not to murmur, as they murmured in the wilderness and were destroyed by the destroyer.

To murmur because of the hardness of the way, to complain about our circumstance, is to actually murmur against God. To murmur is to stop the flow of God's creative power. Instead of multiplying our resources, we tend to lose even that which we thought we had.

Remember, it is God's will for us to give thanks to Him in all things.

> *'Give thanks in all circumstances, for this is God's will for you in Christ Jesus.'*   (1 Thessalonians 5:18 NIV)

If we are going to speak creative words, we must cleanse our hearts and make them free from all murmuring.

> *'But the righteousness which is of faith, speaketh on this wise: "Say not in thine heart, who shall ascend into heaven?" (that is, to bring Christ down from above) or "Who shall descend into the deep?" (that is, to bring Christ up from the dead). But what saith it? The Word is nigh thee, even in thy mouth, and in thy heart; that is, the word of faith, which we preach.'*   (Romans 10:6–8)

To murmur is to harden one's heart in unbelief. The Greek word for heart is *'kardia'*; the seat of the intellect and emotions. The Scripture attributes to the heart: thoughts, reasoning, understanding, will, judgement, affections, love, hatred, fear, joy and anger.

The heart is used for the mind in general: the will, the memory, the intentions, affections or desires, and the conscience.

If the word we speak is to become creative, the Word has to be established in our intellect and affections – in our heart. The Word will be held in captivity in our lives until this is accomplished.

Further insight will be gained by studying the traumatic incident the disciples experienced after the miracle of the loaves and fishes.

Jesus had sent them in a boat to cross over to Bethsaida on the other side. A great storm arose and the wind was contrary to them, causing them to shrink in terror.

After Jesus stilled the storm, the Word says:

> *'For they considered not the miracle of the loaves and fishes; for their hearts were hardened.'*   (Mark 6:52)

The key word to this text is 'considered' (*suniemi*); from *'sun'*, together and *'hiemi'*, to send or put. When the word is confined to the sphere of mental perception, it means to hear, perceive, to put it all together and make sense out of it.

They could not understand the lesson they should have learned from the blessing and breaking of the loaves and fishes.

We must realise that the Word of God is as incorruptible seed. It will not bear fruit until it takes root in our minds and emotions, however, for our negative emotions will choke out its life. Fear possessed the hearts of the disciples for the Word had not become logos to them. Because of this, they operated in fear instead of faith.

The young man, Gideon, is another example of circumstances creating negative responses. When the angel spoke to Gideon: *'The Lord is with thee, thou mighty man of valour'*; Gideon's response was: *'If God be with us then where are all the miracles?'*

It is hard for us to understand that God could use negative circumstances to create inner peace, in order for us to have a platform for the word of faith to operate in power.

In Psalm 17, David recognises that the men of the world, even wicked men, are instruments in the hand of God to reprove him and bring him into a place of righteous communion with God.

> *'Rise up, O Lord, confront them, bring them down; rescue me from the wicked by Your sword.'*
> (Psalm 17:13 NIV)

> *'And I – in righteousness I will see Your face; when I awake, I will be satisfied with seeing Your likeness.'*
> (Psalm 17:15 NIV)

Psalm 56 shows the outworking of this. David's enemies were threatening his life. His human response was to be afraid; but he used his fear to stimulate his faith through praising God's Word.

Abraham's response to the negative factors surrounding the promises of God was to have hope. He was empowered and grew strong as he gave praise and glory to God.

We understand that faith comes from hearing and hearing from the Word of God (*rhema*). But *'rhema'*, a word spoken or uttered, must be established in our hearts for the word to bring forth fruit. Much emphasis has been placed on *'rhema'* by those who teach faith, but we need to see that the *'rhema'* be established into the good soil (the good heart) to be productive.

Let us look at the word *'logos'*. *'Logos'* is the articulate utterance of human language. *'Logos'*, when it refers to discourse, is regarded as the orderly linking and knitting together, in connected arrangement, words communicating inward thoughts and feelings of the mind.

Jesus, when He interpreted the parable of the sower to His disciples, said that the seed sown on stony ground represents those who, when they have heard the Word, immediately receive it with gladness, yet have no root in themselves. That is, they lack depth of character. When persecution and afflictions come because of the Word, they are offended (Matthew 13:3–9).

An example of this truth can be seen in a study of the tabernacle at Shiloh.

> *'So that He forsook the tabernacle of Shiloh, the tent which He placed among men; and delivered His strength into captivity, and His glory into the enemy's hand.'*
>
> (Psalm 78:60, 61)

The sons of Eli were called the sons of Belial. The expression, 'sons of Belial', is a term denoting nature and character, not title. In application to the sons of Eli, it denotes the worthless and wicked nature of their character. They were base and unteachable, for they held the truth in unrighteousness and incurred God's judgment and wrath.

> *'Eli's sons were wicked men; they had no regard for the Lord.'*
> (1 Samuel 2:12 NIV)

Those who are fully conversant and understand the truth of God's Word know that God is rich in goodness, forbearance and longsuffering; but His wrath is revealed from heaven against all ungodliness and unrighteousness.

The sons of Eli were conversant with and understood the repercussions of their wrong doing; but they disregarded the Lord's rebuke. They ministered spiritual, holy things; but did it out of corrupt hearts.

Look at a contrasting term found in Romans 8:14:

> *'For as many as are led by the Spirit of God, they are the sons of God.'*

A more accurate translation would read: 'For as many are led by the Spirit of the Lord manifest the qualities of a son.'

What a contrast is seen between Eli's sons and Samuel. Samuel wore a linen ephod, the garment of kings and priests and symbolic of the righteousness of the saints.

Fine linen is the product of the flax plant. It is beaten and washed and the more of this refining process it goes through, the finer the quality of linen that will be produced.

God's method of building righteousness within us is based on our faith in the Lord and our obedience to His commands. This is what brings love to perfection.

God's method of bringing us into maturity of love is through suffering and affliction. Both of these words define the word *'pathema'*. This word indicates that the emotions, whether good or evil, are regarded as being subject to external influence exerted upon the mind. Suffering and affliction is the psychological and emotional stress caused by outside pressure.

Samuel was a man of impeccable character. In his address to the nation of Israel, when Saul was appointed king, he challenged the people:

'Behold, here I am: witness against me before the Lord, and before His anointed: whose ox have I taken? or whose ass have I taken? or whom have I defrauded? Whom have I oppressed? or of whose hand have I received any bribe to blind mine eyes therewith? And I will restore it you.

And they responded, "Thou has not defrauded us, nor oppressed us, neither hast thou taken aught of any man's hand".' (1 Samuel 12:3–4)

Such was the integrity of Samuel's heart that God did not allow one word that he spoke to fall on the ground.

We are to count it all joy when we go through temptation; for temptations are allowed by God to perfect our endurance, so that we may be complete and perfect, lacking nothing. Then we, too, as Samuel, can ask without wavering, knowing that God will honour our word when we pray.

'Speak and act as those who are going to be judged by the law that gives freedom.' (James 2:12 NIV)

Chapter 11

When I Was a Child

The affirmation or confession of our faith is a very important aspect in the development of the new nature of Christ placed within us when we are born again of the incorruptible seed, the Word of God.

> *'Who have been chosen according to the foreknowledge of God, the Father; through the sanctifying work of the Spirit, for obedience to Jesus Christ and sprinkling by His blood: Grace and peace be yours in abundance. Praise be to the God and Father of our Lord Jesus Christ! In His great mercy, He has given us new birth into a living hope through the resurrection of Jesus Christ from the dead.'* (1 Peter 1:2–3 NIV)

In his letter to Philemon, Paul expresses the importance of *'epignosis'*; acknowledging or fully recognising every good thing which is in us in Christ Jesus.

> *'That the communication of thy faith may become effectual by the acknowledging or fully recognising every good thing which is in you in Christ Jesus.'*
>
> (Philemon 6)

The 'good thing' or *'agathos'* is character energised, which expresses itself outwardly in active goodness. This good thing is profitable and useful.

In contrast, the old nature is corrupt; for the natural

unregenerated man seeks to do only his own will. Being selfish, he walks in lasciviousness. He acknowledges no restraints and gives himself over to a readiness for all pleasure. He walks in lust (*epithumia*) or *'pathos'* (passion, the lust of desire), a diseased condition of the soul from which a variety of lusts spring.

> *'So I tell you this, and insist on it in the Lord; that you must no longer live as the Gentiles do, in the futility of their thinking. They are darkened in their understanding and separated from the life of God because of the ignorance that is in them due to the hardening of their hearts. Having lost all sensitivity, they have given themselves over to sensuality so as to indulge in every kind of impurity, with a continual lust for more.'*
>
> (Ephesians 4:17–19)

> *'For you have spent enough time in the past, doing what pagans choose to do – living in debauchery, lust, drunkenness, orgies, carousing and detestable idolatry.'*
>
> (1 Peter 4:3)

We are commanded in the Word to put off our sinful nature. This is accomplished by being renewed or spiritually revitalised in our mental attitude and perception by the Holy Spirit.

The diseased or lustful soul of man must go through a metamorphosis. By taking upon himself the manifested qualities of Christ's own nature, which is righteous and holy, man is then made acceptable to God in word, thought and deed.

The maturity of our character in love is important if our faith is going to produce creative words. To speak without being mature in character would cause our words to be a sounding brass and tinkling cymbals.

> *'If I speak in the tongues of men and of angels, but have not love, I am only a resounding gong or a clanging cymbal.'*   (1 Corinthians 13:1 NIV)

'When I was a child, I talked like a child, I thought like a child, I reasoned like a child. When I became a man, I put childish ways behind me.'

(1 Corinthians 13:11 NIV)

Let us look at the great love chapter of the Bible, 1 Corinthians 13, for further confirmation of this truth.

'If I (can) speak in the tongues of men and (even) angels, but have not love (that reasoning, intentional, spiritual devotion such as is inspired by God's love for and in us), I am only a noisy gong or a clanging cymbal.

And if I have prophetic powers, that is, the gift of interpreting the divine will and purpose; and understand all the secret truths and mysteries, and possess all knowledge; and if I have (sufficient) faith so that I can remove all mountains, but have not love (God's love in me); I am a useless nobody.'

(AMP)

Paul likens a person who lacks character to a child (*nepios*: from *'ne'*, *'not'* and *'epos'*, to speak): a person who is not able to speak fluently. This person, because of a lack of endurance, steadfastness and patience, will be as one who is also weak in faith. Endurance (fortitude) develops maturity of character, that is, approved faith and tried integrity.

We will now study God's method of bringing us into maturity of character and approved faith. A single Greek word, *'pathema'*, translated into two English words, suffering and affliction, gives us insight into the way God establishes character within us.

This word, *'pathema'*, as previously explained, means to experience psychological and emotional stress caused by outside circumstances.

When various trials and temptations come upon us, it is vital that we respond correctly to them in order to reap a benefit rather than to allow them to defeat and destroy us.

> *'Consider it pure joy, my brothers, whenever you face trials of many kinds.'*   (James 1:2 NIV)

Jesus said to count it all joy, *'chara'*, and to be exceedingly joyful when we fall into diverse temptations.

Paul said in Romans 5:3–4:

> *'Moreover, let us also be full of joy now! Let us exult and triumph in our troubles and rejoice in our sufferings, knowing that pressure and affliction and hardship produce patient and unswerving endurance, and endurance (fortitude) develops maturity of character; that is, approved faith and tried integrity. And character (of this sort) produces (the habit of) joyful and confident hope of eternal salvation.'*   (AMP)

As we study the parable of the prudent man, who built his house upon the rock, we should understand that the very same rain, flood, and wind which came upon the house built upon the rock also came upon the house built on the sand, by the foolish man.

> *'Therefore, everyone who hears these words of Mine and puts them into practice is like a wise man who built his house on the rock. The rain came down, the streams rose, and the winds blew and beat against that house; yet it did not fall, because it had its foundation on the rock. But everyone who hears these words of Mine and does not put them into practice is like a foolish man who built his house on sand. The rain came down, the streams rose, and the winds blew and beat against that house, and it fell with a great crash.'*   (Matthew 7:24 NIV)

The storm was the same; but the response to it by each individual was different.

If we look at the adverse circumstances of life, our trials and temptations, and consider them as God's reproofs, we will see that the temptation (*peirasmos*, proof) is used by

God for the purpose of proving one's faith. It is never for the purpose of causing one to sin.

> *'Blessed is the man who perseveres under trial, because when he has stood the test; he will receive the crown of life that God has promised to those who love Him. When tempted, no one should say: "God is tempting me." For God cannot be tempted by evil, nor does He tempt anyone.'*
> (James 1:12–13 NIV)

> *'Then Jesus was led by the Spirit into the desert to be tempted by the devil.'*
> (Matthew 4:1 NIV)

God tested the children of Israel in the wilderness for the purpose of teaching them that man does not live by bread alone, but by every Word proceeding from the mouth of God.

Jesus was driven by the Holy Spirit into the wilderness, where He was tempted of the devil for 40 days. The temptation (*peirazo*) Jesus suffered was, from the devil's point of view, for the purpose of soliciting Jesus to sin. Satan tempts in order to show someone as unapproved.

God's testings are to prove that we are acceptable to Him. When God tests, *'dokimos'*, it is in the same manner as metal being tried by fire. Hence, to be approved as acceptable means to be tried in the furnace of adversity.

> *'Because you know that the testing of your faith develops perseverance.'*
> (James 1:3 NIV)

> *'I counsel you to buy from Me gold refined in the fire, so you can become rich; and white clothes to wear, so you can cover your shameful nakedness; and salve to put on your eyes, so you can see.'*
> (Revelation 3:18 NIV)

The lukewarm church at Laodicea was counselled to buy gold tried in the fire. Peter said that the trying of our faith is more precious than gold, which perishes.

Not to be chastened or to be disciplined by God would mean that we would remain in spiritual infancy. Many today are denying themselves the privilege of inner transformation and growth because of their inability to reconcile adverse circumstances to their concept of God and His presence.

> *'And you have forgotten that word of encouragement that addresses you as sons: "My son, do not make light of the Lord's discipline, and do not lose heart when He rebukes you, because the Lord disciplines those He loves, and He punishes everyone He accepts as a son. Endure hardship as discipline; God is treating you as sons. For what son is not disciplined by his father? If you are not disciplined (and everyone undergoes discipline), then you are illegitimate children and not true sons. Moreover, we have all had human fathers who disciplined us and we respected them for it. How much more should we submit to the Father of our spirits and live! Our fathers disciplined us for a little while as they thought best; but God disciplines us for our good, that we may share in His holiness."'*

(Hebrews 12:4–10 NIV)

The story of Gideon and the Midianites is a good example of this. The Midianites (meaning 'confusion' and 'contention') were invading and harassing Israel, impoverishing them by robbing them of the rewards of their labours.

When the angel spoke to Gideon *'The Lord is with thee, thou mighty man of valour'*, he responded: *'If the Lord be with us, then where be all His miracles?'* (Judges 6:12).

In Jeremiah 48:11 it says:

> *'Moab hath been at ease from his youth and he hath settled on his lees, and hath not been emptied forth from vessel to vessel, neither hath he gone into captivity. Therefore his taste remaineth in him and his scent is not changed.'*

Moab was at ease; that is, he was undisturbed, restful

and quiet. He had not endured any testing, trials or harassment. He was inactive, doing nothing.

The expression: *'Not been emptied from vessel to vessel'* when used in conjunction with *'settled on his lees'* is a wine-making term. Wine has to be poured from vessel to vessel in order to remove the dregs.

The Scripture does not intimate that Moab had no dregs, but these dregs, lees, had not been dealt with. He had not been emptied (*ruwq*, to pour out, to make empty).

'Neither hath he gone into captivity'. This word, captivity, *'gowlah'*, has a special meaning to us for it comes from a root word which means to denude, to make naked. He lacked transparency and, therefore, no healing or restoration had taken place within his life.

To confess our faults to one another and pray means to be healed and restored to a spiritual tone of heart and mind.

> *'Therefore, confess your sins to each other and pray for each other so that you may be healed. The prayer of a righteous man is powerful and effective.'*
>
> (James 5:16 NIV)

Because Moab had lived a life free from stress, he was unchanged, inactive. Hence his taste (*ta'am*: to taste, to perceive) remained in him and his scent (*reyach*: savour, scent, smell) had not changed.

The tastebuds cause us to discern the many different flavours of food we eat. If we spiritualise this, it means that Moab had no spiritual perception, no discernment. He was unable to judge righteously.

Let us expand this truth further. Remember the story of Abraham and Lot? Because their flocks were increased, there was division among Abraham's and Lot's shepherds.

Abraham came to Lot and suggested a separation of ways between the two families, giving Lot the first choice of the land. Lot looked toward the regions of Sodom and

Gomorrah and saw that the fields were green and lush like the Garden of Eden.

Little did he realise that his choice one day would lead to the death of his wife and the loss of his family, for he failed to see the repercussions that the sinfulness of this city would have upon his family. The name, 'Lot', means veil or veiled and implies that there was a veil over his perception; he was judging according to outward appearances.

Abraham, on the other hand, was a man of deep humility of mind and heart, for he, although he was the elder, exhibited the same mind which was in Christ, who set Himself as being secondary. God's reward for Abraham's humility was to give him the north, the south, the east, and the west.

To be in spiritual infancy or to be one who has not developed the nature of love means that the mysteries of God's kingdom and the cross of Christ is veiled.

> *'Do nothing out of selfish ambition or vain conceit, but in humility consider others better than yourselves. Each of you should look not only to your own interests, but also to the interests of others.'* (Philippians 2:3–4 NIV)

Moab's scent had not changed: that is, he was still emanating the sorrow of his old, unregenerate life.

> *'One who is loved and/or loves God, however, is more than a conqueror over death, life, angels, principalities, things impending and threatening, and things to come, and powers, and heights, and depths and anything else in all creation.'* (Romans 8:38–39)

> *'Now thanks be unto God, which always causeth us to triumph in Christ, and maketh manifest the savour of His knowledge by us in every place. For we are unto God a sweet savour of Christ, in them, that are saved, and in them that perish.'* (2 Corinthians 2:14–15)

Our victory of faith is a sweet offering, a scent unto God.

Many have, because of a lack of understanding, responded negatively to the sufferings and afflictions of life and have allowed the adverse circumstances to cause inner feelings of depression and oppression.

David, in Psalm 42, reveals to us a godly principle that will bring us out of defeat and despair into thankfulness and praise.

> *'My tears have been my food day and night, while men say to me all day long, "where is your God?" These things I (earnestly) remember, and pour myself out within me: how I went slowly before the throng and led them in procession to the house of God (like a bandmaster before his band, timing the steps to sound of music and chant of song), with the voice of shouting and praise, a throng keeping festival.'* (AMP)

'When I remembered these things' – what things? The things that had caused him to grieve. this word, remember, *'zakar'*, means to recollect, to bring to remembrance, to confess.

When he remembered these things, he poured out (*shaphak*: to spill forth, to cast up, to gush out) his soul within him, for he had gone with the multitude to the house of God. With the voice of joy and praise (*tow-dah*: an extension of the Lord, thanksgiving), he kept the holy day with the multitude.

David remembered (to recall, to recollect, to confess) 'those things', the wrong attitudes that brought him deep depression and inner conflict. He cast these things from his soul.

The New Testament would have exhorted him to 'put off' these things from his diseased soul by confessing, for confession brings catharsis, cleansing and healing. More precisely, 'catharsis' means to be made clean from defilement, to be made without spot or wrinkle by a process of purification and purging.

Consequently, after this process, David leads the congregation and he is able to express joy and thanksgiving.

How different is this teaching, as set out in Psalm 42, than what is often taught in our pulpits today. People are being encouraged to deny feelings and emotions, to forget the past, and merely concentrate on positive thinking and confession.

Yet the Word of God clearly teaches that there is a definite sequence which must be followed before proper thanks can be given to God for all things. Without an acknowledgment of the truth, so that responsibility can be taken, cleansing cannot take place through confession and the soul is not free to thank God.

> *'Give thanks in all circumstances, for this is God's will for you, in Christ Jesus.'* (1 Thessalonians 5:18 NIV)

> *'Always giving thanks to God the Father for everything, in the name of our Lord Jesus Christ.'*
> (Ephesians 5:20 NIV)

We must acknowledge the truth. If we deceive ourselves, it means to exalt a lie and believe it to be truth. As we acknowledge the truth, God will give us repentance. This is accomplished by remembering in order that accountability and responsibility can be taken. Thus, through confession, the precious blood of Jesus can cleanse us from all unrighteousness.

> *'Those who oppose him, he must gently instruct, in the hope that God will grant them repentance leading them to a knowledge of the truth, and that they will come to their senses and escape from the trap of the devil, who has taken them captive to do his will.'*
> (2 Timothy 2:24–26 NIV)

When this cleansing, this transformation, has taken place, we then can give thanks to God for all things; and, like Joseph, we can say as he said to his brothers: *'What you intended for evil, God has used for my good'.*

After this comes the joy and thanksgiving, not only because we now experience the release from the conflict, but also the freedom which comes from inner cleansing and change.

> *'Behold, Thou desirest truth in the inward parts: and in the hidden part Thou shalt make me to know wisdom. Purge me with hyssop, and I shall be clean: wash me, and I shall be whiter than snow. Make me to hear joy and gladness; that the bones which Thou hast broken may rejoice. Hide Thy face from my sins, and blot out all mine iniquities.*
>
> *Create in me a clean heart, O God: and renew a right spirit within me. Restore unto me the joy of Thy salvation; and uphold me with Thy free Spirit. Then will I teach transgressors Thy ways; and sinners shall be converted unto Thee. Deliver me from bloodguiltiness, O God, Thou God of my salvation, and my tongue shall sing aloud of Thy righteousness. O Lord, open Thou my lips and my mouth shall show forth Thy praise.'*
>
> (Psalm 51:6–10, 12–15)

Chapter 12

Purifying Ourselves

The development of Christian character, sanctification, holiness and purity is very much linked with the hope of the coming of the Lord Jesus Christ.

When Peter shares on the coming of the Lord Jesus Christ, his emphasis is not on the signs of the coming of the Lord, but on the character of the Lord:

> *'The Lord is not slack concerning His promise, as some men count slackness; but is longsuffering to usward, not willing that any should perish, but that all should come to repentance.'*
> (2 Peter 3:9)

He then goes on to share that this period of longsuffering should be taken as a time of preparation for us:

> *'Seeing then that all these things shall be dissolved, what manner of persons ought ye to be in all Holy conversation and godliness.'*
> (2 Peter 3:11)

'Eusebeia', godliness, has the general sense of a pious life which is morally good. The word holy is *'hagios'*, which means to be separated, sanctified and consecrated; not only separated ceremonially, but also morally.

John, in his first Epistle, also gives an emphasis on making oneself ready:

> *'Beloved, now we are the sons of God, and it doth not yet appear what we shall be: but we know that, when He shall appear, we shall be like Him; for we shall see Him as He is. And every man that hath this hope purifies himself, even as He is pure.'*   (John 3:2–3)

'Hagiazo' means to consecrate, to dedicate. It is from a root word which means to be free from defilement and infirmities and is used to express the everlasting sanctity of the marriage relationship.

As we study the word 'purifies', we begin to understand the connection between the coming of Jesus and the heart preparation of those who are of the Body of Christ.

> *'Let us be glad and rejoice, and give honour to Him: for the marriage of the Lamb is come and His wife hath made herself ready. And to her was granted that she should be arrayed in fine linen, clean and white: for the fine linen is the righteousness of the saints.'*
>
> (Revelation 19:7–8)

Righteousness, *'dikaioma'*, is the product or result of being justified by God; thus, it is the legal right which the child of God has by faith through Jesus Christ. This should be translated: 'For the fine linen is the legal rights of the saints'.

In Luke's gospel, it says:

> *'Likewise, also, as it was in the days of Lot; they did eat, they drank, they bought, they sold, they planted, they builded; but the same day that Lot went out of Sodom, it rained fire and brimstone from heaven, and destroyed them all.'*   (Luke 17:28–29)

> *'Even thus shall it be in the day when the Son of Man is revealed. In that day, he which shall be upon the house top, and his stuff in the house, let him likewise not come*

down to take it away: and he that is in the field, let him
likewise not return back. Remember Lot's wife...'

(Luke 17:30–32)

Lot had moved into Sodom (burning with lust) and his
family had integrated with the inhabitants.

When Lot urged his sons-in-law to flee from the impending judgment, they considered that he mocked (*tsachaq*, to
laugh or scorn). This is taken from a root word to laugh
outright.

As Lot, his wife and two daughters fled they were
warned not to look back. Lot's wife looked back and was
turned into a pillar of salt (Genesis 19:17, 26).

To look back after having escaped the pollutions of the
world and become desirous to be entangled in them again
and thus be overcome, creates a last condition which is
worse than the first.

Jesus said:

'No one who puts his hand to the plough and looks back
(to the things behind) is fit for the Kingdom of God.'

This was said in response to the man who desired to
become a disciple but wanted to first say goodbye to those
at his home. The man was still emotionally linked with his
past and his family in an inordinate way.

Lot's wife looked back and brought herself under the
same judgment which had been pronounced against
Sodom.

I do not feel that we should try to interpret the account
of Lot and his family fleeing from Sodom as being the
rapture of the church, although it could be a spiritual type;
but rather, that unless we separate ourselves from the
world we will incur the judgment of God which is already
upon the world.

'For God sent not His Son into the world to condemn the
world; but that the world through Him might be saved.'

(John 3:17)

> *'He that believeth on Him is not condemned, (**krino**: to try to pass sentence, to condemn) but he that believeth not is condemned (**krino**: under sentence) already because he hath not believed in the Name of the only begotten Son of God.'*　　　　　　　(John 3:18)

The world is already under the sentence of condemnation because of its rejection of Christ. A part of that judgment is manifested in the toil, strife, discord, poverty, and sickness which abounds so greatly in this world system.

How then can these Scriptures relate to us? Let us turn to Paul's exposition on the Lord's table:

> *'But let a man examine (**dokimazo**: to test, to examine, to discern) himself and so let him eat of that bread, and drink of that cup, for he that eateth and drinketh unworthily (**anaxaios**: unfit, unworthily) eateth and drinketh damnation (**krima**: the suffix, 'ma' indicates the result of; **krino**: to share in what already has been pronounced or judged) to himself, not discerning the Lord's body.'*　　　　(1 Corinthians 11:28–29)

Sodom already had a sentence of judgment upon it. Lot's wife came under the pre-announced judgment of God.

For us to participate unworthily in the communion, that is to participate with a wrong attitude of heart, would mean to bring oneself under the judgment, the sentence, the condemnation that is already upon the world.

What does it mean when it says: *'Not discerning the Lord's Body'*? The word discerning is *'diakrino'*, from *'dia'* which denotes separation. This could imply that we are not separating ourselves from fellowship with those things that are forbidden by God.

We are not to be unequally yoked (to fellowship, to be in concord or harmony or agreement with). These words express deep emotional bonding.

For us not to separate ourselves from the world unto Christ would bring us under the pre-existent judgment which is upon the world; hence, many are sick, weakly and dead before their time.

For if we would judge ourselves (*diakrino*), we should not be judged (*krino*); but when we are judged by the Lord, we are chastened (*paideuo*: to educate by discipline or punishment) of the Lord that we should not be condemned (*katakrino*: to pronounce sentence against) with the world.

If we examine ourselves or judge ourselves, we will not be judged and chastened by the Lord. This kind of discipline from the Lord is for our good and is an act of responsible love on the part of God toward us, His children.

This has nothing to do with our salvation or standing before God in new birth. We are saved by grace, through faith, and sealed by the Holy Spirit until the day of redemption. God's discipline is to set us free from the condemnation that is upon the world and to develop within us the peaceable fruit of righteousness.

God does not want us to come under condemnation, or be judged with the world. He does not want us to be partakers of the condemnation which came upon Lot's children, nor does he want us to look back as did Lot's wife.

God's chastening is not to punish us for our sins or mistakes, for He has already accomplished atonement by the death of His Son, Jesus, on the cross. Rather, His rebuke and discipline is to bring forth within us the nature and character of Christ, and to change our mental and emotional attitudes.

In Hebrews, we are told that our earthly fathers corrected us because of their love for others. Parental discipline is for a short period of time, but our heavenly Father will keep on disciplining us for our profit (*sumphero*: our benefit).

Affliction and suffering are the emotional and mental reactions that are caused by outside pressures. These outside pressures are, ultimately, in the hands of God for chastening. Chastening is something we must endure, could cause us to faint, and is not pleasant but grievous.

If we do not see reproofs as instruments from God's point of view, we can allow bitterness to come. This root of bitterness will spring up and defile many.

Many leave the family, marriage and the church because of offences and stress. Those who go in bitterness only carry their wrong attitudes into the new relationship, the new marriage or the new church fellowship.

To be in a comfort zone, to escape the pressure that the Lord allows, would mean that we would remain in spiritual infantilism.

Many times the Lord chastens to keep us from sin. This is the experience of Paul in 2 Corinthians 12:7:

> *'And lest I should be exalted above measure through the abundance of the revelations, there was given to me a thorn in the flesh, the messenger of Satan to buffet me, lest I should be exalted above measure.'*

Notice that twice Paul mentioned that his buffeting by the messenger of Satan was to keep him from being exalted, from being egotistical, and from pride. This Scripture is generally interpreted as Paul being dealt with because he had pride. But look closely at what the Scripture says. He was being dealt with in this manner, not because he had pride, but in order to keep him from becoming exalted in pride.

In conclusion, let us study the word 'meekness'. Comprehension of this godly attribute will help us to understand and react correctly to the pressures of life.

The word meek is *'prautes'*, the inner disposition or grace of the soul expressing a right attitude toward God and man.

It is the condition of heart, demonstrating gentleness – not in weakness, but in power. It is the attitude of spirit in which we accept God's dealing with us as good and do not dispute or resist. To develop meekness, we must first understand and accept the sovereignty of God.

Jesus said He was meek and lowly. If we would learn of Him we would find rest for our souls.

In His humiliation He was: *'Like a sheep before his shearers is dumb'*, in that He did not strike back, retaliate or justify Himself. Rather, He committed Himself into the hands of ungodly men, knowing that His Father would judge righteously over Him.

When Pilate marvelled at His (Jesus') lack of self-justification, he said, *'Don't You know that I have power to crucify You or the power to release You?'*, Jesus responded with: *'You have no power unless it is given to you from above'*.

Meekness is knowing that God is Sovereign and will judge righteously over us.

We are to know that His desire toward us is for us to come into a likeness of His character, demonstrating all the fruits of the Holy Spirit. In meekness, we shall cease from striving but learn from the hand of the Lord those things which would bring purity into our lives.

> *'Lord, my heart is not haughty, nor mine eyes lofty: neither do I exercise myself in great matters, or in things too high for me. Surely I have behaved and quieted myself, as a child that is weaned of his mother: my soul is even as a weaned child.'*   (Psalm 131:1–2)

A child who has been weaned is now content to wait for provisions more adult in nature. The rooting of the infant has ceased, and the ability to trust in his mother's provision has been nurtured and comes into maturation. Let us trust in Him that those things which befall us are for our perfection, not our destruction. As the Psalmist says in conclusion, *'Let Israel hope in the Lord from henceforth and forever'*.

'*But we know that, when He shall appear, we shall be like Him; for we shall see Him as He is. And every man that hath this hope in him purifieth himself, even as He is pure.*'
(1 John 3:2–3)

Chapter 13

Blessed Are They That Mourn

One of the greatest enemies to our faith is double-mindedness. This term was used by the Jews of a man who attempted to worship God, but who still loved the creation, who wished to secure both worlds. He would not give up the world here and yet was loath to give up heaven.

To exalt that which is created above the creator is idolatrous. To worship the creature is to exchange the truth for a lie. For this reason, God gave them over and abandoned them to vile and degrading passions.

> *'Put to death, therefore, whatever belongs to your earthly nature: sexual immorality, impurity, lust, evil desires and greed, which is idolatry.'*
>
> (Colossians 3:5 NIV)

A double minded, or *'dipsuchos'*, person is one who is torn between carnal and spiritual things (James 1:8).

In the days of Hosea, the prophet (which can be interpreted as a spiritual type of the last days), we see the Lord blessing Ephraim with great financial prosperity. But the more He poured out His blessing upon them, the more they turned to idolatry. Although with their mouth they worshipped God, their hearts were toward material possessions until they had more faith in their riches than they did in the faithfulness of God, their Provider (Hosea 11:1–2, 7).

If the Laodicean church is dispensational in interpretation, we can see somewhat of a similar spiritual condition prevailing today, as in the days of Hosea the Prophet. The confession of the Laodiceans was that they were rich and increased with goods and wealth and in need of nothing. Yet they were falling short of true spirituality. Thus, in God's eyes, they were poor, blind and lukewarm (Revelation 3:14–18).

The Spirit said to the Laodiceans: *'I know your works'* (*ergon*, meaning specific work). Their works were not of faith and, therefore, they were spiritually naked. The confession of their mouth was different from their actions. Because their works were of the flesh, produced not by faith (works not of faith are sin), they were naked; they were not covered with fine linen, the righteousness of the saints.

They put more credence in their finances (*'I am rich and increased with goods and have need of nothing'*) than they did in their faith towards God.

The word *'laodicea'* means 'to do the will of the people'.

One of the major problems with the church today is subjectiveness; that is, our decisions and actions and behaviour are initiated and nurtured by self-interests rather than by the leading of the Spirit of God.

The will of man, many times, is dramatically opposed to the will of God. This can be seen in the incident from Matthew 16 when Jesus rebukes Peter. When Jesus had asked the disciples whom men said He was, they replied:

> *'Some say that Thou art John the Baptist; some, Elias; and others, Jeremias, or one of the prophets.'*
>
> (Matthew 16:13–20)

When Jesus pressed them for an answer, Peter replied:

> *'Thou are the Christ, the Son of the living God. And Jesus answered and said unto him, "Blessed art thou Simon Barjona; for flesh and blood hath not revealed it*

unto thee, but My Father which is in heaven. And I say also unto thee, that thou art Peter, and upon this rock I will build My church; and the gates of hell shall not prevail against it".'

Then in verse 21,

'Jesus began [clearly] to show His disciples that He must go to Jerusalem and suffer many things at the hands of the elders and high priest and scribes, and be killed, and on the third day be raised from the dead.'

(Matthew 16:21 AMP)

'Then Peter took Him aside to speak to Him privately, and began to reprove and charge Him sharply, saying: "God forbid, Lord! This must never happen to You!"'

(Matthew 16:22)

Jesus' response to Peter's reproof is important, for it reveals the conflict that can exist between our will and the will of God.

But Jesus turned away from Peter and said to him:

Get behind Me, Satan! You are in My way – an offence and a hindrance and a snare to Me; for you are minding what partakes not of the nature and quality of God, but of men.'   (Matthew 16:23)

Israel as a Type

The history of Israel points to the fact that many times the will of the people was in conflict with the will of God. This polarisation is demonstrated clearly in the days of Elijah. His challenge to the people was:

'How long halt ye between two opinions? If the Lord be God, follow Him! But if Baal, then follow him.'

(1 Kings 18:21)

After this challenge, Elijah built an altar in the Name of

the Lord. He made a trench around it, put the wood in order, sacrificed a bullock and laid it on the wood. then he commanded his servants to pour water on the altar until even the trench was filled.

> *'And it came to pass at the time of the offering of the evening sacrifice, that Elijah the prophet came near and said: "Lord God of Abraham, Isaac, and of Israel, let it be known this day that Thou art God in Israel, and that I am Thy servant, and that I have done all these things at Thy Word." '* (1 Kings 18:36)

Works Make Our Faith Alive

Faith by itself, without corresponding works and actions of obedience, is destitute of power, inoperative, and dead.

> *'Was not our forefather, Abraham (shown to be) justified – made acceptable to God – by (his) works when he brought to the altar as an offering his (own) son Isaac? You see that (his) faith was co-operating with his works, and (his) faith was completed and reached its supreme expression (when he implemented it) by (good) works.'* (James 2:21–23 AMP)

> *'For as the human body apart from the spirit is lifeless, so faith apart from (its) works of obedience is also dead.'* (James 2:26 AMP)

To confess with our mouths without corresponding good works of obedience is also to be double-minded.

The Principle of Two Witnesses

For with our lips we made confession, and in our hearts we believe.

> *'For with the heart a person believes (adheres to, trusts in and relies on Christ) and so is justified;(declared*

righteous, acceptable to God) and with the mouth, he
confesses, declares openly and speaks out freely his
faith.' (Romans 10:10 AMP)

To make confession with our mouth without the corresponding witness of the conscience is the condition as
described by John.

'In whatever our hearts in [tormenting] self-accusation
make us feel guilty and condemn us. For [we are in
God's hands]; He is above and greater than our
consciences (our hearts), and He knows (perceives and
understands) everything – nothing is hidden from Him.
And beloved, if our consciences (our hearts) do not
accuse us – if they do not make us feel guilty and
condemn us – we have confidence (complete assurance
and boldness) before God.' (1 John 3:20–21 AMP)

To illustrate the importance of this principle, let me
again share the testimony of the healing of the young lady
from a severe head cold. She had requested prayer as we
were seated around the dinner table.

Later in the meeting, she nudged me and said: 'I was not
healed when you prayed.' My response was to ask her: 'Did
you have faith?' to which she responded: 'How do I know?'
I then asked her to confess the Word: 'By the stripes of
Jesus I am healed.'

After she repeated this confession, I asked her what the
response of her conscience was. She said: 'My conscience
says I am lying, I am not healed.'

I encouraged her to keep on confessing until her heart
was in agreement with her mouth. suddenly she said: 'I am
healed.' And she was!

Unless our mouth and hearts are in agreement, it is
difficult to put our faith into action and produce good
works.

The Development of Character and the Healing of Double Mindedness

Our response to temptation and trials are important in developing endurance, steadfastness, and patience. For the development of the characteristics of endurance and steadfastness and patience means that we will be a people perfectly and fully developed, with no defects and lacking nothing (James 1:2–4).

We then will not waver, hesitate or doubt when we pray.

> *'For the one who wavers (hesitates, doubts) is like the billowing surge out at sea; that is blown hither and thither and tossed by the wind. For truly, let not such a person imagine that he will receive anything (he asks for) from the Lord, (for being as he is) a man of two minds – hesitating, dubious, irresolute – (he is) unstable and unreliable and uncertain about everything (he thinks, feels decides).'* (James 1:6–8 AMP)

God's method of bringing us to repentance, as revealed to the Laodicean church, is to rebuke and chasten. Rebuke (*elegcho*) speaks of verbal reproof and admonition; while chasten (*paideuo*) is to discipline as a loving parent corrects his children.

If we fail to heed His verbal reproofs, He will chasten us with reproofs that cause affliction and suffering. The need for this kind of discipline reveals the deep nature of double-mindedness: a condition of heart that needs to be cleansed; and the established wrong mental attitudes of mind, a condition which needs to be changed and renewed.

The cure for double-mindedness is the cleansing and renewing of our hearts.

James gives us further illumination:

> *'Draw nigh to God, and He will draw nigh to you. Cleanse your hands, ye sinners; and purify your hearts, ye double-minded. Be afflicted, and mourn, and weep;*

let your laughter be turned to mourning, and your joy to heaviness. Humble yourselves in the sight of the Lord.'

(James 4:8–10)

The Amplified Bible expresses this passage as:

'Come close to God and He will come close to you. (Recognise that you are) sinners, get your soiled hands clean; (realize that you have been disloyal) wavering individuals with divided interests, and purify your hearts (of your spiritual adultery). (As you draw near to God) be deeply penitent and grieve, even weep (over your disloyalty). Let your laughter be turned to grief and your mirth to dejection and heartfelt shame (for your sins). Humble yourselves – feeling very insignificant – in the presence of the Lord, and He will exalt you. He will lift you up and make your lives significant.'

This word, *'pentheo'*, denotes to grieve as for the loss of a friend. This same word is also used in Matthew 5:4:

'Blessed are they that mourn; for they shall be comforted.'

A deeper expression of mourning is used by Paul in 2 Corinthians 7:10:

'For godly sorrow worketh repentance to salvation not to be repented of: but the sorrow of the world worketh death.'

The word sorrow, *'lupeo'*, speaks of a grief which is inward and cannot be released of despondency, depression, and anger towards self. It produces the sense of a need to be punished because we feel responsible for our inner attitudes and failures.

This kind of mourning is called godly sorrow and leads to repentance which causes an inner transformation and reconstruction. A reconstruction of the personality takes place in order for the original source of deep despondency or depression to be healed.

Because this kind of profound experience of grief, dejection, and sorrow which is self-contained leads to purification, renewing and cleansing of the heart and mind, those who mourn this way can be congratulated or called blessed (Matthew 5:4).

We will understand why such profound grief is necessary to accomplish change as we study the different words that are used in Scripture for repentance.

In Matthew, we see Judas in deep remorse over his act of betraying innocent blood.

> *'Then Judas, which had betrayed Him, when he saw that He was condemned, repented himself, and brought again the thirty pieces of silver to the chief priests and elders, saying: "I have sinned in that I have betrayed the innocent blood".'*
> (Matthew 27:3–4)

The word repent used in this text is *'metamellomai'*, which implies a change of mind and heart without taking responsibility for the lack of character or weakness which motivated Judas to sell Jesus for thirty pieces of silver. This caused his deep guilt feelings. The Scripture says: *'He repented himself'* (Matthew 27:3).

If we study carefully the Scripture, we will see the basic attitude of character which caused Judas to yield himself to Satan's temptation to betray Christ.

When Mary took a pound of ointment of spikenard and anointed Jesus for His burial, the Word says Judas complained about the waste this had been and suggested that the ointment should have been sold and the proceeds given to the poor.

An interesting observation is made by John:

> *'This he said, not that he cared for the poor; but because he was a thief, and had the bag, and bare what was put therein.'*

In other words, he was a covetous man concerned with the control and power of money! (John 12:3–6).

When Judas repented, he repented himself; that is, he was sorry and felt guilty when he realised that he had betrayed an innocent man. He even tried to make restitution by returning the silver to the High Priest, but he did not take responsibility or accountability for his weakness which had motivated him to commit such an act. Judas, in remorse, hanged himself.

The nation of Israel also provides us with an example of a change of mind and heart without taking responsibility for the sin which caused their unbelief. After being swayed by the negative report of the ten spies and refusing to be obedient to God, they desired to turn back into the wilderness.

Then, when they were worried that impending death would be their portion if they turned back, they decided to enter into the promised land. However, they had missed their chance and were stricken by their enemies.

This seemed to be a paradox, a 'no win situation' for the same reason as Judas many centuries later. Both failed to ask forgiveness for the sins which had caused them to be stiffnecked and hard of heart. They were sorry for the pain caused to themselves and to others, but not truly repentant for the sin itself and its effect on their relationship to God.

The repentance mentioned in 2 Corinthians 7:10 is 'metanoia', which means conviction for guilt, reversal of decision; this expresses not only removal, but remission of the sin which caused the sense of remorse and guilt.

However, true mourning will cause us to feel the need of being punished. As we confess our transgressions, we will receive cleansing of heart. Then the focus of punishment turns from self unto the cross of Jesus.

Romans 8:31–39 reinforces this concept:

> 'What shall we then say to these things? If God be for us, who can be against us? He that spared not His own son,

*but delivered Him up for us all, how shall He not with
Him also freely give us all things?*

*Who shall separate us from the love of Christ? Shall
tribulation, or distress, or persecution, or famine, or
nakedness, or peril, or sword? As it is written, "For thy
sake we are killed all the day long; we are accounted as
sheep for the slaughter". Nay, in all these things, we are
more than conquerors through Him that loved us. For I
am persuaded, that neither death, nor life, nor angels,
nor principalities, nor powers, nor things present, nor
things to come, nor height, nor depth, nor any other
creature, shall be able to separate us from the love of
God, which is in Christ Jesus our Lord.'*

'He that spared not His own Son' – the word 'spared' is
used in various places in Scripture in conjunction with
God's judgment. He spared not the angels that fell; He
spared not the ancient world that sinned; He spared not
the cities of Sodom and Gomorrah.

He spared not His Son, that is, He fully punished His
Son for our sins.

*'He was wounded for our transgressions. He was bruised
for our iniquities, the chastisement of our peace was
upon Him and with His stripes we are healed.'*

(Isaiah 53:5)

In verse 10 of the same chapter the Amplified version
gives us a graphic description of the Father, causing His
son to be sick with our sins.

*'Yet it was the will of the Lord to bruise Him; He has
put Him to grief and made Him sick. When You and He
make Him an offering for sin (and He has risen from the
dead, in time to come), He shall see His spiritual
offspring. He shall prolong His days, and the will and
pleasure of the Lord shall prosper in His hand.*

*He shall see the fruit of the travail of His soul and be
satisfied; by His knowledge of Himself (which He*

possesses and imparts to others) shall My (uncompromisingly) righteous One, My Servant, justify and make many righteous – upright and in right standing with God; for He shall bear their iniquities and their guilt (with the consequences, says the Lord).'

As we take responsibility for the inner weaknesses of our nature, we will grieve or feel depressed because we know that we have failed to measure up to God's standard of righteousness.

As we confess these failings and shortcomings, the focus of punishment is taken off self and placed upon Jesus our substitute. This not only sets us free from self-condemnation, but the act of repentance grants us the deeper inner transformation of soul.

Our mourning is then turned to joy as we experience the comfort of the Holy Spirit who gives us beauty for ashes, the oil of joy for mourning, the garment of praise for the spirit of heaviness (Isaiah 61:3).

Congratulations then to those who mourn, for *'they shall be comforted.'*

Chapter 14

The Yoke is Broken by the Anointing

As we continue our study in the development of a Christ-like nature, we need to take note of the differences between our humanity and the humanity of Jesus. We have been predestined to be conformed into the image of the son of God, who is the first born from amongst the dead.

> 'For those God foreknew, He also predestined to be conformed to the likeness of His Son, that He might be the firstborn among many brothers.'
>
> (Romans 8:29 NIV)

The Calling of Sonship

The Greek word, *'teknon'*, or child is related to *'tikto'*, to beget or bear. It is used both in the natural and the figurative senses, giving prominence to the fact of birth.

'Huios', the word son, is used in the title the Son of God, and primarily signifies the relationship of offspring to parent and not simply the birth, as indicated by *'teknon'*.

The difference between believers as children of God, *'teknon'*, and as sons, *'huios'*, is brought out in Romans 8:14–18:

> 'For as many as are led by the Spirit of God, they are the sons of God. For ye have not received the spirit of bondage again to fear; but ye have received the Spirit of

adoption, whereby we cry, Abba Father. The Spirit itself beareth witness with our spirit, that we are the children of God: and if children, then heirs; heirs of God, and joint-heirs with Christ; if so be that we suffer with Him, that we may be also glorified together. For I reckon that the sufferings of this present time are not worthy to be compared with the glory which shall be revealed in us.'

'Tekna' refers to those who are born of God, while *'huios'* refers to those who show maturity; who are acting as sons. When referring to the basic relationship as a born-again child of God, it is expressed as *'tekna'*.

> *'The Spirit itself bears witness with our spirit, that we are the children of God.'* (Romans 8:16)

The word 'children' in this reference is *'tekna'* and is used for a new believer.

When *'huios'* is used, it give evidence of the dignity of our relationship and likeness to God's character. An example is used in 1 John 1:3, 7:

> *'That which we have seen and heard declare we unto you, that ye also may have fellowship with us: and truly our fellowship is with the Father, and with His Son Jesus Christ. But if we walk in the light, as He is in the light, we have fellowship one with another, and the blood of Jesus Christ His Son cleanseth us from all sin.'*

The expression Son of God, *'huios theos'*, is used of Jesus to manifest His relationship with the Father, or in the expression of His character. The Lord Jesus is never called *'teknon theou'*, a child of God, as believers are.

Acts 13:33 says:

> *'God hath fulfilled the same unto us their children, in that He hath raised up Jesus again; as it is also written in the second Psalm, Thou art My Son, this day have I begotten Thee.'*

Psalm 2:7 says:

> *'I will declare the decree: the Lord hath said unto Me, Thou art My Son; this day have I begotten Thee.'*

The birth of Christ in His humanity and His sinless conformity to the Father's character is expressed not with *'teknon'* but with *'huios'*, speaking of a son in a genuine sense.

We mention the difference between the birth of Christ in His humanity and our rebirth in the spirit because of the traditional teaching of many fundamental evangelicals: that when we are reborn of the spirit, we are perfect; therefore, there is no need of a second work of grace to be accomplished within that will bring us from *'teknon'*, new believers or new sons, unto *'huios'*, used in reference to those who show maturity and act as sons.

> *'Praise be to the God and Father of our Lord Jesus Christ! In His great mercy, He has given us new birth into a living hope through the resurrection of Jesus Christ from the dead.'* (1 Peter 1:3 NIV)

The Calling to Glory and Virtue

Furthermore, our calling as Christians is to glory and virtue.

> *'According as His divine power hath given unto us all things that pertain unto life and godliness, through the knowledge of Him that hath called us to glory and virtue.'* (2 Peter 1:3)

The word glory, or *'doxa'*, means to exhibit character. Not the outward glorious appearance which would attract attention to the person or thing itself: but that glory shown from within. It is the manifesting of acts of honour. The word 'virtue' is *'arete'*, or moral excellence, and moral goodness as that which gives man his worth.

173

It is only through God's generosity in giving us the gift of His Son, and His exceeding great and precious promises that we inherit the divine nature.

Thus, it will be only as we yield personal rights to those things which might be of natural gain to us, and have the mind of Christ, that we then escape from intentional sin. We are no longer living to please ourselves and the world, but to please God and do what God wills.

> *Forasmuch, then as Christ hath suffered for us in the flesh; arm yourselves likewise with the same mind: for he that hath suffered in the flesh hath ceased from sin; that he no longer should live the rest of his time in the flesh to the lusts of men, but to the will of God.'*
>
> (1 Peter 4:1)

As we are able to count as loss those natural benefits of life, we will desire a more close and intimate fellowship with the Lord.

The Calling to the Preciousness of the Word

As we become more deeply acquainted with and acquire more knowledge of the Lord Jesus, we will be able to add to our faith Christian virtue. It is as the Word becomes precious to us that we will have the inner motivation to lay aside our will in order to be obedient to His will.

> *'For this very reason, make every effort to add to your faith, goodness; and to goodness; knowledge; and to knowledge, self-control; and to self-control, perseverance; and to perseverance, godliness; and to godliness, brotherly kindness; and to brotherly kindness, love.'*
>
> (2 Peter 1:4–7 NIV)

The word 'precious' has a special spiritual meaning for us. Remember in Samuel's time: *'The Word was precious in those days'*.

*'The boy Samuel ministered before the Lord under Eli.
In those days, the word of the Lord was rare; there were
not many visions.'* (Samuel 3:1 NIV)

Jesus describes seeking the Kingdom of Heaven as:

*'Like unto treasure hid in a field; the which when a man
hath found he hideth, and for joy thereat goeth and sell-
eth all that he hath, and buyeth that field.'*

(Matthew 13:44)

The Kingdom of Heaven is:

*'Like unto a merchantman, seeking goodly pearls: who,
when he had found one pearl of great price, went and
sold all that he had, and bought it.'*

(Matthew 13:44–46)

As we internalize the Word, we possess inner power or
motivation to become obedient to it. As we meditate upon
it, our minds are renewed and our inner personality and
character is transformed into the likeness of His image.

*'Do not conform any longer to the pattern of this world,
but be transformed by the renewing of your mind. Then
you will be able to test and approve what God's will is –
His good, pleasing and perfect will.'*

(Romans 12:2 NIV)

*'You were taught, with regard to your former way of
life, to put off your old self, which is being corrupted by
its deceitful desires; to be made new in the attitude of
your minds; and to put on the new self, created to be
like God in true righteousness and holiness.'*

(Ephesians 4:22–24 NIV)

We are, by giving all diligence, to add to our faith virtue;
and to virtue, knowledge; and to knowledge, temperance;
and to temperance, patience; and to patience, godliness;

and to godliness, brotherly kindness; and to brotherly kindness, charity.

We are then told that if these things are in us and abound, we will never be barren.

To be barren, or *'argos'*, means to be inactive, lazy or useless. Nor will we be unfruitful in the knowledge, *'epignosis'*, or our Lord Jesus Christ. *'Epignosis'*, is to become fully acquainted with our Lord Jesus Christ.

Peter tells us if we fail to develop these Christian virtues, then we are blind (opaque, or discoloured) and have forgotten that we have been purged from our old sins. The word purge is *'katharismos'*, which means a working off, absolution, or expiration of our former sins.

As we develop in character, our psychological and emotional responses to the sins, mistakes, and the traumas of the past are healed.

As we experience freedom from the repercussions of sin, the turbulence, guilt, and remorse, we gain total liberty to express the fruit of our new nature.

Let us look at three aspects of a lack of character from the parable of the sower in Matthew 13:3–6:

> *'And He spake many things unto them in parables, saying: "Behold, a sower went forth to sow; and when he sowed, some seeds fell by the way side and the fowls came and devoured them up: some fell upon stony places, where they had not much earth: and forthwith they sprung up, because they had no deepness of earth: and when the sun was up, they were scorched; and because they had no root, they withered away. And some fell among thorns; and the thorns sprung up, and choked them." '*

Firstly, when Jesus later interpreted this parable to His disciples, He said: 'The seed sown on the pathway was the person, who, upon hearing the word of the Kingdom, could not grasp or comprehend it: The evil one came and snatched away what was sown in the heart.'

Similarly, the seed sown among the rocks represents those who hear the message without hesitation, accepting it joyfully. However, they have no real root or depth of character, and when affliction or persecution arises because of the Word, they are offended (*skandalizo*). That is, they stumble and are enticed to sin. Becoming apostate, they fall away.

Lastly, the seed sown among thorns refers to those who hear the Word, but allow the cares of the world and the pleasures and delight and deceitfulness of riches choke and suffocate the Word. They yield no fruit.

Inner Fatness

To develop the character of Christ (which is referred to as the fruit of the Spirit in Galatians 5:22–23) is to be free, for against such there is no law to hold us into bondage.

The prophet Isaiah refers to the development of inner Christlikeness as the anointing, and it is this anointing which breaks the yoke of oppression. For the prophet said: *'The yoke shall be broken by the anointing'.*

> *'His burden shall be taken away from off thy shoulder, and His yoke from off thy neck, and the yoke shall be destroyed because of the anointing.'*   (Isaiah 10:27)

The word 'anointing' is used in different forms in the Bible; but in this text it means 'inner fatness'. The symbolism is that of fitting a yoke on a young bullock. As the bullock grows and the yoke is not changed, the growth of the bullock's neck will burst asunder the yoke.

This prophecy was given in relationship to the nation of Assyria, which was being used by God to chasten Israel for her disobedience. The yoke of oppression which had been brought upon Israel would be broken through much fatness, or inner spiritual growth.

Summary

God's method of bringing us to inner spiritual growth is through our responses to the reproofs of life. We are to love our enemies, bless those that curse us, pray for those who despitefully use us, do good to those who hate us.

> *'But I tell you: Love your enemies and pray for those who persecute you!'* (Matthew 5:44)

Reproofs come to us in many ways. The Word has several examples of responses to these reproofs of life.

Firstly, it could be that our expectations of others are cut off.

John the Baptist was a man of deep integrity and holiness, a prophet who saw things only in black or white. He was the forerunner of Christ, and at the River Jordan declared Jesus to be the Lamb of God, who was to take away the sins of the world.

> *'The next day, John was there again, with two of his disciples.'* (John 1:34–36 NIV)

After Jesus began His public ministries, He was branded a winebibber and glutton, one who sat and ate with the publicans and sinners. This offended John, for Jesus was not measuring up to John's ideal of righteousness.

From prison, he sent two disciples to ask: *'Are You the one who was to come, or should we expect someone else?'*

Jesus, after healing the sick, turned around and said to the emissaries:

> *'Go back and report to John what you have seen and heard: The blind receive sight, the lame walk, those who have leprosy are cured, the deaf hear, the dead are raised, and the good news is preached to the poor.'*
>
> (Luke 7:22–22 NIV)

In the context of our Scripture, Jesus then said:

> *'And blessed is he, whosoever shall not be offended in me.'* (Luke 7:23 KJV)

Secondly, our own personal weaknesses and failings can be reproofs.

David considered the men of the world and his enemies to be instruments in the hand of Saul to bring reproof and correction to him.

> *'He rescued me from my powerful enemy, from my foes, who were too strong for me.'* (Psalm 18:17 NIV)

When he fled Jerusalem from his son, Absalom, Shimei cursed David and threw dust and stones at him. His response shows true humiliation and brokenness.

> *'...so let him curse, because he hath said unto him, curse David ... and that the Lord will requite me good for his cursing this day.'* (2 Samuel: 16:10, 12)

As we begin to understand God's method of transformation, we will be as Paul: able, therefore, to say:

> *'And He said unto me: "My grace is sufficient for thee; for My strength is made perfect in weakness". Most gladly therefore will I rather glory in my infirmities, that the power of Christ may rest upon me. Therefore, I take pleasure in infirmities, in reproaches, in necessities, in persecutions, in distresses for Christ's sake: for when I am weak, then am I strong.'* (2 Corinthians 12:9–10)

Paul was able to turn each stumbling block into a stepping stone.

As we, too, respond to the reproofs of life, we will be able to turn all things to our good because we love God and are called according to His purpose.

> *'And we know that in all things God works for the good of those who love Him, who have been called according to His purpose.'* (Romans 8:28 NIV)

179

SECTION D:

Psychology of Man

Chapter 15

Introduction to the Psychology of Man

Psychology is the science which deals with the mind and mental processes, feelings, and desires. The science of human and animal behaviour, it has been stated, is truly a product of the nineteenth and twentieth centuries.

Psychology had its primary origin in philosophy. There is no denying that Plato, Aristotle, and other early scholars speculated our problems associated with the basic nature of man.

It is only in the last hundred years that psychologists have defined their subject matter and established its foundations.

Although there are over two hundred different psychological disciplines, there are four major paradigms:

1. **Psychoanalytic paradigm**: The focus on the analysis of the psyche. Major adherents: Sigmund Freud, Carl Jung.
2. **Sociocultural paradigm**: The focus on social and cultural factors influencing the personality. Major adherents: Alfred Adler, Karen Homey, Erik Erikson.
3. **Existential paradigm**: The humanistic paradigm with the focus on problems of existence. Major adherents: Carl Rogers, George Kelly, Abraham Moslow.
4. **Learning paradigm**: The focus on the learning process which related to personality disorders. Major adherents: B.F. Skinner, John Dollard, Neal Miller.

Most psychological disciplines are based on humanistic concepts: namely, that man is innately good and, placed in the right environmental circumstances, has the self motivation and power of self-recovery.

We must not confuse pastoral counselling with humanistic psychology and psychiatric care.

Although relatively new in its modern concept, *'cura animarium'* or the care of the soul, is as old as the believing community itself.

Clebsch (1974)[1] has identified four pastoral care functions from the pages of church history. They are:

1. **Healing**: a pastoral function that aims to bring or restore wholeness to the person.
2. **Sustaining**: helping a hurting person to endure and to transcend the circumstances by seeing those circumstances through a godly perspective and making a Christlike response to them.
3. **Guiding**: assisting a confused and perplexed person to make or to choose a godly solution to his problem.
4. **Reconciliation**: seeking to re-establish broken relationships, either between man and fellow man; or between man and God.

We would like to add a further function to those described by Clebsch and Jackle, and that is:

5. **Redeeming the time**: that is, to regain, through the redemptive power of the cross, lost opportunities. Each one of our lives is an epistle, known and read of all men. Through the redemptive power of Christ, expedited through forgiveness, let us rewrite the pages of our life history where we have sinned or responded negatively to the reproofs of life.

The Restoration of Many Generations

The Shepherds of Israel had failed in four basic pastoral areas. The following indictment was issued against them for their manipulation and use of the flock for their own gain:

> *'The diseased and weak you have not strengthened, the sick you have not healed, the hurt and crippled you have not bandaged, those gone astray you have not brought back, the lost you have not sought to find; but with force and hardhearted harshness you have ruled them.'*

(Ezekiel 34:4 AMP)

A beautiful promise was given to the sheep:

> *'For thus saith the Lord God: Behold, I myself, will search for my sheep and will seek them out.'*

(Ezekiel 34:11)

A deeper insight is given to us to the fulfilment of this promise through Zechariah 13:1:

> *'In that day there shall be a fountain opened to the house of David and to the inhabitants of Jerusalem for sin and for uncleanness.'*

We know the fountain which was opened was the Lord Jesus, shedding His precious blood to cleanse sin and uncleanness.

The word, 'uncleanness', means hurts, bruises, and wounds – the effects of sin. Jesus not only cleanses from all unrighteousness, but cleanses us from the effects and repercussions of sin. Not only of our own personal sins, but He heals those who are the victims of sin.

The Identity Generation

Marshal McLuhan stated:

> 'This generation, from Tokyo to Paris to Columbia, youth mindlessly acts out its identity quest in the theatre of the streets, searching not for goals, but for roles, striving for an identity that eludes them.'

This generation has been called the identity society.

Many children have been raised in a loveless environment which produces a failure complex within. Drugs, alcohol, sex, violence, and rebellion are but symptomatic of the deep inner infantile anger which is the root of self-rejection.

A girl receives her self-esteem from her father. In turn, a mother who shows little support of her son's capabilities can produce a lack of self-respect.

Parents who abuse their children are themselves often victims of childhood mistreatment. Since they do not love themselves, it becomes impossible to truly love others; thus, the vicious cycle continues from generation to generation.

> *'The wheel of birth (the cycle of man's nature), being itself ignited by hell.'* (James 3:6 AMP)

Our Introduction to the Ministry of Inner Healing

Our family came to the Lord through miracles of physical healing. It was our testimony of these miracles that led us to yet another area of the Lord's compassionate restoration.

At the time, I was pastoring an Assemblies of God Church in Central Western New South Wales, Australia. While prayerfully seeking a spiritual awakening for the area, the Lord spoke to my spirit and said He was going to bring renewal through the local Anglican Diocese.

I was shocked. We had had no association with the Anglicans in our community whatsoever.

It took two years of heart preparation for the Lord to be able to use me for His purpose.

After this time, the Lord instructed me, during prayer, to visit the local Anglican priest and testify to him of our experience of finding Christ through physical healings in our immediate family.

Much to my amazement, when I knocked on the door of

the church and introduced myself, explaining why I had come, the vicar was very receptive. He asked me to share in a Bible study he was conducting on the subject of divine healing.

As a result of the first meeting in his church, in which a man was miraculously healed, a great move of the Holy Spirit started in that parish. Many found Christ in new dimensions of salvation and the Baptism of the Holy Spirit.

Many years later, I found out how gracious the Lord had been to my Anglican brother. The very morning I had been led by the Holy Spirit to visit him and testify of Christ's healing power, he had written a letter of resignation to his bishop. He had determined to leave the ministry because he was not seeing the signs and wonders as recorded in the Book of Acts.

As a result of our early association, we established a healing service in the Anglican Church where countless scores of people attended for healing.

One day, my priest-friend's wife called and requested counsel. In her words, she had sought the reality of Christ's presence through the sacraments of the church, and then evangelically by responding to altar calls to receive Christ as her personal Saviour. All to no avail. She still could not find tranquillity of heart or peace of mind.

As we prayed together, I was prompted of the Lord to inquire as to what her reaction had been to the death of her first-born child. Her response was: 'I accepted it as the will of God.'

I then responded, 'I feel you have repressed your grief by denial, and this has become a wall between you and the Lord.' I asked her to bring to remembrance the time when the doctor had entered the room and told her of her baby's death (the child had died two hours after birth). As she did this, she confessed her feelings of grief to the Lord and instantly went through a catharsis; (literally, the Greek word for cleanse).

Pent-up grief was released with deep agonizing cries.

Suddenly, a beautiful tranquillity and peace settled within her spirit and was reflected on her face.

Her husband later testified that there was no need to verbalize the healing upon returning home as he saw it written all over her face.

A few days after that encounter in counselling, she said to the Lord, 'You promised to fill me with your Holy Spirit.' Immediately, she began to speak gently in an unknown tongue, as the Spirit gave her utterance.

Since that initial experience with healing of the memories, the Lord has allowed us to minister healing to thousands of wounded Christians who, through some trauma of life, had been bruised mentally and emotionally.

Many of us still hold, framed in our minds, experiences and reactions which hinder the fruit of the Spirit from being fully manifested in our lives. Love, joy, peace, faith, etc., are diminished by our painful imaginations or memories.

We understand from our study of Scripture the importance of casting down these imaginations and high things which exalt themselves above the knowledge of God (2 Corinthians 10:4–5).

The word 'imagination' is *'logismos'* and means those considerations and intentions of the mind which are hostile to the Gospel and would thus prevent us from knowing and receiving our full inheritance and restoration in Christ.

The Ministry of Inner Healing

Inner healing has been described as a contemporary form of spiritual healing. Its advocates define it as the process wherein the Holy Spirit restores health to the deepest aspects of life by dealing with the root causes of hurts and pains. Basically, it involves a twofold procedure in which:

1. The power of evil is broken and the heritage of wholeness that belongs to Christians is restored.
2. Memories of the past are healed by prayer.

This belief has been severely criticized by those who are fundamentalistic in theology. However, I feel the main problem is a confusion of biblical truth with methodology and technique.

Let us look at the Scripture and determine the biblical validity of inner healing from the two approaches given above.

1. *The power of evil is broken*

Paul, when testifying to King Agrippa, tells of his encounter with the Lord on the road to Damascus.

> *'And I said: "Who art Thou, Lord?"*
>
> *And He said: "I am Jesus whom thou persecutest. But rise, and stand upon thy feet: for I have appeared unto thee for this purpose, to make thee a minister and a witness both of these things which thou hast seen, and of those things in the which I will appear unto thee; delivering thee from the people, and from the Gentiles, unto whom now I send thee, to open their eyes and to turn them from darkness to light, and from the power of Satan unto God, that they may receive forgiveness of sins, and inheritance among them which are sanctified by faith that is in me."'* (Acts 26:14–18)

Here, Paul related his commission: to open their eyes from darkness to light, to turn them from the power of Satan unto the power of God, to receive forgiveness and an inheritance sanctified by faith.

In Colossians 1:12–14, Paul again relates the power of the Gospel:

> *'Giving thanks unto the Father, which hath made us meet to be partakers of the inheritance of the saints in light; who hath delivered us from the power of darkness, and hath translated us into the kingdom of His dear Son: in whom we have redemption through His blood, even the forgiveness of sins.'*

The Father hath delivered us (*rhuomai*). This word denotes to draw with force and violence, to drag, to pull, meaning to deliver or to draw out of danger or calamity and to liberate from the power of darkness. The word darkness is (*skotos*) meaning spiritual darkness. This implies ignorance or error, sin, and misery; and the place of infernal spirits.

To be loosed from Satan and this place of darkness is the right of each child of God.

When Jesus healed the woman who was bowed over eighteen years with a spirit of infirmity, He responded when criticized:

> '*Should not this daughter of Abraham be loosed from this infirmity which Satan has bound her, lo, these eighteen years?*' (Luke 13:16)

In Ephesians the Word describes us thus:

> '*. . . aliens from the Commonwealth of Israel, and strangers from the covenants of promises, having no hope and without God in the world.*'

Galatians 3:13–14 tells us:

> '*Christ hath redeemed us from the curse of the Law, being made a curse for us: for it is written, "Cursed is everyone that hangeth on a tree", that the blessing of Abraham might come on the Gentiles, through Jesus Christ; that we might receive the promise of the Spirit through faith.*'

Deliverance from unclean spirits is called by Jesus the children's bread (Mark 7:27).

> '*. . . And from the days of John the Baptist until the present time the kingdom of heaven has endured violent assault, and violent men seize it by force [as a precious*

> *prize] – a share in the heavenly kingdom is sought for with most ardent zeal and intense exertion.'*
>
> (Matthew 11:12 AMP)

> *'. . . But if I drive out demons by the Spirit of God, then the kingdom of God has come upon you.'*
>
> (Matthew 12:28 NIV)

2. The healing of memories

Possibly the first reference to God's working in this unique way is portrayed in Genesis 41:50–52:

> *'And unto Joseph were born two sons before the years of famine came, which Asenath the daughter of Poti-pherah, priest of On, bare unto him. And Joseph called the name of the firstborn Manasseh: for God, said he, hath made me forget all my toil, and all my father's house. And the name of the second called he Ephraim: for God hath caused me to be fruitful in the land of my affliction.'*

Now, let us look closely at verse 51:

> *'And Joseph called the name of the firstborn Manasseh: For God, saith he, hath made me forget all my toil, and all my father's house.'*

Joseph's reaction to the rejection by his brothers, and his falsely caused imprisonment, is described in Psalm 105:17–19:

> *'He sent a man before them, even Joseph, who was sold for a servant. His feet they hurt with fetters, he was laid in chains of iron and his soul entered into the iron; until his word (to his cruel brothers) came true, the word of the Lord tried and tested him.'* (AMP)

There are two major Hebrew words for the word 'forget': *'shakeach'*, which means to be oblivious of, from want of memory; and *'nashah'*, which means to remit or to remove. The word in our text is the word *'nashah'*, to remit.

The Greek word for remit is *'aphiemi'*. Sins are remitted as we ask for forgiveness or make confession which cleanses the unrighteousness.

Association that Reawakens the Conscience

Perhaps Peter's denial of Christ is a good biblical example of someone being remorseful over past memories.

> *'Then began he to curse and to swear, saying, I know not the man. And immediately the cock crew. And Peter remembered the word of Jesus, which said unto him, "Before the cock crows, thou shalt deny me thrice." And he went out and wept bitterly.'*

(Matthew 26: 74, 75)

The 'cock crow' is what is termed psychologically as association. Association is the theory used to explain complex mental processes, such as learning and memory, in terms of associative links formed between one idea and another.

Associative links are established when two individual sensations are experienced together and, as a result, when one of them is later experienced, the other is called for. For example, rain and wetness are experienced together: therefore, when one thinks of rain, wetness is also thought of.

Peter, upon hearing the rooster crow, remembered the words of Jesus, *'Verily I say unto thee, that this night before the cock crows thou shalt deny me thrice.'* An associative link was formed, the painful memory recalled, and thus, Peter *'went out and wept bitterly.'*

Summary

We have touched on a number of different subjects in this introduction. To understand the full context of inner healing, we need to explore the formation of the personality. All of these topics mentioned will be covered in detail in the following lessons. This promises to be one of the most powerful expositions in understanding truly the depth of the ministry of the Holy Spirit to our innermost being.

Even as *'My frame was not hidden from You, when I was being formed in secret and intricately and curiously wrought (as if embroidered with various colours) in the depths of the earth'* (Psalm 139:15 AMP); knowing us in the most intimate details so does He long to have us fully healed from the wounds and scars of sin. His promise to us is,

> *'as the Son has given life, even so does He give life abundantly.'* (John 10:10b)

> *'And whom the Son has set free, he has set free indeed!'* (John 8:36)

Reference

1. Clebsch, W. (1974). *Christianity in European History*. Oxford University Press

Chapter 16

Structure of Basic Personality

The Psychological Concept

The term 'personality' has its etymological and conceptual origin in the Latin infinitive '*personare*', which referred to the mouthpiece or hole in a mask through which an actor spoke. The classical Latin term '*persona*' began as a theatrical term describing the mask the actor wore in the role he played.

Eventually the meaning of persona spanned a continuum ranging from surface external to the deep identity of the individual. The English term 'personality' spans the same range.

Legend has it that the theatrical mask was invented by a vain actor who designed it to cover up his squinting. When a play was performed, it was common practice for one actor to play several different roles which were designated by different masks, thus persona took on the idea of presenting a fãcade, or acting a role which might belie one's inner thoughts or feelings.

Jung's analytic theory made a distinction between ego and persona. He stated that the ego was the centre of consciousness which was composed of perceptions, feelings, thoughts and memories.

The ego provided for the basis of the individual's identity and continuity while persona was the mask the person adopted as a reaction to social convention. Persona thus reflected the public behaviourism accepted by society and roles demanded in society.

Persona presents humans as social animals. If ego identified too strongly with persona, one's true feelings or inner nature became a mere reflection of society instead of an autonomous identity.

Many sociological approaches to personality have taken the view whereby personality represents an individual's 'social-stimulus value'. Yet behind each of the actors' masks stood a person, an individual with individual thoughts and feelings beyond those demanded by the role.

It was possible that the actors personal thoughts and feelings might affect how the role was played. This belief developed into an approach viewing the personality as something internal, underlying, or latent to actual behaviour.

This absence of the drama might question whether the words expressed by the actor, and their mode of expression, indicated the role demands or the actor's inward inclinations. This mode of thought remains a source of variation in the definition of personality (Stagner, 1974).

The Soul of Man: A Biblical Perspective

As we have stated in our introduction to the study on the Psychology of Man, psychology is the study of the soul of man, or the reaction between emotions and mind.

If we do not have an understanding of the formation and development of man's nature and character, it will be difficult for us to relate all sections of Scripture to our spiritual growth, maturity, and healing.

Man is God's unique creation, created out of the dust of the earth, after the image and likeness of God Himself. He then breathed into him the breath of life and man became a living soul.

God's ultimate intention was to have an extended family

of many sons ruling and reigning with Him throughout the eternal ages.

Man was given the power of pro-creation to reproduce after his kind, for God said to Adam, *'Be fruitful and multiply'* (Genesis 1:22–28).

In the Old Testament, man is considered to be a dichotomy: an inward and external man. Thus, the word soul and spirit are sometimes used interchangeably.

In the New Testament, we see soul and spirit more clearly defined.

> *'For the Word of God is quick, and powerful and sharper than any two-edged sword, piercing even to the dividing asunder of soul and spirit, and of the joints and marrow, and is a discerner of the thoughts and intents of the heart.'*   (Hebrews 4:12)

Peter, in his Epistle, called the spirit the hidden man of the heart; while Jesus, when speaking of the infilling of the Holy spirit, said:

> *'Out from His innermost being springs and rivers of living water shall flow.'*   (John 7:38)

Paul exhorts the Christians in 1 Thessalonians 5:23 to be wholly sanctified in spirit, soul and body.

> *'And the very God of peace sanctify you wholly; and I pray God your whole spirit, soul and body be preserved blameless unto the coming of our Lord Jesus Christ.'*

It is the spirit that makes man uniquely different from all the creation of God and elevates man above the animal kingdom.

The Conscience: The Inner Eye

The psychoanalytical term for the ethical component, the conscience, is called the super ego. According to Freudian theory, the super ego's function is to provide the standards by which the ego operates. Freud believed that this was a split-off portion of the ego with its basic organization taking place gradually and unconsciously during the first five years of life, arising out of the demands and the intro-projections of parental prohibitions and input.

Other theorists believe that the ego-ideal, with its positive aspirations, stems primarily from the identification of a loving, caring mother, while the conscience, with its prohibitions, stems primarily from the feared father and anxiety over castration.

They further assume that the super-ego is not wholly formed during early childhood but continues to develop, largely on a sub-conscious level, as we communicate on a personal, social level with our social, cultural group.

When the super-ego is violated or is too severe and rigid, the individual becomes inhibited, anxious, and unhappy. If it is too permissive, it generally leads to immature, irresponsible behaviour and an egocentric personality.

J. Finis Dake,[1] in his Bible commentary, defines the conscience as the inner eye and judge of our thoughts, actions and affections, either condoning or condemning them.

All psychological theorists agree that there is a part of man's personality which exercises moral judgment over thoughts, feelings and actions.

We need, therefore, to study very carefully from the Word of God the development of the conscience and its effect upon the human personality.

The Pauline Psychology of the Conscience

There is no equivalent in the Hebrew language of the Greek word *'suneidesis'*, or conscience.

Paul speaks of his own conscience, the conscience of Christians and the conscience of the Gentiles. The conscience is the faculty of moral judgment. The word *'suneidesis'* means knowledge shared with one's self. It is man's consciousness of his conduct as his own and his judgment as to whether it is right or wrong.

Paul said: *'I am not aware of anything against myself.'* He meant that his conscience was clean, it did not condemn him of having done anything wrong. However, he goes on to say, *'But I am not thereby acquitted.'*

George Eldon Ladd,[2] in *A Theology of the New Testament*, states:

> 'The conscience, at best is, therefore, a guide to relative value. One could have a clear conscience, and yet be guilty of wrong in the sight of God.'

Bible teachers agree that the conscience has a vital role in our walk in faith and that a clear conscience is paralleled to faith. It affects our relationship with God, and is essential for spiritual, emotional, and physical wellbeing.

For this reason, the Apostle Paul exercised great discipline over his body, mortifying and deadening carnal affections, bodily appetites and worldly desires, endeavouring in all respects to have a clear conscience void of offence toward God and man. He walked in 'humility of mind' toward his brethren lest he should cause a weaker brother to stumble and sear his conscience, therefore sinning against Christ.

To understand the principles relating to a clear conscience, it is important to have a comprehension of how the conscience is developed.

It would appear from Scripture that all men have a basic conscience which is the result of the universal law of God being written in their hearts.

This God-inspired conscience makes men inexcusable in God's sight, for God's holy wrath and indignation are revealed from heaven against all ungodliness and unrighteousness of men, who in their wickedness repress and hinder the truth and make it inoperative.

For that which is known about God is evident to them and made plain to them in their inner conscience, because

God Himself has shown it unto them, for God's invisible nature and attributes, His eternal power and divinity are discernible in and through the things that have been made.

It would appear that the 'God-inspired conscience' comes from a knowledge of God which is revealed to us either through 'the things that have been made' and/or through personal knowledge of God's moral character (gleaned through personal fellowship) with Him or by a study of the revealed character of God – either through the personality of Christ or the law of God).

A violation of man's 'God-inspired conscience' brings a conviction of sin which leads to true godly repentance, and a right standing with God through faith.

The negative conscience is a direct result of man's disobedience toward God.

In the original, primal temptation, Satan said:

> ' "*Ye shall not surely die for God doth know that the day you eat thereof then your eyes shall be opened and ye shall be as gods knowing good and evil.*" *After man's disobedient act, God said, "Man now has become as one of us, knowing the difference between good and evil."* '
>
> (Genesis 3:5, 22)

Man, then, through his self or moral conscience, had become a 'Law unto self'. Paul speaks of this by saying:

> '*When the Gentiles, who have not the divine law do instinctively what the Law requires, they are a law unto themselves, since they do not have the Law. They show that the essential requirements of the law are written in their hearts and are operating there, with which their conscience (sense of right and wrong) also bears witness: and their (moral) decisions, their arguments of reason, their condemning or approving thoughts will accuse or perhaps defend and excuse them.*'
>
> (Romans 2:14–15 AMP)

Man, who is ruled by his negative, self-moral conscience, then becomes a law unto himself, being led by conscience instead of the Holy Spirit.

The conscience is then the linking facility between the *'psuche'* (soul) and the *'pneuma'* (spirit) giving man a primal awareness of God and is the restraining influence that warns him of evil, becoming the motivator for him to do good.

The innate quest for wisdom and truth originates in this instinct.

It is when the conscience is smothered by the flame of sensual desire and greed that the subtle voice of sin stills the voice of the conscience. This becomes a 'seared conscience'.

The seared conscience then becomes fertile ground for deviation from universal truth. Repressed guilt 'feelings' lead to many neurotic, psychotic, and psychosomatic conditions.

It is when man become void of conscience, or reprobate, that he degenerates and falls as low as the animal kingdom. The driving lust for carnal gratification and earthly goods kills the thirst for the living waters of life, and man becomes unworthy of the Creator who created him.

God's Transforming Power through Confession – Release from Guilt

A very vital part of the spirit of man is his conscience. Only when our consciences (our hearts) do not accuse us – in that they do not make us feel guilty and condemn us – do we have complete boldness and assurance toward God.

A clear conscience is parallel to faith and affects our relationship towards man and God. It is essential for spiritual, emotional and physical freedom. It is only when our consciences (our hearts), do not accuse us – in that they do not make us feel guilty and condemn us – that we have complete boldness and assurance toward God.

It is when the conscience is violated that we feel guilt. Because the conscience is developed through the law of God written on our heart together with our social, cultural, and religious upbringing and environment, there are different types of resultant guilt created through violation. These each need a different approach and insight when attempting to obtain release.

These different types of guilt can be classified as follows:
1. Godly conviction
2. False guilt
3. Sub-conscious guilt

Sub-conscious guilt is caused by the removal of the incident from conscious thought patterns by trauma, rationalization, blame-shifting, shock, drugs or hypno-therapy.

A person can remove guilt from the conscious mind by the above methods, but the guilt will remain in the sub-conscious area, causing fear, anxiety, depression, anger. Many times, because of the emotional energy which is created, it will manifest itself through psychosomatic illnesses or abnormal behavioural traits.

The deadening, or searing, of the conscience leads men to become reprobate. That state will cause men to give themselves over to all manner of uncleanness while others become spiritual shipwrecks.

A mature Christian (who is able to take in the meat of the Word of God) is one whose senses and mental faculties are trained by practice or able to discriminate and distinguish between what is morally good and noble and what is evil and contrary, either to divine or to human law.

Our Responses Come from the Conscience

Under pressure we are prone to respond to life's situations from our conscience. This is amplified by Uriah's response to David, who tried to cover his adultery with Bathsheba by recalling Uriah from the battlefield. When David wined and dined him, even causing him to be drunk, Uriah still would not violate his conscience, but said:

> *'Why should I sleep with my wife and be at ease when the mighty men of Israel and the ark of God are out on the battlefield?'* (2 Samuel 11:11)

The following testimony of a man convicted of manslaughter after a hit-and-run accident shows clearly how we behave according to our conscience.

As a child, this man was afraid of his father, and particularly afraid of punishment. One day, without permission, he took his father's new gold watch to school. As he was displaying the watch to his friends at school, he accidentally dropped and broke it. He took the watch home and replaced it in his father's drawer without telling anyone what had happened. Because of his fear, he would not confess to breaking the watch, even though he felt guilt.

Later in life, he became a successful businessman. One night on his way home from work, a young child ran out in front of his car and was crushed under the wheels. In a moment of panic, he sped away from the scene of the accident without stopping to render aid. A journalist, reporting the accident and court sentence, investigated the man's life, amazed at such behaviour from a supposedly 'respectable citizen'. How could such a mature, successful man react in this irresponsible manner? He was responding according to his conscience.

Sub-conscious guilt is possibly the hardest to define and deal with. Many times it is only as the spirit of God re-awakens the conscience that we can deal with it and be free. Remember, the only evidence of sub-conscious guilt in many cases will be anxiety, depression, anger, fear, or in some cases, abnormal behaviour traits and psychosomatic illnesses.

The Re-awakening of the Conscience

Joseph's brothers had sold him into slavery, lying to their elderly father to cover their sin. Joseph had, after many severe testings, been promoted to governor of Egypt, and was in charge of distribution of food during the famine years.

God was planning to use the ten brothers of Joseph as foundation members of Israel, but He had to heal them from the inner moral weaknesses caused by their guilt. To do this, He had to re-awaken their consciences.

Let's pick up the story from Genesis 42. Jacob saw that there was corn in Egypt, and sent the ten brothers on a journey to acquire grain. The ten brothers were recognized by Joseph, who did not reveal himself to them, but rather, in a very subtle manner, was used by the Holy Spirit to bring them under conviction.

> ' "Ye are spies; to see the nakedness of the land ye are come." And they said unto him, "Nay, my lord, but to buy food are thy servants come. We are all one man's sons, we are true men, thy servants are no spies." And he said unto them, "Nay, but to see the nakedness of the land ye are come." And they said, "Thy servants are twelve brethren, the sons of one man in the land of Canaan; and, behold, the youngest is this day with our father, and one is not." '

Joseph then tells them that their words have to be proven, and puts them in prison for three days. They said to one another:

> 'We are verily guilty concerning our brother in that we saw the anguish of his soul, when he besought us, and we would not hear; therefore, is this distress come upon us.'

Guilt will always carry with it the sense of punishment. The Lord did not allow this incident to happen to condemn them, but rather that they should be redeemed, and reconciled to their brother. Remember, it is desirable to have a clear conscience both toward God and man.

David, also, is a good biblical example of someone who had to deal with guilt from the past.

This is revealed to us in Psalm 32. Here he is in a deep state of anxiety (moisture dried up) and depression. His bones felt as though they were wasting away. He was groaning all the day long, and was in deep despair.

In this psalm, David reveals to us how to deal with this kind of problem. He acknowledges his sin to God and made confession (continually unfolding the past until all was told). God then instantly forgave him all the guilt and iniquity of the past.

Inner Weakness Causes Defeat

David exhorts all the Godly to pray for this kind of release, for when the pressures of life come they will not affect the Spirit within. If we have victory of freedom within, we will have mastery over all the pressures and circumstances from without.

And the Lord said to Cain:

'Why are you angry? And why do you look sad and dejected? If you do well, will you not be accepted? And if you do not do well, sin crouches at your door; its desire is for you, and you must master it.'

(Genesis 4:6–7 AMP)

Some paraphrased translations render this verse to indicate that the anger (weakness) within was an open door for the evil one to enter.

He had to master his spirit or he would be overpowered by the evil one from without.

Certainly this keeps in teaching with Proverbs 25:28:

'He that hath no rule over his own spirit is like a city that is broken down, and without walls.'

Note also the following Scripture:

> *'When angry, do not sin; do not ever let your wrath,*
> *your exasperation, your fury or indignation, last until*
> *the sun goes down. Leave no (such) room or foothold*
> *for the devil, give no opportunity to him.'*

(Ephesians 4:26–27 AMP)

It is important to be free in spirit if we are to bind things without and be masters over them. Many times unrecognised and unresolved guilt from the past will cause neurotic conditions in later life. If we cover our sins, we shall not prosper.

On one occasion as I visited a lady on an emergency pastoral counselling call, I found her under deep depression, unable to speak because of the hypertension. She was a woman of about sixty years of age. As I looked at her, the Holy Spirit said to me that she had sub-conscious guilt which was now coming forth through anxiety, fear and depression. This was being caused by guilt feelings which had developed when she was a young child of about ten years.

At that time of her life, she had been involved with some form of sexual activity related to her young brothers. As she grew older, her mind had forgotten the incident. She lived a well-adjusted life until her grandchildren grew to be around ten years old. This triggered the awakening of the conscience: and, as a result, the emotional syndrome started.

Another lady had repeated mental breakdowns throughout a twenty year period. These breakdowns would occur during the month of November. She would be hospitalized and given shock treatment. This syndrome was broken when the Holy Spirit revealed subconscious guilt which had come in because of a teenage abortion occurring in the month of November.

One man was afraid to go out of his home because he feared policemen. He had never been arrested or had any record of convictions. He became paranoid and deeply distressed by his condition. In counselling it was revealed by the Holy Spirit that as a boy of thirteen a policeman had knocked on the door of his home. He was masturbating at the time this happened. Years later, the mere sight of a policeman triggered sub-conscious guilt which was the root cause of his paranoia and depression.

Space will not permit the sharing of all those who have found release, some neurotic, some psychotic, some, after years of intermittent hospitalization and medical care, now being surrounded with songs and shouts of deliverance when the guilt and sin are uncovered, confessed, and cleansed by the blood of Jesus through the eternal Spirit. They are released now and free to serve God in new dimensions of freedom, joy, and peace, through and in the Spirit of the Lord Jesus.

Not only will repressed guilt cause neurotic and psychotic emotional problems, but false guilt has a similar effect on our behaviour, particularly towards others.

One man found it difficult to relate to people on a one-to-one personal basis. This inability to share and show emotions was a great hindrance, not only to him but to his friends also. As he was seeking God one night for an answer to this problem, a scene from his early childhood flashed before his mind. He saw himself as a child listening to his mother chat with her friends and relatives, saying how traumatic her son's birth was to her, recalling the physical agony and pain she had gone through.

As a child hearing these things, he considered himself the cause of his mother's hurt and pain. In his childish mind, he felt guilty that he had hurt his mother and had nearly caused her death. This false guilt was the cause of his inability to express or receive love, for logically (or with a lack of true logic), he concluded, 'Since you hurt the one you love: don't get too close in a relationship, or you might cause the one you love (or the one who loves you) pain.'

After this false guilt was dealt with, a new found liberty

came into his relationships with others, and he was able to freely give and receive love without fear. False guilt is a basic and established attitude of the mind. False guilt can only be dealt with as the attitude is re-established by the renewing of the mind. Remember, attitudes affect behaviour and behaviour affects feeling. The behaviour will not alter or the feeling change until the attitude is adjusted.

A couple once came for marriage counselling. The husband was not able to show love; he seemed cold in emotional and physical responses. The wife, who was very emotional and used to displaying emotions and affection prior to her marriage, found herself hurt by the lack of emotional response from her husband, although she confessed that for some unknown reason she was frigid.

In counselling, parental attitudes were dealt with, and, in this case, this was the key to release. The man, as a child, had been told that it was wrong for 'little men' to cry, and had been scolded by his parents for doing so. The wife had been told that sex was dirty and not to be enjoyed. These attitudes, established through the parents, were causing false guilt, which was in turn, blocking the emotions.

When the attitudes of the man and woman were re-established from the Word of God, the behaviour and feelings of both partners were changed and they began to enjoy a natural, free response to one another, both emotionally and physically.

There is no greater bondage than that of a pseudo-religious nature, or the false guilt which can be a result of such.

One young lady had married at seventeen years of age, and, because of severe incompatibilities in the marriage, had divorced. Later on, she remarried, and then found Christ as Saviour. She attended church but began to experience heavy depression and anxiety, resulting in hypertension headaches. The depression seemed to intensify when she attended church.

Counselling revealed that a strong emphasis had been

placed on divorce, re-marriage and adultery. Her conscience, under false premises, was causing false guilt.

As we shared from 1 Corinthians 7:22, concerning the reality of Christ's acceptance of us in the state or condition we are in when we come to Him, her guilt and attitudes were dealt with and her conscience was freed. Relating to the release of the emotions, the hypertension headaches disappeared.

Guilt can result in fear, and fear certainly has torment.

A crisis call was received to counsel a young woman about to be recommitted to an institution because of uncontrolled fear. The Holy Spirit began to reveal the root cause. Her real problem was guilt which triggered off the fear.

Her mother had been a stern woman. One day she caught the daughter in the act of childish bodily exploration and masturbation. The child had been whipped and made to feel extremely guilty. She had continued the practice of masturbation even though she had been threatened with a further beating if she was caught again. This developed a fear of being caught and punished. This escalated until any form of guilt would trigger the fear. As confession was made, the guilt was removed and the fear dissipated, resulting in perfect freedom.

Man has many ways of trying to release guilt feelings: shock therapy, drug therapy, blameshifting, psychotherapy, etc. Rationalization, too, has been used widely, but only the blood of Jesus and His Word can bring release. The cleansing, healing power of Christ is released as we make confession.

It is interesting to note that man, from the very beginning, has tried to escape taking responsibility for his sin and has shifted blame onto others. In the garden when God confronted Adam, he blamed Eve, and she in turn blamed the serpent.

Cain failed to take responsibility for the murder of Abel and became a vagabond. Many people today are unsettled

– insecure simply because they will not take responsibility for their actions. Adam, Eve and Cain would have received God's instant grace if they would have taken responsibility for their actions, for God's eternal nature is that of grace and mercy.

Many people find it particularly difficult to gain a clear conscience when there has been a problem in one of the following four areas:

1. Adultery
2. Fornication
3. Abortion
4. Death before restitution can be made with the offended person

A minister's wife was hyperactive and very tense, unable to rest physically or emotionally, lacking peace of mind. She had rebelled as a teenager against her parents, particularly her father who was a Godly minister for Christ. He was so distressed because of the shame and hurt of his daughter's behaviour that he died with a broken heart.

The daughter, herself now a minister's wife, cried, 'How can I make restitution? How can I make confession or receive forgiveness, now that he is dead?' The Holy Spirit led in a unique way. I felt impressed to say to her, 'As you know, we are forbidden by God to communicate with the dead. But, do you believe that Jesus is the God of the living and the dead?' Her response was, 'Yes!' I continued, 'Then ask Jesus to take a message to your father and ask him to forgive your behaviour.' She prayed a simple little prayer, 'Dear Jesus, would you please tell my daddy that I am sorry for my behaviour and please forgive me.'

As she prayed, the flow of tears stopped and a beautiful tranquillity and peace came over her. The guilt was removed. I felt reluctant to share this story, concerned that some would misunderstand, thinking that we had made the Gospel mystical, but I was reminded of the words of a ministry friend: 'That which we don't know or understand is much safer committed to the care and safe keeping of Jesus.'

Many times guilt will not be released until confession is made to the person involved, or restitution is made. One must always be careful in making confession to others. Spend time in seeking guidance from the Holy Spirit. We can take example from the prodigal son in planning what we should say, taking full responsibility and not entering into debate, argument or blameshifting. Our confession should be simple and concise, but always ending with the most important, 'Will you please forgive me?' Regardless of the other party's response, we have then done as the Bible tells us, and the guilt will be removed.

The following are four basic confessions relating to the release of guilt:

1. *'Confess with your mouth the Lord Jesus.'*
(Romans 10:9–10)

2. *'Confess your sins, and He is faithful to forgive and cleanse.'* (1 John 1:9)

3. *'Confess your faults to one another and pray for one another.'* (James 5:16)

4. *'Make Christ the High Priest of our profession (confession)'* (Hebrews 3:1)

or in simple words, 'Say what God says.'

In conclusion, let me relate one more testimony of God's mercy and grace and His enduring love and kindness.

An elderly lady sought counsel, being much distressed in mind. Each time she would pray or try to partake of the Lord's table, some sin from the past would come and cause her great shame and guilt.

Forty years prior she had been forced into an adulterous relationship by her husband. this had never been confessed or dealt with. As confession was made, cleansing came and

211

she was free. how well this typified David's expression, *'My sin was ever before my face.'*

Conclusion

We don't have to become introspective as we draw closer and closer to the Lord; that which is in our hearts hindering our spiritual growth will come under the searchlight of the Holy Spirit. The gentle conviction of His Word and Spirit will increase the sensitivity of our conscience and our relationship with Him will deepen and become more secure, leading to boldness in his presence, faith in His Word and security in His love.

References

1. Dake, F.J. *Dake's Bible Commentary*
2. Ladd, G.E. *A Theology of the New Testament*. USA: Erdmans

Chapter 17

Primal Forces

Much of what we teach is the result of personal ministry of the Holy Spirit as we have sought to draw nearer to the Lord in sanctification.

Other than my conversion and baptism in the Holy Spirit, the greatest spiritual experience I can recall came at a time when I felt the Lord leading me into service. The feeling of powerlessness and unworthiness caused me to travail for hours for a clean heart and upright spirit in order that I might teach transgressors the way of the Lord.

In a sense, my experience in the baptism of the Spirit was a disappointment, for although I could pray and worship in the Spirit, I still had areas of my life which seemed to be uncontrollable. I felt something of the anguish Paul must have experienced in describing himself as a wretched man, one who had certain areas holding him in continual bondage although he had a heart's desire to be free.

One Sunday morning a young visiting speaker expounded the text from John 3:14:

> 'As Moses lifted up the serpent in the wilderness, even so must the Son of Man be lifted up.'

This, he explained, was Christ identifying Himself with our sinful humanity. He further stated that our baptism in water actually identified us with Christ in His crucifixion, death, burial and resurrection.

Surely a circumcision made without hands in the putting away of the sins of the flesh, the circumcision of Christ. Being buried with Him in baptism, wherein also ye are risen with Him through the faith of the operation of God, who hath raised Him from the dead (Colossians 2:12).

As I then, through faith in Christ's redemptive work, appropriated this truth, I felt a great sense of inner cleansing and a tremendous anointing of His Spirit.

Because some teach that sanctification is a mortifying of self, the question to then ask would be: is it an annihilation of the self to mortify the dictates of the flesh, or is it something quite different?

An Historical Perspective

Paul, in his letter to the young church at Colosse, refutes false teachings which were poisoning the church community. These teachings were firstly: the universe contained a number of beings of various degrees of power and importance; and second: the gnostic teaching which was an extreme asceticism.

The Gnostics taught that the human body was sinful and, in order to attain to spiritual enlightenment, the body had to be mortified by rigorous denial.

Such was the extreme of this teaching which had crept into the doctrine of the young churches, that its adherents believed Christ could not have been born with a natural physical body but rather He had a mystical spiritual body.

John said that this was the doctrine of the spirit of antichrist. to expose this false doctrine, a simple test was to ask: *'Has Jesus come in the flesh?'* The spirit which denied this would also deny the Father and Son.

Modern Day Gnostics

The Krishna Consciousness Movement is, in a word, ascetic. Its devotees live a highly disciplined life of self-denial.

In addition to this disciplined life, their very attire and beads are designed to help the devotee forget the physical realm so that they can dwell upon Krishna. Asceticism is crammed into every area of their being.

The extreme asceticism of the Eastern religions and philosophies have been westernized for acceptance in the United States. One such example is Eckankar.

Eckankar was founded by Paul Switchell and is based on Tibetan Buddhist philosophy. This cult teaches the viewpoint that the world is one essence, composed of spirit. It has many of the hallmarks of the first century heresy called gnosticism, a system of belief which denied the existence of the physical realm. Followers of Eckankar believe Jesus is simply an advanced ECK master.

There are two all-inclusive world views which have been predominant in twentieth-century thinking:

1. **Atheistic world view**: the atheist or materialist claims basically the only things which truly exist are those things in the material world which can be detected through the five natural senses. Therefore, there is no supernatural, no spiritual reality, no God.

2. **Pantheistic world view**: the pantheistic world view is the one which prevails in the East. Pantheism teaches one level of reality: God and the material world are one. God then becomes the sum total of all there is; He is not a separate being somewhere beyond the world: rather, all of the material world, everyone and everything, is a part of the divine.

The Christian viewpoint, or **theistic world view**, stands in sharp contrast to the materialistic and pantheistic world views.

The theist says that there is a material world which can be detected by use of our five senses, but there is also a spiritual reality beyond the material world – a Creator and a creation which are distinct and separate.

Rightly Dividing the Word of Truth

Paul warns us of vain philosophies and traditions of men which divert our faith away from Christ and His atoning work.

> *'For by grace are ye saved through faith, and that not of yourselves: it is the gift of God, not of works, lest any man should boast.'* (Ephesians 2:8–9)

The believer is to be set apart unto God; this is sanctification. His body is to be separated unto God as a living sacrifice, holy and acceptable. This cannot be done by our own works, strength, and self-effort, but must be done through the grace of God.

Separation from the unfruitful works of darkness is mentioned by Paul in 2 Corinthians. This term for separation (*aphorizo*), means to set off by a boundary. It speaks of separation from something unclean in order to be bonded to the Lord in service and fellowship.

The Primal Drives

Fearfully and wonderfully made

When the Psalmist David reflected on man, he praised God, for he recognized that man was fearfully and wonderfully made.

God created the inner man by breathing into him the breath of life and man then became a living soul.

His body was formed out of the dust of the earth and made in God's own image (*tselem*, shape, figure, bodily form). The Greek word *'eikon'* confirms the idea of bodily image and likeness. The body, *'soma'*, wonderfully made and consists of various chemicals: iron, sugar, carbon and so forth.

In the body we have the five senses: sight, smell, hearing, touch and taste; these give us our world consciousness.

Let us look at the term body, or *'soma'*, as it is used in Scripture.

When the Greek word *'soma'* is used, it speaks of the body as a whole, the instrument of life, whether it be a man living (Matthew 6:22) or dead (Matthew 27:52). It is used for beasts (Hebrews 13:11), grain (1 Corinthians 15:37), and heavenly hosts (1 Corinthians 15:40).

Sometimes the word stands, by synecdoche, for the complete man (Matthew 5:29, 6:22; Romans 12:1).

The body is not the complete man, for he (the spirit man), himself, can exist apart from his body (2 Corinthians 12:2–3).

The body is an essential part of the man, however, The redeemed are not perfected until the resurrection (Hebrews 11:40), for no man will be in his final state without his body (John 5:28–29; Revelation 20:13).

The word is also used for physical nature as distinct from spirit, *'pneuma'* (1 Corinthians 5:13), and from soul, *'psuche'* (1 Thessalonians 5:23).

'Soma', (body) and *'pneuma'* (spirit) may be separated; *'pneuma'* and *'psuche'* (soul), can also be distinguished.

Self-preservation

The linking faculty between the physical flesh (*soma*) of the body and the soul (*psuche*) are the innate primal drives or natural instincts. The first of these basic instincts we will call self-preservation, or the primal instinct to live.

It is this instinct which causes the baby, as it comes out of the birth canal, to take its first breath of life, *'pnoe'*, the breath of beginning. Modern natural childbirth methods instruct the expectant mother and father about the physiology of birth, stressing natural childbirth without drugs. Many babies instinctively breathe without the traditional slap on the bottom when no drugs are involved in the childbirth process.

The maturation of natural self-preservation has many

ramifications as it develops into rational self-preservation. Natural anger and/or fear motivates this instinct when our lives are threatened.

Hunger and Thirst

The next primal force to develop is hunger and thirst. We will understand more clearly this motivating drive if we realize that God's purpose of placing it within our lives is to bond us emotionally and spiritually to the natural world. This is particularly so in the case of hunger and thirst.

When a little baby gets hungry or thirsty it actually experiences physical pain, causing it to cry. When the mother lovingly and gently satisfies this need, a deep emotional and spiritual bonding takes place between the two. This creates comfort and security.

This bonding is particularly pronounced if the mother is breast feeding her child. She might be miles away from home; yet, when her child gets hungry, her breasts engorge with milk.

The significance of this bonding can be seen in the life of Moses. Because Moses was an exceedingly beautiful child, his mother hid him for three months rather than follow Pharaoh's decree of death. She then made an ark of bulrushes and put the child therein, placing him at a strategic spot among the rushes by the edge of the Nile River.

When the daughter of Pharaoh came to bathe at the river's edge, she saw the child and commissioned Moses sister, who lingered nearby, to call a Hebrew woman (his true mother) to nurse the child for wages. Later, when he grew, his mother took him back to Pharaoh's daughter and he was then raised in all the wisdom of Egypt, becoming mighty in word and deed.

When he had grown to maturity, he refused to be called the son of Pharaoh's daughter. He chose instead to suffer affliction with the people of God rather than to enjoy the pleasures of sin for a season. This reversal was a result of his early childhood bonding to his mother and the culture of his family.

Until recently, social behavioural scientists thought that the child's development was primarily social-environmental conditioning. If this were true, then Moses would have no desire to return to his spiritual heritage. In those early years when he was being tenderly raised on his mother's breast, a deep emotional and spiritual bonding had taken place.

In the New Testament, we see the importance of the Lord's table in the Love Feast of 1 Corinthians 11. The breaking of bread was a vital part of the life style of the early Christian community. To eat unworthily was to eat and drink damnation to one's self.

Paul warns the Corinthian church not to keep company with any man who is called a 'brother' and yet is a fornicator, or covetous, or an idolater, or a railer, or a drunkard, or an extortioner.

With such a one they were not to eat. The Scriptural implication is that 'not to eat' means not to partake with that person around the Lord's supper.

In these examples, to eat with a degenerate disciple would mean being bonded to them in their sin.

Jude also gives a strong admonition relating to those who have gone in the way of Cain or run greedily after the error of Balaam for reward.

'Woe to them! For they have run riotously in the way of Cain, and have abandoned themselves for the sake of gain (it offers them) to the error of Balaam, and have perished in rebellion (like that) of Korah! These are (elements of danger), hidden reefs in your love feasts, where they boldly feast sumptuously – carousing together (in your midst) – without scruple providing for themselves (alone)winds; trees without fruit at the late autumn gathering time, twice (doubly) dead, (lifeless and) plucked up by the roots; wild waves of the sea,

> *flinging up the foam of their own shame and disgrace;*
> *wandering stars for whom the gloom of eternal darkness*
> *has been reserved forever.'* (Jude 11–13 AMP)

Many parents today allow their children to eat separately from the family as they watch television, and they wonder why the children relate and respond more to TV characters than family members.

It is important for a family to set aside at least one meal a day where they can eat together in harmony and peace. Those who do so will find a deep emotional and spiritual bonding existing between each other.

We have ministered to many with deep rooted problems of insecurity, loneliness and self-rejection. Tracing their problems back, we find wrong nurturing, the trauma of wrong weaning or illness which caused isolation from the mother while being breast-fed.

Each of us needs to fully absorb the fact that the Lord was watching over us as we were being formed in our mother's womb. He will never leave us or forsake us. He, that in redemptive rejection by His father, called: *'I am a worm and no man,'* now can offer comfort and consolation through the Holy Spirit to those who sense deep rejection.

He, who holds us in the hollow of His hand, will dangle us on His knee, and take those of us who feel forsaken by our parents, up in His arms.

The Sexual Drive Forces

Freud ultimately stated that all of man's basic neuroses stem from the sexual libido. We mention this hypothesis to draw attention to this powerful, primal force which can cause a man to be consumed with lust; even as Solomon states, to take fire to his bosom.

Sexual forces begin to develop prior to puberty, generally starting with a fixation on the same sex. Many psychologists consider the homosexual to be one who became fixed at this stage of developmental patterning.

At puberty a young person has all the sexual feeling of an adult. Current day dating principles wrongly allow permissiveness in sexual foreplay. Young people pairing off before they are emotionally, psychologically or spiritually mature enough to handle their sexual feelings can easily lead to promiscuity.

Paul exhorts the young man Timothy to flee youthful lusts and shares with him God's standard of conduct towards those around him. Older men are to be treated and respected as fathers; older women as mothers; and the younger women as sisters, with all purity.

As we study Paul's exposition to the Corinthian church, rife with carnality, he states the principle that the body is not for fornication but is to be a temple of the Holy Spirit.

In verse 15, he states that our bodies are members of Christ. He then asks this question:

> *'Know ye not that your bodies are members of Christ? Shall I then take the members of Christ and make them the member of an harlot? God forbid. What? Know ye not that he which is joined to an harlot is one body? For two saith he, shall be one flesh.'*

> (1 Corinthians 6:14–16)

He goes on to say that he that is joined to the Lord is one body. To be joined to the Lord in spirit is to be one body with Him. On the same token, if a Christian has intercourse with a harlot, he joins Christ's Spirit to the harlot. Fornication then becomes a sin against one's own body, and directly, against Christ.

When we touch the opposite sex in a sexual way we are not just merely touching their physical bodies, but are bonding with them emotionally and spiritually.

This God-given primal instinct has been given to us for the purpose of a bonding into one flesh with the sharing of mutual comfort and pleasure as well as for procreation.

However, this must take place in the sanctity of marriage where it will be nurtured to the fullness of the perfection God intended. Anything outside the sanctity of marriage has far reaching negative repercussions.

The power of this drive, when out of control, can only be broken by repentance and an acknowledgment of God's forgiveness. This will bring release and cleansing from unrighteousness and guilt.

Classified Sexual Deviate Behaviour

In his book, *The Encyclopedia of Human Behaviour*,[1] Robert M. Golderson said:

> 'The sex role is a major ingredient of the self-concept, and persistent confusion over sex identification is bound to have drastic effects on the individual's attitude towards himself, as well as his relationship to others. It not only gives rise to feelings of insecurity and inadequacy, but deprives him of a definite place in society. On the other hand, a clear concept of one's sex role is a foundation for self-acceptance, emotional security, and confidence in dealing with other people.'

The acceptance of humanism has given our culture the philosophy of relativity, which is faith in reason. Relativity teaches that there are no absolutes: therefore, we have changing standards of morality.

These changing standards in the sexual role of teenagers has thrown our younger generation into confusion and conflict. Confusion because, without absolutes, there is no real balance between freedom and licence; conflict because of the difference between the theories which are taught by parents and churches and those of secular education.

The result is self-gratification without responsibility or restraint. This is hedonism

The Bible is absolute, for its laws and precepts are unchangeable. Because man has three basic areas of motivation (spiritual, emotional/psychological and physical), we must discern and understand God's ideal for the sexual area.

This can be stated as: 'God wants the emotional, psychological and physical drives to find their motivation and control through the spiritual'.

To repeatedly sin against our moral conscience would lead to reprobation, in which state man can pursue his passions without restraint. The ultimate end of a seared conscience is expressed by Paul in Romans 1:24–32:

> *'Wherefore God also gave them up to uncleanness through the lusts of their own hearts, to dishonour their own bodies between themselves: Who changed the truth of God into a lie, and worshipped and served the creature more than the Creator, who is blessed for ever. Amen. For this cause God gave them up unto vile affections: for even their women did change the natural use into that which is against nature: And likewise also the men, leaving the natural use of the woman, burned in their lust one toward another.'*

The Spirit of Harlotry

In a series of meetings in the South Pacific region, I called a gentleman from the congregation and through a word of knowledge discerned a spirit of murder within him. His response was to say, 'This is possible, for I have written letters to all of our politicians threatening to murder them.'

I then discerned that this spirit of murder had entered into him through intercourse with his wife who was an unrepentant prostitute.

He became violent when this was discerned as the spirit of darkness reacted to the truth. However, he was gloriously released from this bondage through the power of Jesus's Name.

According to Solomon, a true prostitute is one who has a

deep hatred for men and seeks to destroy their soul through sexual intercourse. Those who have had intercourse with a prostitute have come into a spiritual bonding with that spirit of murder.

The Act of Sodomy

Pope Paul, at a general audience in Rome on 13 November, 1979, said,

'Evil is not merely a lack of something, but an effective agent, a living spiritual being, prevented and preventing. A terrible reality, mysterious, frightening. We know that this dark and disturbing spirit really exists and that he still acts with treacherous cunning: he is the secret enemy that sows errors and misfortunes in human history. It is not a question of the devil and the influence he can exert on individual persons but as well as on communities, whole societies and events, and is a very important chapter of Catholic doctrine.'

Timothy Winn, when writing on the subject of sodomy, said:

'Most people are in agreement that all curses are evil, but there are evils that cannot be prosecuted as crimes. Few would deny that the spiritual power of evil is the greatest enemy of humankind. Although there are some who refuse to recognize the reality of evil, as an entity outside of our being, capable of affecting our being in many different ways, I am not of that number.'

Cain was warned that evil was lurking at his door, ready to pounce.

'And in the process of time it came to pass, that Cain brought of the fruit of the ground an offering unto the Lord. And Abel, he also brought of the firstlings of his

224

*flock and of the fat thereof. And the Lord had respect
unto Abel and to his offering: but unto Cain and to his
offering He had not respect. And Cain was very wroth,
and his countenance fell. And the Lord said unto Cain,
"Why art thou wroth? and why is thy countenance
fallen? If thou doest well, shalt thou not be accepted?
and if thou doest not well, sin lieth at thy door. And unto
thee shall be his desire, and thou shalt rule over him."'*

(Genesis 4:3–7)

To yield oneself to sin is to become a slave to it. The
Webster's new *Universal Unabridged Dictionary*[2] defines
sodomy as any sexual intercourse regarded as abnormal, as
between persons of the same sex, especially males, or
between a person and an animal.

The New Testament says:

*'Know ye not that the unrighteous shall not inherit the
Kingdom of God? Be not deceived: neither fornicators,
nor idolaters, nor adulterers, nor effeminate, nor
abusers of themselves with mankind.'*   (Ephesians 5:5)

This word abusers of themselves is *'arsenokoites'*, or a
sodomite.

In the Old Testament, the word sodomite is *'qadesh'*,
which means a sacred person, a (oracle) devotee (by prostitution) to licentious idolatry: sodomite, unclean. This is
taken from the root word *'qadash'*, meaning to consecrate,
dedicate, defile, hallow.

The word 'sodom' is a word which means to burn or,
literally, to burn with lust.

It would appear from the Old Testament that the word
'sodomite' was used for a person who was dedicated as a
temple prostitute, particularly a male. However, in the
New Testament, the word has been defined as any abnormal deviant sexual behaviour which, according to Colossians 3:5, is idolatry:

> *'Therefore, consider the members of your earthly body as dead to immorality, impurity, passion, evil desire and greed, which amounts to idolatry.'* (NAS)

In the Book of Romans, Paul says that when a person begins to exalt the created above the Creator, that God will give that person over in the lusts of their hearts to impurity, that their bodies might be dishonoured among them. The act of sodomy many times is included in rape, child molestation, incest, prostitution, bestiality, and the sex life of homosexuals and lesbians.

The Effects of Sodomy

Possibly the most common effect of sodomy is the destruction of self-esteem and human respect, which results in depression, nervous disorder, lack of emotional control (especially fear or anger), anxiety attacks, which lead to hopelessness and despair with suicidal tendencies. When human respect is destroyed in a relationship, there is nothing to hold back violence. This has definitely contributed to the ever increasing problem of battered women and children.

Pornography

The US Attorney General's Commission on Pornography showed only too clearly the relationship between sexual perversion portrayed in photographs and writing with violence. The Greek word for pornography is *'pornographlos'*, meaning the uniting of harlots.

Pornography, then, is depicting, with photographs and words, the acts of sodomy.

The proliferation of sodomy is not only found in the homosexual community but is especially found in the heterosexual society of today – largely due to the several billion dollar pornographic industry.

James Dobson, who was one of the commissioners on the US Attorney General's Commission on Pornography, said:

> 'For a certain percentage of men, the use of pornographic material is addictive and progressive: like the addiction to drugs, alcohol or food, those who are hooked on sex become obsessed by their need. It fills their world, night and day. And too often their families are destroyed in the process.'

Father Bruce Ritter said,

> 'The greatest part of pornography degrades sex itself and dehumanises and debases a profoundly important, profoundly beautiful, sacred relationship between man and woman, who seek in sexual union not the mere satisfaction of erotic desire, but the deepest slavery of their nuptial vows, and committed and faithful love.'

Pornography, which is the fruit of sodomy, leads many men to be tempted into having extra marital affairs, or even to enter into prostitution where the oral genital acts can be classified as sodomy.

Whatsoever a Man Soweth

Evil will reap evil, and two of the most common and perplexing venereal diseases of this generation can be related basically to sodomy. I speak, of course, about Herpes II and the fatal disease known as AIDS (Acquired Immune Deficiency syndrome).

When we realize that evil is a power, a force, then we will begin to understand the political power of the gay movement and why a minority can have such influence over the majority.

Parental Responsibility

Few parents realize the powerful influence for good and for evil they have on their children.

Parents must take more responsibility in sexually educating their children and teaching them biblical foundations of sexuality, dating, and the responsibilities of marriage.

If parents do not outwardly express their deep commitment to one another in the marriage relationship, then their children get a wrong message and consider sexuality only in the light of the sexual act which can be enjoyed and used outside of commitment.

To again quote Father Bruce Ritter:

> 'Parents must assume greater responsibility for educating their children about sexuality ... our paralysis fear of talking about sex with our kids is the strongest weapon in the sex industry's arsenal. The bosses of organized crime are more than ready to take over the sex education of America's children.'

References

1. Golderson R.M. *The Encyclopedia of Human Behaviour*
2. Webster's. New Universal Unabridged Dictionary

Chapter 18

Soul Bondages

Man has been uniquely designed by his Creator to be conformable.

> *'For those whom He foreknew – of whom He was aware and loved beforehand – He also destined from the beginning (foreordaining them) to be moulded into the image of His Son (and share inwardly His likeness), that He might become the first-born among many brethren.'*
>
> (Romans 8:29 AMP)

The word *'summorphos'* (conformable) in a paraphrased sense means 'that which we are emotionally bonded to, we become like as unto'.

Paul prays for the early Christians' hearts to be knit together in love:

> *'(For my concern is) that their hearts may be braced (comforted, cheered and encouraged) as they are knit together in love, that they may come to have all the abounding wealth and blessings of assured conviction of understanding, and that they may become progressively more intimately acquainted with, and may know more definitely and accurately and thoroughly, that mystic secret of God (which is) Christ, the Anointed One.'*
>
> (Colossians 2:2 AMP)

The word 'knit' is the Greek word *'sumbibazo'* which means to drive together, to form or forge a union. In the context of the text used, this union is to be motivated by love.

In Philippians 2:2, Paul writes:

> *'Fill up and complete my joy by living in harmony and being of the same mind and one in purpose, having the same love, being in full accord and of one harmonious mind and intention.'* (AMP)

The King James version uses the words 'of one accord'. The Greek word for this is *'sumpsuchos'*, or to be joined in soul.

> *'Now the company of believers was of one heart and soul, and not one of them claimed that anything which he possessed was (exclusively) his own, but everything they had was in common and for the use of all.'*
>
> (Acts 4:32 AMP)

Man has the capacity to become knit together (or to be joined in soul) to one another.

Because the emotions are a bonding agent, any joining together, outside of agape love, can lead to a wrong, negative, and destructive soul tie.

Bondage Through Emotional Domination and Control

Adverse or traumatic circumstances can cause bondage through emotional control. A good example from the Scriptures would be Mary's parental control over Jesus, which He found necessary to sever.

Because of Mary's unmarried state at the time of the conception of Jesus, and the most unusual circumstances, we can see how this would lead to an abnormal focus by Mary upon Jesus.

At the time of the Baby's dedication to the Lord, an important prophetic word is given to Mary by Simeon:

> *'And a sword will pierce through your own soul also, that the secret thoughts and purposes of many hearts may be brought out and disclosed.'* (Luke 2:35 AMP)

When Jesus was twelve years old, He had gone to Jerusalem with his parents for the Passover feast. he remained behind in Jerusalem without His parents' knowledge. Observe how Jesus handled the very subtle emotional control expressed by Mary:

> *'But supposing Him to be in the caravan they travelled on a day's journey, and (then) they sought Him (diligently, looking up and down for Him) among their kinsfolk and acquaintances.*
>
> *And when they failed to find Him, they went back to Jerusalem, looking for Him (up and down all the way). After three days they found Him (came upon Him); in the (court of the) temple, sitting among the teachers, listening to them and asking them questions.*
>
> *And all who heard Him were astonished and overwhelmed with bewildered wonder at His intelligence and understanding and His replies. And when they (Joseph and Mary) saw Him they were amazed, and His mother said to Him, Child, why have You treated us like this? Here your father and I have been anxiously looking for You – distressed and tormented.*
>
> *And He said to them, How is it that you had to look for Me? Did you not see and know that it is necessary (as a duty) for Me to be in My Father's house, and (occupied) about My Father's business?*
>
> *But they did not comprehend what He was saying to them. And He went down with them and came to Nazareth, and was (habitually) obedient to them; and his mother kept and closely and persistently guarded all these things in her heart.'* (Luke 2:44–51 AMP)

The word of the Lord, as the Sword of the Spirit, began to pierce Mary's soul as prophesied in Luke 2:35. No doubt the words of Simeon came to Mary's remembrance as she guarded all these things in her heart.

At the wedding at Cana of Galilee, we see again Mary directing Jesus:

> *'And when the wine was all gone, the mother of Jesus said to Him, They have no more wine?*
>
> *Jesus said to her, (Dear) woman, what is that to you and to me? (What have we in common? Leave it to Me). My time (hour to act) is not come yet.'*

Mary persists, however:

> *'His mother said to the servants, Whatever He says to you, do it.'* (John 2:3–5)

Jesus had not come to do the will of His earthly mother, but of His heavenly Father. The final thrust of the sword came later, and the bondage was broken.

As Jesus's ministry of power and authority began to come forth, it evoked an interesting response from His family:

> *'And when those who belonged to Him (His kinsmen) heard it, they went out to take Him by force, for they kept saying, He is out of His mind – beside Himself, deranged!*
>
> *Then His mother and His brothers came, and standing outside, they sent word to Him, calling (for) Him. And a crowd was sitting around Him, and they said to Him, Your mother and Your brothers and Your sisters are outside, asking for You.*
>
> *And He replied, Who are My mother and My brothers? And looking around on those who sat in a circle about Him, He said, See! Here are My mother and My*

> *brothers, for whoever does the things God wills is My brother, and sister, and mother!'* (Mark 3:31–35 AMP)

From this time on, we read nothing further about Mary attempting to influence Jesus.

While on tour in the South Pacific, a young married woman came for prayer with multiple physical and emotional problems. As we prayed together, I felt prompted to say, 'Does your mother control or dominate you in any way?' Her response was, 'Oh, yes! Each time I refuse to comply with my mother's wishes, she accuses me of not loving her and threatens to kill herself!'

My second question to her was, 'Does your mother suffer the same emotional and physical conditions as you do?' Her reply: 'Yes, exactly the same'.

I explained how the mother had joined herself together with her (the daughter) through the 'soul bonding' and then began to break the ties in prayer. As a result, the young woman was totally delivered, not only from the physical conditions, but also from the emotional.

Another woman, who had served for twenty five years as a missionary had become manic depressive and homosexual. The Holy Spirit revealed that it was her father who had the missionary call, but had projected it to his daughter because he was unable to follow the calling himself. The daughter's hatred was the bonding agent, or soul tie, to her father. When the hatred was released, she experienced healing and deliverance.

The Projection of Our Will Onto Others

Possibly the most subtle form of all domination and soul ties comes from the parental attempts to live their frustrated life ambitions out through their children. I've experienced this in my own life. Several years ago, a friend confided to me that I was controlling and dominating my eldest son. My first reaction was denial. True, I had a very heavy spiritual burden for his welfare and Christian walk. He had an executive position in Australia before coming to the United States to be with us. In the US, however, he was unable to secure a position in which he had expertise. He had been trained by a major corporation in Australia as a management auditor.

The death of his mother in a head-on collision a few weeks after his arrival in the US was a tremendous personal loss and grief to us, and as a caring, concerned father, I spent many hours in personal prayer for him.

That Christmas, the Holy Spirit directed us to spend the day together as a family – the first time we had been able to do so for years. Around a family communion table the Lord spoke clearly into my spirit that I had dominated my son.

Then, the Holy Spirit began to unveil how this had taken place. Even as a child, I had an interest in business. My childhood games were not 'cops and robbers' or 'cowboys and Indians' – but rather, I played 'trading posts' and other finance or sales related games.

When I was called into the ministry, I left the farm with crops standing unharvested on the vine, so intense had the call of God been.

When Kerry (my son) finished his college education, he came to me requesting permission to go to Bible College. My response was, 'No, you're too immature now. It's not the right time. You need to get involved in business.'

To please me, he surrendered his will to my will and started as an office boy, attending night school to qualify as an accountant. He quickly advanced in his work. By the time he was twenty-one years old, he was a chief accountant for the Textile Division of Dunlop Australia.

As we prayed together around the communion table, I asked forgiveness, releasing him from my control. A beautiful miracle of deliverance took place. Shortly thereafter, Kerry was able to find suitable employment and a new freedom was manifested in his life.

Thousands of people are held in captivity through parental domination.

This kind of soul bondage can be so subtle that it takes revelation and discernment from the Holy Spirit to identify the intrusion.

The apostle Paul said: *'I am free from all men, that I may be a servant to all.'*

Any type of control exercised over another in an ungodly manner can cause bondage.

Psychic Bonding Through the Occult

Because 90% of people have weaknesses in the spiritual intuition areas, psychic bonding is quite common – particularly with those who are involved in drug taking and occult.

The best way for me to illustrate this point is through testimony.

A beautiful sixteen year old teenager was very close to her grandfather. He had terminal cancer of the stomach. The day after his death, the young girl experienced severe pain in the same region of her body where his cancer had been.

When the pains persisted, she was taken by her parents for a medical check-up. No physical evidence existed that would explain the stomach pains.

After a few weeks, the granddaughter began to experience psychic phenomenon; she heard voices telling her not to eat.

The concerned parents took her for a psychological evaluation. She was hospitalized for observation in a psychiatric unit of a local hospital.

The parents then sought counsel from our drop-in counselling centre, although they were not Christians. At three o'clock that Sunday afternoon, one of our counsellors led the parents to Christ, broke the curse of witchcraft off their lives, and shared the promise from the Lord that a lamb was sufficient for the whole household.

At exactly three o'clock that afternoon, their daughter, who had been sitting on her hospital bed tormented with the voices speaking to her and suffering severe stomach pain, was instantly healed. The voices ceased, the pain ceased, a miracle had taken place.

Sickness Transferred by Emotional-Psychic Bonding

'Transferral neurosis' is the psychological term used to describe the transferral of the psychic, one to another.

We know that fear and unbelief can be transferred. The whole nation of Israel turned back into the wilderness because fear and unbelief was transferred to them by the ten spies with a negative report.

Another story is that of Gideon's battle with the Midianites. The army commanders of Israel were asked to challenge those with fear to return home, lest they transfer their fear to the other soldiers. Hence, Gideon's challenge to the men who had responded to his trumpet call:

> '*So now proclaim in the ears of the men, saying, Whoever is fearful and trembling, let him turn back and depart from Mount Gilead. And 22,000 of the men returned, but 10,000 remained.*' (Judges 7:3 AMP)

Just recently I was ministering in a Christian facility for girls. One of the residents had contracted a severe kidney infection. As we spoke to her, I noticed that she seemed to be overly attached to a giant toy teddy bear. I was then prompted by the Holy Spirit to ask who had given her the bear, and had the giver of the gift suffered with a kidney infection.

The response to my question was affirmative. Her mother had given her the toy just prior to the mother's death from a kidney condition. As we broke the psychic soul ties, the young woman was instantly healed.

236

A few weeks after this incident, the same girl was in a state of catatonic depression for several days. She had lost all contact with reality, and was in a trance-like condition.

I felt impressed to ask the supervisor of the house if she had been bonded to anyone who had died tragically. The supervisor informed me that the girl's best friend had committed suicide two weeks prior by hanging herself.

As we again broke a psychic bonding, the girl instantly awoke, looked around, and said: 'Where am I? How long have I been here?' The depression had totally disappeared when the bonding was broken.

Strong Emotional Feelings Can Bond Us to Iniquities

As the sorcerer of the city of Samaria, Simon had mystified the people with his magic practices. When Philip went down to Samaria preaching Christ, his words met with a ready and sympathetic response from the large crowds who listened to him and saw the miracles that he performed.

Simon, seeing the power of God demonstrated through the anointing of the Holy Spirit upon Philip, came to conversion and baptism.

When the church at Jerusalem heard that Samaria had received the word of God, they sent down Peter and John, who had the ministry of laying on of hands, to receive the Holy Ghost.

When Simon saw that through the laying on of the Apostle's hands the Holy Spirit was imparted, he offered them money that he, himself, might impart the gift.

The Phillips translation of the New Testament expresses the strong language used by Peter in response to Simon's request:

> *'To hell with you and your money! How dare you think you could buy the gift of God for money!'*

Peter goes on to say,

> *'For I can see inside you, and see a man bitter with*
> *jealousy and bound with his own sin!'*
>
> (Acts 8:23, Phillips translation)

In the Amplified Bible, Peter's words are translated as:

> *'For I see that you are in the gall of bitterness and a*
> *bond forged by iniquity (to fetter souls).'*

Simon was bonded by his bitterness to the iniquities of the past.

Perhaps I could use another illustration to explain how strong emotional feelings can bond us together, especially to those negative traits we may despise in others.

'Wally' was a social misfit, a drop-out from society. We first made contact with him through our drop-in centre in King's Cross in Sydney. Wally was not only a drop-out, but an alcoholic. After a real conversion experience, we began the spiritual battle of seeing Wally released from the power of alcohol.

In counselling one day, Wally was asked about his relationship with his father. He confessed that the relationship was virtually non-existent, and that his father was an alcoholic. When I asked him how he felt towards his father (were there, perhaps, any strong unresolved emotional feelings) Wally's response was: 'I hate his guts!'

Because of his father's abuse to him as a child, Wally had grown up to hate his father and had made an oath never to be an alcoholic like his father. Why, then, one might ask, did he become like the person he hated and despised, and had vowed never to become like?

The answer is simple. The scriptural principle is as follows: Man is conformable, and if we are in emotional intimacy with someone, we will become like as unto that person. The truth is real and binding.

Grief Can Bond Us to Pathogenetical Sicknesses

A lady diagnosed as terminally ill with cancer came to me for counselling and prayer. As we shared together, the Holy Spirit prompted me to ask if some loved one had died of cancer and whether she had resolved her grief about the death.

She began to tell how her son had contracted cancer in the stomach, and that the family, being strong charismatic Christians, were believing and confessing his healing.

One morning they went into his room to waken him, only to discover that he had passed away in his sleep during the night.

The mother's grief was two-fold. She grieved at the loss of her son, but also that the Lord seemingly had not responded to their prayers.

A few months after the son's death, the mother began to experience discomfort and pains in her stomach – which was later diagnosed as cancer.

The healing power of the Lord was manifested to her as she renounced the grief and broke the emotional soul tie between herself and her son.

Spiritual Transference Through Soul Ties

One of the most bizarre stories of soul ties unfolded when we were ministering in New England (Boston, Massachusetts area) in 1979.

The Holy Spirit had given me a vision of a woman who had an abnormal attachment to a cat. The call brought a ripple of laughter from the congregation, but a woman responded and shared a strange story with us.

Her mother had lived in an apartment alone. Although the mother had suffered from a heart condition, she preferred to be independent.

One day the daughter visited her mother and found the

woman dead in her bed. Her pet cat was walking up and down over the dead body. The daughter did not really consider the cat's behaviour at the time but took the cat home with her to care for it, since it had been the mother's much loved constant companion.

Months after the mother's funeral, the daughter was wakened one morning by the cat walking up and down over her body. She experienced a severe heart attack, very similar to that which had been responsible for the death of her mother. Since the daughter was young and physically strong, the attack was not fatal – but a strong fear of death began to obsess her mind.

We explained briefly to her the concept of soul ties, and had her renounce the spirit of death that had been transferred to her through the tie with the cat. As we prayed, she was released from the spirit of death, and experienced physical healing in the process.

Summary

Soul ties can represent emotions or objects; they are the medium by which we become bonded together to other people or objects.

It is important as we minister to people in prayer counselling to be very sensitive to the Holy Spirit's promptings; otherwise, we can counsel and minister in vain. The Lord brings healing and release through the knowledge of the truth; but the knowledge must be precise and accurate.

> *'And you will know the truth, and the truth will set you free.'* (John 8:32)

> *'My grace (God's favour) and peace, (which is perfect well-being, all necessary good, all spiritual prosperity and freedom from fears and agitating passions and moral conflicts) be multiplied to you in (the full, personal, precise and correct) knowledge of God and of Jesus our Lord.'* (2 Peter 1:2 AMP)

SUPPLEMENTARY MANUAL:

Emotions and Health

Supplementary Manual

Emotions and Health

Emotions are a Physical Event

Every emotion you feel is a physical event. When you have a strong emotional reaction, even one generated by watching a movie, hormones are secreted and your body chemistry is altered. When the feelings are particularly strong, the physical reactions are likely to be equally extreme.

Emotions can alter your endocrine balance, your blood supply and your blood pressure. They can also inhibit your digestion, change your breathing and alter the temperature of your skin. A sustained state of emotional upset may cause changes that lead to disease. Your psyche may trigger the over-reaction of hormones which may produce a disease process.

Your body tries continually to be in a state of equilibrium, maintaining a precarious balance between too much of a substance and too little. If stress or other factors upset this seesaw, the body will seek to adapt by altering its chemistry. This alteration can be damaging to the rest of the organism, causing so-called diseases of adaptation.

One source of stress is external change. Big events, good or bad, in your private life may make you vulnerable to illness. Social change, war-time pressures and job tensions are often accompanied by sharp rises in disease. The chronic stresses of fast-paced everyday life take their toll.

What makes a person develop a specific disease? To some degree his personality makeup is the determining factor. Researchers are finding that people with certain character traits are likely to suffer from certain diseases.

For example, people with neurodermatitis, a type of skin affliction, usually have a craving for close physical contact. A hereditary vulnerability, or one acquired through illness or injury, may combine with emotional factors to produce a disease. Thus, someone with an inherited predisposition to diabetes may develop symptoms of the disease during a stressful period.

Virtually all illnesses have emotional components.

Your susceptibility to micro-organisms of disease, for example, the common cold, or the bacilli of tuberculosis, may fluctuate with your state of mind. Gastrointestinal conditions, sexual disturbances, heart disease and countless other ailments have been found by investigators to have strong psychological factors.

Even cancer has recently been linked to emotion. Researchers are finding that cancer victims are people who have long felt hopeless, who have believed their lives are doomed to despair. The onset of the disease, in many cases, is associated with a series of overwhelming losses which have caused the person to give up entirely.

You already know from your own experience that your body chemistry is interwoven with your emotional state. Merely recall the last time you had a bad cold. It is likely you were gloomy and short-tempered. You may have lost your enjoyment of food, reading and company. These mental effects were as much a part of the cold as the runny nose.

Tuberculosis is sometimes marked by lassitude, fatigue and vague aches and pains. These symptoms are so non-physical in the traditional sense that doctors may not initially regard the symptoms as genuine and consequently overlook TB in its early stages.

A similar problem is posed by pyelonephritis, a kidney

infection. Victims may be dismissed as 'depressed' or 'bored' before their physical condition is recognized.

Some types of cancer also mimic psychiatric illness. Dr Z.J. Lipowski of the Psychiatric Faculty of McGill University tells of having three patients referred to him over a brief period, each supposedly a psychotic suffering from depression. In each case Dr Lipowski found the depression psychosis was a result of undetected cancer of the pancreas.

Nutritional disorders may also affect behaviour in bizarre ways. Pellagra results from a dietary deficiency of niacin, a compound of the vitamin B complex. The first cases in the United States were found in institutions for the insane. The patients were psychotic, disoriented and suffering from hallucinations and delirium. Once niacin was added to their diet their symptoms disappeared.

You have in your brain some ten million interconnected nerve cells. When a cell receives a stimulus, it produces a molecule of substance called ribonucleic acid (RNA). This molecule causes the cell, upon receiving a given impulse, to respond in a certain way – such as varying in its chemical makeup, releasing certain compounds, or taking part in an electrochemical circuit. Such responses constitute your mental activity. Thus, RNA may prove to be an essential unit of memory.

Proprioceptive Sensations

A 'charley horse' is a proprioceptive sensation, as is a stomach ache. For that matter, so is an orgasm. A general sense of well-being is such also.

Your emotions are proprioceptive sensations. If this surprises you, where do you feel that surprise? In the back of the neck? In your stomach? The precise spots vary from person to person. But for every emotion you feel, you do just that; you feel it. Physically, you feel it in specific locations.

In the same manner as your intellectual ability to

multiply 2 by 3, emotions exist in your body cells. Tune into yourself the next time you feel in a particular way – happy, sad, whatever. You will essentially experience the same set of proprioceptive sensations which have come to constitute the feeling you have labelled happiness or sadness. Happiness may in part be a lightness in your chest; sadness may be a leaden weight in the same place. From such proprioceptive locations come the figures of speech 'lighthearted' and 'heavyhearted'.

Painful feelings, such as anxiety and depression, are literal pains. They are hurtful, proprioceptive sensations. When you say, 'My feelings are hurt', you mean exactly that. The ache of rejection is no less an ache than that of a crushed finger.

Common sense suggests that first you should have an emotional experience followed by your bodily expression. Presumably you are sad, that is why you cry. You are afraid and so your heart beats faster. You become enraged, and in response to your rage, your adrenal glands pump the hormone adrenaline into your bloodstream. According to a popular belief, a stimulus (S) produces an emotion (E), which leads to psychological responses (PR), such as tears, or an increased heartbeat or adrenaline in your bloodstream.

Subsequent studies have also shown that adrenaline pours into your bloodstream in dozens of circumstances other than those provoking rage. Can the same amount of adrenaline in one situation be experienced as rage, in another as excitement, in a third as ecstasy? By itself, it cannot. Such a bodily reaction alone is too indiscriminate to account for the subtle range of emotions we are capable of experiencing.

Finally, experiments have demonstrated that there is a component to emotion over and beyond outpourings of hormones. subjects were injected with fear-related hormones. In a detached way, many of them felt as if they were afraid. But few experienced the actual feeling of fear.

A current view of emotion holds that it is largely a function of the **limbic** system. *'Limbic'* means 'border'. The structures comprising the system extend from the fringe of the brain to the centre of the brain.

The limbic system is a primitive part of the brain. Its counterpart is found in the brains of lower animals. This is contrasted with the cerebral cortex, found only in more complex animal brains. Intellectual activity is centred in the cerebral cortex.

The limbic system has a strategic relationship with other areas of your brain. It provides clues to the interplay between your conscious awareness and your bodily feelings.

Tracings show that through circuitry from your sense organs, the limbic system can receive external stimuli, i.e. sights, sounds, tastes, smells and touches which can evoke emotion. Through other nerve connections the limbic system can respond to your body sensations and can work in close association with centres of consciousness in your cerebral cortex.

Your emotions, then, are physical phenomena, existing in your body as proprioceptive sensations. They are products of a complex interplay between portions of your brain: the cerebral cortex, the centre of conscious interpretation; the limbic system, which serves as a clearing house; and the hypothalamus, which regulates the autonomic nervous system.

The Endocrine System

When you are relaxed, your parasympathetic nervous system predominates. Your brain functions at a moderate state of arousal. After a meal, you are likely to become somewhat drowsy as blood is shunted from your brain and muscles to your digestive tract. You breathe easily. Your heart beats regularly and slowly. Your skin is warm and dry.

Let us, then, suppose there comes a menacing sound from

the next room. As if alerted by a siren, you mobilize your resources. Abruptly your sympathetic nervous system takes over. Your digestion comes to a halt. Blood shifts to your muscles and brain. Your brain becomes highly aroused. You suck in air more deeply. Your heart beats faster. As the peripheral blood vessels contract, your skin becomes cold and clammy. Sugar, a fast burning fuel, is released into your blood from your liver. Fat gets mobilized for fuel. Additional red corpuscles enrich the circulation. White cells, to combat infection, pour from your spleen. Increased platelets increase your blood's ability to coagulate.

Physiologists have named this set of responses the **fight or flight pattern**. In a test on a cat which was fed a meal laced with salts of the element barium so that the cat's stomach could be viewed on X-ray film, researchers found that when the cat was content its stomach went through wave-like digestive motions, now looking like a smooth sausage, now like an hourglass pinched in two or three places.

The instant the cat was angered or frightened, the emotions came to a dead halt. As if paralysed, the stomach remained smooth or constricted for an hour or more. It remained frozen even after the cause for fright was removed and the cat made comfortable.

As an explanation, researchers have advanced the emergency theory, in which adrenaline prepares the animal for fight or flight during times of stress. In an emergency, the animal suspends non-essential tasks such as digestion, and quickly becomes physically capable of meeting its enemy or running away.

In humans, these changes are associated with such elemental emotional experiences as pain, fear and rage. The physical changes you undergo are the results of man's natural instinct for self-preservation.

Adrenaline is secreted from the interior of the adrenal gland, a two-inch long and roughly pyramidal structure straddling one end of each kidney. The adrenal gland is triggered by the sympathetic nervous system, and this nerve-gland system gave experimenters the first clues to the inseparability of mind and body and the causes of psychosomatic ills.

A gland is a collection of cells specialized for the secretion of fluids. The first glands explored by physiologists were the exocrine glands, which release secretions through ducts onto a selected body surface. The salivary glands are exocrine. They send saliva into the mouth through a minute tube. The sweat glands similarly have ducts connecting with the surface of the skin.

The other major group of glands (endocrine, or ductless glands, such as the adrenal) are far more important in the development of psychosomatic disease. These glands release their secretions directly into the blood. The secretions, termed hormones from the Greek horman meaning 'to stir up'), are highly potent. Though greatly diffused, a mere drop may stimulate a certain activity.

A few crystals of adrenaline, dissolved in 100,000 parts of water, can be injected into a cat. In less than a minute the cat will arch its back and bare its claws. Its widened pupils gleam. Its whiskers stiffen. It foams at the mouth. Its tail bushes out to several times its normal size. Its heart is racing, its breathing is rapid, and its blood is overflowing with sugar. All of this occurs from an injection the equivalent of a sprinkle of salt in a bath tub full of water.

It has further been found that adrenaline causes the liver to release amounts of sugar into the blood. A normal cat, when frightened, has abnormal amounts of sugar in its urine; whereas in cats whose adrenaline glands have been removed, the sugar levels remain the same.

What is the applicability of this to humans? One particular study took urine samples of Harvard students while they were in the midst of difficult examinations. With striking frequency, excessive amounts of sugar were found in their urine due to adrenaline released in response to the emotional strain of their examinations.

Almost any type of emotional strain can raise your

production of adrenaline. Some stressful situations which have been explored are:

Air travel: Investigators found adrenaline levels increased significantly among passengers of military air transport after the plane took off. Even the pilot experienced a marked rise in adrenaline during flight.

Harassment: Volunteers were given a series of tasks and set about doing them diligently. But, when rushed and criticized unfairly, the adrenaline output of the angry, frustrated volunteers skyrocketed.

Tiredness: Lack of sleep can greatly increase the emotional stress of a situation and the consequent secretion of adrenaline. Volunteers suffered the loss of a night's sleep, and this alone caused increased adrenaline. When the volunteers tried to perform routine laboratory tasks following a night of sleep loss, their adrenaline response was even more exaggerated.

Fear: Four-year-old Denise was to undergo the extraction of some baby teeth. She had previously had a bad experience with a local anaesthetic for some stitches in her forehead. Now, screaming, she baulked at sitting in the dentist's chair. It was necessary for the dentist to, first, give her a sedative. Within minutes of the extraction she had a heart attack and was rushed to the hospital. She died two hours later. The coroner found that her heart had stopped because of the adrenaline excess in her bloodstream initiated by fear.

The substance 'noradrenaline' was discovered in 1946. Noradrenaline is secreted by the adrenal medulla. It serves to increase blood pressure during emergencies. Noradrenaline may help to spur you on to vigorous, aggressive behaviour. Studies of African mammals show that aggressive animals (lions and the like) have higher levels of noradrenaline pumping through their circulatory systems than do non-aggressive beasts such as giraffes and antelopes.

The medulla of the adrenal gland is covered by a bark-like cortex, resembling the shell around a nut. The cortex is a gland completely independent of the medulla. similar to adrenaline, the hormones of the adrenal cortex ebb and flow with the changing emotional states. They have been studied primarily in their response to emotional stimuli.

Subsequent investigators have found that the adrenal cortex is essential to maintaining the levels of sodium and potassium in your blood and cells. When the balance is upset because of damage to the cortex, the blood loses water and thickens while the tissues become waterlogged and disabled. Toxic wastes gather in the kidneys, poisoning the body. The body become less and less able to withstand infections, cold and heat. Even a slight injury or illness can cause shock and even death.

Some of the steroids (for example, cortisone and cortisol) raise muscle strength and efficiency and increase blood flow in certain parts of the body. This group, called glucocorticoids, also reduce inflammation and protect the tissue against the effects of injury.

Because of their anti-inflammatory properties, those compounds extracted from animals and those synthesized in labs have wide use in the treatment of conditions ranging from poison ivy to rheumatoid arthritis.

Other corticosteroids, the mineralcorticoids, promote proper sodium and potassium balances in the blood and cells and help regulate the functions of the kidneys.

There is a hormone linkage, a sort of chemical telegraph system, between the brain and the adrenal cortex. This method of sending a message from the brain to a gland is wholly different to the nervous system which connects the hypothalamus of the brain to the adrenal medulla.

The hypothalamus also connects across a bridge of nerve tissue with the pituitary gland, a pea-sized structure which emits at least ten different secretions. The pituitary gland is called the **master gland** of the endocrine system because it produces secretions which trigger other glands, **target glands**, to produce, in their turn, hormones.

On receiving a certain message from the hypothalamus,

the pituitary releases into the bloodstream ACTH, (adrenocorticotropic hormone) – the suffix 'tropic' means 'acting upon'. ACTH acts on the adrenal cortex, causing it to secrete steroids. The pituitary-adrenal cortical system is remarkably sensitive to even subtle psychological factors.

In animals, the housing conditions, the amount of handling, the degree of social activity with other animals, are all reflected in corticosteroid changes. Marked responses are noted in novel experiences. Transferring a monkey from one cage to another, for example, will send its ACTH response up, as will punishing it or placing it in a restraining chair.

Human corticosteroid responses to stress are similar. A young woman showing symptoms of hyperthyroidism had developed the disease just after an accident in which she was badly frightened but suffered very little injury. Studies were initiated to observe how sharp emotional disturbances might influence the thyroid gland and to observe the relationship between psychological trauma and the disease.

Since these early studies, the frequent occurrence of severe emotional distress just prior to the onset of hyperthyroidism has been widely reported.

One researcher found evidence of psychological trauma in 94% of 200 hyperthyroid cases he investigated.

Another investigator reported a 'clear history of psychological trauma as the exciting cause' in 85% of 3,343 cases. Eleven per cent of the total cause involved reactions to surgery or the delivery of a baby. An additional 13% had severe life-threatening crises, such as fires, earthquakes, car accidents, combat experience, or narrow escapes from other accidents. By far the largest category – 61% of the patients – had sustained long periods of emotional disturbances, such as worry, disappointment, or grief.

Hyperthyroid victims often suffered grave threats to their security in early childhood. Many lost their mothers early in life. Others were brought up by parents who were unhappily married. Still others felt rejected by one or both parents, or felt displaced by a brother or sister. Commonly, the hyperthyroid victim is the eldest child in a family that was deprived both economically and emotionally.

In such situations the child may be left with feelings of being deserted. This can lead to pronounced fears of death from violence or neglect. This child may perceive an actual threat to his physical being.

What often characterized hyperthyroid patients is their negative pattern of handling anxiety. Commonly, a person with thwarted dependency needs shows manifestations of regression. he turns to infantile patterns of reacting. The person likely to develop hyperthyroidism takes the opposite tack; he seeks to become excessively mature.

Hyperthyroidism can explode in a person. **Shock Basedow** (named after the physician who first described it) is the term for the onset of hyperthyroidism a few hours after a severe emotional jolt, such as the catastrophic loss of a relative or a narrow escape from death.

By far the most common precipitant, however, is a series of stressful events which the patient senses as calamitous to his emotional security. This may be the gradual dissolution of a marriage upon which a person has placed his complete emotional stability. Another frequent precipitant is the death of an ageing mother and father within a short period of time, to which the patient responds by thinking: 'Now I am really alone. I can no longer feel protected.'

General Adaptation Syndrome

Your total being strives to maintain a precarious balance

Diabetics may suffer impaired circulation. Heart ailments and amputations among diabetics are not uncommon. In rare cases, the blood, which is normally faintly alkaline, becomes acidic, and this condition can kill quickly.

Conversely, if blood sugar is too low over a long period of time, the cells get too little food and fuel. The nervous system is affected first, and the victim of hypoglycaemia, (from the Greek meaning 'low sugar in the blood') may be confused and have hallucinations. Convulsions, and ultimately coma, may also result.

Internal mechanisms continually try to maintain your delicate balance of blood sugar, so that the concentration remains essentially the same no matter how much sugar you consume or how much energy you expend.

The body is, thus, in a state of perpetual physical adjustment. that is why if any hormone goes awry, illness is likely to occur. Insulin is the obvious example in this illustration. If too little insulin is secreted, diabetes develops. If too much is secreted, hypoglycaemia results.

The picture is never simple, since no hormone acts alone. For example, the normal response to hypoglycaemia is a massive outpouring of adrenaline.

Thus, in addition to the symptoms of too little sugar, the victim suffers those symptoms of adrenaline excess: over-rapid heart actions, a rise in blood pressure, anxiety, sweating, and pallor. Any of these in turn can lead to further complications.

Each person meets the challenge of stress in his own way. The family quarrel which triggers a heart attack in one may make another resentful, while for a third it may serve as a goad to useful and productive work. Whatever the response, it involves the whole individual. Inseparably, the body and mind both play a part in dealing with the stresses of life.

Everyone recognises the influence of emotion upon the flow of tears, the secretion of sweat, the colour of the face, or the temperature of the hands.

'Everyone knows the racing heart of excitement, the gasp of horror, the panting of passion. In a resentful man, the effect of the situation which rouses his resentment will be portrayed in his nose, his stomach, his urinary tract, his posture, and the sour look on his face. The entire organism reacts to an environment which it has interpreted as threatening.'

(Cornell University internist, David P. Barr)

The late Dr F. Harold G. Wolff advanced a theory that the body reacts to stresses, emotional as well as physical, by choosing from a limited repertoire of mechanisms of response: changes in heart rate, respiration, hormone flow, and so forth. Then, since these responses may be related to the immediate situation, they may disturb homeostasis (i.e. organic equilibrium were there is a tendency for an organism to maintain a uniform psychological stability between and within its parts) rather than restore it. They may even be more damaging than the original threat. Disease is often primarily the manifestation of such an unsuitable response, particularly when this response is prolonged or frequently repeated.

In one study to determine if stress makes rats more susceptible to illness and death, the researchers used three groups of rats. One group was administered electrical shocks. The second group got shocks preceded by a warning signal. The third group received neither shocks nor signals.

The group that became ill and died earlier had been exposed to shock plus warning signals – **double stress**, since the signals caused anticipation in addition to the actual pain. In contrast, the group exposed to neither shocks nor signals had the lowest incident of death and sickness.

Adrenal enlargement, gastrointestinal ulcers, and thymolymphatic shrinkage are the omnipresent signs of damage to the body when disease attacks.

Whatever was done to the animals in experiment, whether adrenaline or insulin was shot into them, whether they were exposed to cold or heat, or to X-rays, or to physical injuries, they always underwent the same physiological changes, following the same pattern. In addition to the specific reactions (burns or injuries, for example), this complex sequence of responses could always be seen.

The study showed that this syndrome could be brought about by any stressful situation, by emotional tension as well as physical distress. The conclusion was drawn that disease is not just suffering, but is a fight to maintain the homeostatic balance of our tissues when they are damaged.

No organism can exist continuously in a state of alarm. An agent, so damaging that continuous exposure to it is incompatible with life, causes death within hours or days of the alarm reaction. However, if survival is possible, the alarm reaction gives way to the stage of resistance.

What happens in the resistance stage is, in many instances, the exact opposite of events in the alarm reaction. For instance, during the alarm reaction, the adrenal cortex discharges hormones into the bloodstream. Consequently, the gland depletes its stores. In the resistance stage, the gland accumulates an abundant reserve. Again, in the alarm reaction, the blood volume diminishes and body weight drops. But during the stage of resistance the blood is less concentrated and body weight returns to normal.

Curiously, after prolonged exposure to any noxious agent, the body loses its ability to resist. It enters the third stage, that of exhaustion. This stage always occurs as long as the stress is severe enough and is applied long enough, because the adaptability of a living being is always limited.

This entire response is called 'The General Adaptation Syndrome' (GAS). **General**, because it is produced only by agents that have a general effect upon large portions of the body; **adaptive** because it stimulates defence and thereby helps insure the body against hardship; **syndrome** because its signs are coordinated and partly dependent on each other.

This whole system is an evolution through three stages:

1. the alarm reactions;
2. the stage of resistance;
3. the state of exhaustion.

The important role in the resistance stage is played by the

hormone ACTH, which stimulates the adrenal cortex to produce secretions.

Derangements in the resistance stage lead to diseases of adaptation. These diseases are caused not by any particular agent but by the body's normal response to the stress produced by the agent. For example, the excessive production of ACTH in response to some mild local irritation could damage organs far from the original site of the injury. In this sense, the body's own reactions seem to encourage various maladies. This could include emotional disturbances, headaches, insomnia, sinus attacks, high blood pressure, gastric and duodenal ulcers, certain rheumatic and allergic afflictions, and cardiovascular and kidney troubles.

With sustained stress the adrenal cortex hormones tend to constrict blood vessels in the kidneys. If the stress is sufficiently prolonged, hypertension and damage to the kidney may result.

If, within a year, your spouse runs off with another person, you've been swindled by a favourite aunt, your business goes bankrupt, and you lose your house through foreclosure, look out! These disasters indicate the imminence of something perhaps even worse. Within twelve months you are almost sure to come down with a major illness.

On the other hand, if, in one year you wed a dreamboat, discover a cure for an ill beleaguering mankind, win the National Lottery, and master the glockenspiel, again beware. Such triumphs also point us to the serious possibility of illness within twelve months.

Another survey gave some 400 people a list of 43 major 'life events', such a marriage, personal achievement, change in financial status, son or daughter leaving home, or divorce. The 400 subjects were asked to rate the life events as to the relative degree of adjustment needed for each. The top ten came out in this order; death of a spouse, divorce, marital separation, jail term, death in the family, personal injury of illness, marriage, being fired from a job, marital reconciliation, and retirement.

Next, the subjects were asked to list by year, for the previous ten years, any major life events which had happened in their lives. Afterwards, their lists were compared with their medical histories. In case after case, the year in which several major life events occurred was followed by a year in which the person was stricken with serious illness.

The connection between stressful life events and disease is based on the function of the body's immunity system. Fear, excitement and strain may well weaken it. Stressful events may also upset emotional balance by affecting hormone production. Either way, big events in your life may mean that you will subsequently be ill.

The death of a spouse is especially likely to bring on illness. A widower, in the first six months following his wife's death, is half again as likely to die of coronary disease than other men of his age.

Sharp changes can evidently make children, as well as adults, more susceptible to disease. In one study, it was found that in the six months before becoming ill, every sick child had experienced at least one major life change. These changes tended to pose a considerable threat to the child's well-being. A close family member may have been seriously ill or died. The child's best friend may have moved away. The child may have been permanently placed in another home.

The severe changes such as death, severe illness or separation tended to be compounded by still further disruptions. The child's school situation may have been radically altered. Under the tension of the change, family members may have related differently to the child.

Moving to a new residence is a major life change which sometimes precipitates illness. Even to well-off families, moving to a new house may precede severe emotional illness, with many psychosomatic symptoms.

Complaints of heart palpitations and constant tension

headaches were reported to a medical doctor by a number of husbands involved in household relocations. The disorder and upheaval of the move to a new home, the long drawn out legalities in preparation for the move, the new mortgage payments, and the competitive feelings toward the new neighbours, were part of the extreme stress imposed upon them.

Sexual problems for both men and women became underscored by a move. For some couples, having children had been delayed until the couple had a house. Now, with a newly acquired home, the husband and wife were confronted with the inadequacy of their sexual relations and the threat of assuming parent roles.

Of the two major causes of occupational stress, work that is beyond your own capacity is the more troublesome. If difficulties arise through organizational shortcomings, you can always argue for organizational change or increased resources. Your personal reputation is not at stake, the shortcoming is outside you.

But when the cause of difficulty is your own inability to cope with the situation, you are likely to alternate between being anxiously indecisive and being unwise and rash in your decision making. To do badly in your job is to expose the fact that your abilities are lower than your level of responsibility calls for.

Shift work apparently increases the job holder's problems. Men working afternoon and night shifts have greater strain and tension in marriage than do day workers. Men working the night shift report difficulties with their roles as protectors of their family and as husbands. They are disturbed by sexual incompatibility with their wives.

Shift workers are also commonly bothered by problems of body function which ordinarily are influenced by the clock; sleep, appetite, moving the bowels. They are more likely to suffer colds, headaches, infectious diseases, ulcers and rheumatoid arthritis.

Early physicians commented that diabetics are fond of

the pleasures of the table, that heart disease most often occurs among the anxious, that peptic ulcer sufferers are frequently hard-driving go-getters.

Expressions such as 'melancholia' reveal the intuitive knowledge that depressed people suffer from gall bladder disturbance. Melancholia, a term for severe depression, is derived from the Greek *'melas'*, meaning 'black', and *'chole'* meaning 'gall'.

It has been observed that personality types not only exist, but fall into three broad categories. In some diseases the typical sufferer is excessively apprehensive. He readily expresses his thoughts and freely reacts to his feelings of fear or anger. In nearly all his spheres of living, he is physically and verbally active.

This first personality type was asked, among other questions, 'If you were sitting on a park bench and a stranger – just your size, age and sex – walked up and kicked you in the shins, what would you do?' Most such patients, instead of saying they would demand a reasonable explanation, replied: 'We'd have a showdown', or 'I'd beat the heck out of him'. This type of patient is termed the 'excessive reactor'. In this category fell nearly all of the victims of coronary occlusion, degenerative arthritis and peptic ulcer.

Another type of patient is much the opposite. He tends to suppress his fear and anger, indeed is not even aware he has such feelings. He inhibits his actions and holds back his thoughts.

If kicked in the shins by a stranger, what would such people do? Most of them reply: 'Nothing.' Nearly all the sufferers of neurodermatitis, rheumatoid arthritis and ulcerative colitis fall into this group of 'deficient reactors'.

A final group are the 'restrained reactors'. They are aware of their fears and anger but rarely act on or express them. A characteristic response to a kick in the shins is: 'I'd be pretty mad' or 'I might hit him'. In this group are most sufferers from asthma, diabetes, hypertension, hyperthyroidism and migraine.

Also studied were the accident prone. Typically, accident prone people fit the description 'happy-go-lucky'. They show little of the nervous tension that characterizes most psychosomatic patients, and would ordinarily be envied for their cheerful outlook on life.

However, they have an unstable character. They rarely complete difficult assignments. When the going gets tough or the responsibility heavy, they move on to something easier. Although usually intelligent, the accident prone person generally has little interest in intellectual values and deep thinking.

He usually likes people, however, and people like him. 'Charming' is frequently used to describe accident prone people. They mix well socially, often exuding a devil-may-care manner that many people find attractive. They like adventure and tend to avoid responsibility. They live from day to day, with little concern for tomorrow. The average person often envies tendencies in others because he cannot normally divorce himself from reality to the same extent.

The accident prone are quite casual about many things, including marriage and sex. Their marriages tend to be unstable. Extramarital affairs are relatively common with them.

Impulsive behaviour is a primary characteristic, as well. The accident prone make decisions quickly, often without adequate thought.

A characteristic trait among the accident prone is their resentment of authority: a hostility the person may not be consciously aware of. This resentment often can be traced to a parent who exercised authority in rigid, severe, overwhelming ways. As the child grows, his resentment of his parent attaches to other authority figures, represented by school, employer, spouse, government or church.

Most accident prone people are brought up in a strict religious atmosphere by stern, authoritative parents. A large proportion had neurotic traits in childhood. They walked or talked in their sleep, lied persistently, stole or were truant. These tendencies eventually disappeared, evidently replaced by the accident habit.

The accident prone person and many adult criminals share a number of the same traits, especially resentment of authority and a tendency toward impulsive behaviour. This tension leads one to break the law, the other to break his bones.

Variables

In patients suffering from organic ailments, similar emotional conflicts recurred too frequently to ignore. In such conflicts could lie clues to the cause of a specific psychosomatic disease.

From studies, clear patterns of motivation have emerged. Among them are the following: duodenal ulcer patients have a characteristic conflict about dependency needs. Asthma sufferers frequently fear losing their mother and have difficulty crying. Trouble in handling hostile impulses appears again and again in people suffering from hypertension. Neurodermatitis victims intensely crave physical closeness.

There is considerable evidence that a predisposition to a specific organic disease is inherited. For example someone may have as an X factor (i.e. an inherited variable) a vulnerability in his circulatory system this person may experience a second variable: a basic emotional conflict. His bodily response to this 'psycho-dynamic constellation' may now put a chronic strain on his heart or blood vessels.

As a final variable, this person, his vulnerable organs already under attack by his response to emotional conflict, finds himself in an 'onset' (something approaching) situation. Such an external life event may trigger a full-blown case of hypertension. Likewise, if the X factor was in the lining of his bronchial tubes, and a severe emotional conflict was present, he might develop asthma.

These variables may well be interrelated. A person born

with a vulnerable circulatory system may feel great hostility towards his parents, but never express it because he craves their approval. Unexpressed hostility may affect his internal chemistry, causing a constriction of the arteries and a build up of cholesterol on the artery walls.

His craving for approval may lead him to an onset situation, perhaps driving him to carry on his work dutifully even under unreasonably difficult conditions. Over-conscientiousness is a common trait among hypertensives. A 'beast of burden' may subtly invite heavier and heavier loads. He then may feel even greater unexpressed hostility. This in turn can cause further stress to his vulnerable organs and lead to a case of hypertension.

An inborn bodily defect lies at the root of diabetes. There may be either an inadequate production of insulin by the pancreas or an excessive destruction of insulin by the tissues. Either way, the sugar content of the blood is abnormally high. The condition is believed to exist from birth, though diabetic symptoms may show up only later in life. It is thought that prolonged stress, emotional as well as physiological, may result in a permanent failure of the person's already strained regulatory mechanisms. Then the disease becomes apparent.

Before the disease is discovered, Dr Helen Flanders Dunbar found diabetics have a long history of deprivations, fatigue, weariness and a sense of depression and hopelessness.

The emotional picture may be the result of the unrecognized disorder in metabolism. It is thought, however, that these emotional difficulties represent psychological conflicts that have been boiling beneath the surface. Studies have also shown that diabetics may have an insatiable wish to be fed. One theory is that this craving may cause the release into the bloodstream of large quantities of sugar. Unable to obtain satisfaction for his infantile oral desires, the diabetic may unconsciously release from his sugar reservoirs the food he wants.

The Will to Live

As every doctor knows, one of the most important requirements for recovery in any patient is his will to live.

A great majority of patient hospitalized for physical illness experience a psychological disturbance before they got sick.

Most commonly this was not anxiety, fear or anger – the emotions ordinarily considered to be associated with sickness – but an attitude of 'giving up'.

'What's the use?' patients would ask. Or they would report: 'It was just too much.' 'I couldn't take it any more.' 'I didn't know what to do.'

Giving up takes at least two forms: helplessness and hopelessness.

In helplessness the victim feels let down or left out. Patients recall experiencing such a feeling as the result of a change or an impending change over which they feel powerless and for which they do not feel themselves responsible.

In hopelessness, on the other hand, the victim has a feeling of futility or despair engendered by what he thinks of as his own failure. He feels incapable of compensating in any way for the failure, and he sees no possibility that anyone can help him.

Certain personality traits appear to be associated with each of these aspects of giving up. For the person most likely to experience helplessness, his first response to a situation is often one of anger and fear. He feels chronically deprived.

The person likely to experience hopelessness, on the other hand, often is overactive and selflessly devoted to others. Irrespective of his accomplishments, he has difficulty feeling successful. His feelings of hopelessness are often preceded by feelings of guilt or shame.

A widow fitting the description of hopelessness was informed that her last living sister had died. She bitterly condemned herself for not having visited the sister and helping her, even though this was not realistically possible. An hour later she had a stroke.

If persons who are biologically disposed to a disease, helplessness and hopelessness may provide the climate suitable for the development of the disease. One woman had a normal number of streptococcal bacteria in her throat kept in check by antibodies. When shame and guilt inhibited her from expressing her wishes for protection and loving, the streptococci increased, evidently because her resistance weakened. Conversely, when she was attempting to resolve such conflicts in a realistic manner and found herself a more worthwhile person, her resistance was restored and the bacterial count dropped significantly.

Generally, giving up follows the loss, or threat of the loss, of someone or something close to the patient – a wife or husband, parent, child, home, job or career plan. It is not the loss itself that is significant in the development of illness, but the way the person reacts to the loss.

Such losses may be actual, threatened, or symbolic. An actual loss includes the death of someone in the family or of a close friend, the loss of a husband or wife by divorce, the loss of money, home or job. A threatened loss can be the serious illness of someone close, or an indication that someone close, possibly a child, is trying to break away or an impending operation that is viewed as a threat to life or normal functioning. A symbolic loss may be a reverse, a rejection, or a rebuff. Often such a symbolic loss seems insignificant to an observer. It is important to the victim, however, because it reawakens feelings of despair stemming from a past threat or unresolved conflict.

Fixation

Figures of speech show the natural tendency to focus on just one part of a reaction. A frightened person is said to be 'in a sweat', 'scared stiff', 'weak at the knees' or 'breathless'.

The person himself, if chronically frightened, is likely to

accentuate only one of these responses, and so may experience such conditions as hyperhidrosis (excessive perspiration) or constipation or muscular rigidity. This may come about because one of these reactions has become a 'fixation', an uncontrollable preoccupation. Therein the individual response is magnified and develops into a symptom.

Evidence shows that such a fixation can affect the function of an organ. Patients with psychosomatic disorders typically are preoccupied with the area of their illness, the hypertensive with his blood pressure, the asthmatic with his breathing. The patient would gladly get rid of the fixation, but he finds himself obsessively locked in repetitive rumination which may intensify his symptoms.

Guilt, especially over one's feelings towards one's parents, may also influence the choice of symptoms.

Physicians attuned to psychosomatics often look for 'anniversaries'. Frequently a patient's symptoms appeared on the anniversary of his parents' death or of the parents developing a similar condition. These symptoms can be a form of self-punishment for going against one's parents, perhaps for wishing them dead.

Guilt of another sort can lead to a faulty 'body image', i.e. the way you see your body and what you expect of it. If an infant is loved and fondled, and if he has a secure and predictable environment, he can successfully turn his interest from himself. First, he turns his attention to his mother, then to the outside. A child so brought up generally has a satisfactory body image. He takes the good functioning of his body for granted and views it as a basically dependable and sturdy mechanism.

On the other hand, if his body image is deficient, he may never outgrow an aspect of infancy: a preoccupation with his own body, in a pattern of fixation that can intensify a psychosomatic symptom and disturb normal functioning.

Self-exploration of the body is essential to development of an adequate body image. It enables the child to learn where his body leaves off and the world begins. Inevitably the child explores his genitals and his urine and faeces. If his parents are outraged by this normal curiosity, the child is likely to feel guilty and frightened. He may extend the taboo to his whole body.

Psychosomatic patients are often ignorant of their body and how it functions. They find thinking about their body and its workings distasteful, even frightening. This is usually in marked contrast to the person's sophistication in other areas of knowledge, and is thought to originate in the child's early guilt over self-exploration.

Pain Sensitivity

How much pain you feel depends greatly on what else is occupying your attention.

Boredom and isolation can increase your sensitivity to pain. Patients who are bedridden or housebound for prolonged periods have little sensory stimulation. Their world gets smaller and smaller as the illness continues. They see few people and have few diverting experiences. They become increasingly irritable, restless and anxious. They may begin to hallucinate.

Psychogenic pain is a common symptom of emotionally troubled people. Patients with anxiety states are particularly apt to have bodily pain. Mental work and emotional strain most commonly precipitate the pains. Pain of emotional origin tends to be located in the head and trunk and to last continuously for long periods. It remains constant throughout the waking hours, but barely interferes with sleep. This is in contrast to the pains of organic illness, which tend to rise and fall throughout the day, often interfere with sleep, and sporadically diminish for days or weeks.

A profile of the typical pain-prone individual has been drawn that such a person is likely to have a prominence of conscious and unconscious guilt. Pain serves as a means of atonement.

He generally has had a bitterly unhappy early relationship with his parents. Often he has a masochistic character structure (*masochistic*: the getting of pleasure from suffering physical or psychological pain, inflicted by others or by oneself), marked by a history of suffering and defeat and a fear of, or sometimes a panicked flight from, success. He may have a propensity to solicit pain, as evident by the large numbers of painful injuries, operations, and treatments.

Typically, he has a strong aggressive drive which is not fulfilled, pain being experienced instead. He develops pain when a relationship is threatened or lost. He has a tendency toward a sadomasochistic type of sexual development, with some episodes of pain occurring in conflict over sexual impulses (*sadism*: the getting of sexual pleasure from dominating, mistreating, or hurting one's partner).

The location of his pain is often determined by unconscious identification with a loved one. The pain is suffered by the patient himself, when in conflict with a loved one. It may, in fact, be pain suffered by a loved one, or be in the pain-prone person's fantasy.

'I get real pleasure killing the animal'. 'Hunting is man's place in nature'. 'I love to be by myself in the woods'. 'I never miss'.

The men who made these comments all suffer from unrelievable pain of emotional origin. Most have severe headaches. The rest have backaches, abdominal pains, or pains in the leg. Half have pain in two or more areas of the body. One says simply, 'I hurt all over'. All the men had difficulties controlling their aggressive impulses. In the woods, however, they could be murderous without fear of killing someone else or being injured themselves.

One of the most dramatic examples of largely psychogenic pain is the anguish amputees sometimes feel in an arm or leg that has been amputated. In most cases an amputee reports feeling a 'phantom limb' almost immediately after surgery. At first the phantom limb feels normal in size and shape, so much so that the amputee may reach out for objects with a phantom hand, or try to get out of bed by stepping onto the floor with a phantom foot. Amputees clench missing fists and even try to scratch missing fingers that itch.

Conversion Reactions

Anxiety/Fear/Hysteria

The most widely accepted definition of anxiety is 'apprehension, tension or uneasiness which stems from the anticipation of danger, the source of which is largely unknown or unrecognized.'

Anxiety and fear are accompanied by similar physiological changes. But anxiety is a nameless dread, a looming sense of imminent destruction. Fear, on the other hand, responds to a consciously recognized real life threat.

Anxiety, while painful, is not necessarily bad for you. It can be useful as a signal, keeping you on notice that a threatening situation is afoot.

A study of skydivers, parachutists who jump for sport, reveals how anxiety can be beneficial if respected and treated realistically.

Anxiety may be extremely harmful, however, when present to such an extent that it interferes with your effectiveness, the achievement of goals or reasonable emotional comfort. The pain of chronic anxiety, and the avoidance thereof, is without doubt, the single most common cause of mental illness. Freud called anxiety 'the central problem in neurosis ... What we call psychiatric disturbances are really the abnormal methods some individuals take to avoid anxiety.'

In a conversion reaction, (a neurosis characterized by the presence of bodily symptoms that have no physical cause) sensory organs often go awry. The sufferer may feel numb, as if parts of his body were anaesthetized. Or he may feel extreme unaccountable pain. One 17-year-old girl suffered from sharp pains in the right side of her abdomen. Doctors removed her appendix, which proved to be normal. The pain continued. Earlier, the girl had suffered an hysterical leg paralysis. It was concluded that her abdominal pains too were a conversion reaction.

The victim of a conversion reaction may go completely blind, or suffer from 'peephole blindness', a narrowing of the field of vision. He may become stone-deaf. He may lose his sense of smell or his ability to speak. Imaginary lumps in the throat and stiff necks are common conversion symptoms.

So is writer's cramp, a hand impairment that particularly afflicts people who have to express themselves on paper.

Hysteria refers to an illness resulting from emotional conflict and characterized by immaturity, impulsiveness, attention-seeking and dependency. Most present day psychotherapists discuss hysteria only in terms of its two principal manifestations. One is the conversion reaction. The other is the dissociative reaction (separating a group of related psychological activities into autonomously functioning units) marked by amnesia, sleepwalking dreaminess, and sometimes actual physical flight from one's surroundings, or even the generation of multiple personalities.

In a study of the conversion reaction, Freud and Breuer reported:

> 'We found to our great surprise at first, that each individual hysterical symptom immediately and permanently disappeared when we had succeeded in bringing clearly to light the memory of the event by which it was provoked.'

Reasoning back from the cure to the cause of conversion hysteria, they concluded:

> 'In hysteria, the unbearable idea is rendered innocuous by transmuting the quantity of excitation into some bodily form of expression.'

This discovery was the beginning of the vast research into 'the mysterious leap from the mind to the body' which is the subject matter of psychosomatics.

Hypochondria

Physicians call hypochondriacs 'crocks' and consider them and their ilk the bane of medical practice, to be referred away to a colleague (preferably a newcomer) as soon as possible. Quacks prey on them, providing the reassurance and mental comfort they urgently seek.

The hypochondriac suffers an obsessive preoccupation with his supposed ill health. At the same time, he bemoans his fate and punctuates his self-pitying with expressions of hopelessness. Yet he gives the impression that there is some source of satisfaction for him in being sick.

Hypochondriacs generally follow a series of steps, almost a waltz, as they wend their way through the world of medical care. Their unwitting partner is the doctor and the dance steps go like this:

1. The patient's demands for treatment, met by the physician's determination to examine and reinvestigate.
2. The doctor tries one medication after another to avoid at all cost missing an organic cause.
3. After each trial medication, the patient experiences some relief, followed by worsening. The net result being 'no change'. Wherein;
4. The patient and the physician become frustrated with each other, and the angry doctor labels the patient a 'crackpot' or 'untreatable'. Then the cycle starts again elsewhere.

A Yiddish proverb says, 'If things are too good, it's bad.'

This might well be the slogan of hypochondria, for it often accounts for the hypochondriac's reluctance to surrender his physical symptoms. Even more than sufferers of other psychosomatic conditions, he is protected from a more dreaded punishment. It would thus, in his mind, be dangerous for him to get well.

The hypochondriac's expectation of punishment is generally the result of unconscious feelings of guilt. Since guilt is painful, it is generally repressed from conscious awareness. It does not, however, cease to exist but continues to motivate a need for expiation, perhaps in the form of the hypochondriac's symptoms or, as he desperately fears, something worse.

Guilt, unconsciously believed, can be relieved only by suffering. A principle of paleologic (ancient logic) is the so-called 'law of talion', a concept that guilt of a crime (be it real or imagined) is assuaged only by an identical or similar punishment. Wishing a parent dead, then, can make a person unconsciously convinced that he, too, must die. The hypochondriac, therefore, finds his symptoms welcome. As the Yiddish proverb suggests, if he felt better, he would be worse off.

Most psychosomatic disorders achieve for the sufferer an unconscious primary gain, usually relief from the anxiety or guilt. Almost always there are also unconscious secondary gains: additional advantages made possible by illness. As an example of secondary gain, physical symptoms may be employed as a cover-up for psychiatric difficulties.

From some patients there is a lifelong cry to be taken care of. This is mixed with anger that there has never been enough love, protection or affection. Their symptoms arise evidently as a body language expressing their need to be cared for.

By going from doctor to doctor, they are appealing more for pity than for help. Pity is the coin by which they live in their desperate hunt for care. The women in the group rarely saw themselves in terms of having a future. Their day-to-day concern was for the present, immediate care.

Psychiatrist Charles Wahl offers this advice, adaptable for laymen who must deal with the hypochondriac:

1. **Listen**: A positive willingness to be listened to, rather than being merely tolerated, is what the hypochondriac wants and needs. He seeks a dependable relationship of trust and confidence. As soon as he is reassured of this, his need for unreasonable amounts of attention ordinarily diminishes.

2. **Take his symptoms seriously**: do not tell him that his pains are imaginary. Rather explain how tension can produce the symptoms which frighten him. Use pictures and diagrams to get anatomic and physiological points across.

3. **Focus on feelings**: Encourage him to talk openly about his deep feelings of fear and need. Help him to express other problem areas. Perhaps you can help him see that by concentrating on his health he may be avoiding other areas of difficulty.

4. **Accentuate the positive**: Do not suggest alternative fearful possibilities concerning his symptoms. This can terrify him.

5. **Do not urge new tests**: Hypochondriacs are prone to develop hysterical complications following such procedures as a bronchoscopy or spinal tap.

6. **Do not advise new medicines**: The hypochondriac tends to overdose himself with drugs and become dependent on them.

Anosogosia

The reverse hypochondriac says 'I guess I'm suffering from the tired housewife syndrome'. The following is such an example.

Lisa had four small children and a hectic household. This, agreed her doctor, could account for her fatigue and non-descript low-back pain. Bored, harassed homemakers frequently suffer this set of symptoms. The tired housewife syndrome, as Lisa knew, is nearly always psychogenic.

A less cautious doctor might have simply counselled Lisa

to spend more time on herself and sent her off with a prescription for a mild tranquilliser. Fortunately, Lisa's physician gave her a physical examination. In her left breast he found a substantial tumour.

Lisa was manifesting reverse hypochondria. Whereas the typical hypochondriac uses physical complaints to express an emotional disorder, Lisa was employing psychological symptoms to mask a physical condition.

Technically termed anosogosia, the syndrome is marked by an inability to recognize the existence of a disease. It is potentially far more perilous to the patient than is hypochondria. The typical hypochondriac would do well to be less mindful of his symptoms. The reverse hypochondriac may ignore an organic condition until it is fatal.

Alimentary Processes

Gut reactions are the digestive system reacting to stress, often with stomach pains, diarrhoea, and constipation. Peptic ulcer sufferers commonly hunger for love. In ulcerative colitis the victim may be bursting with unexpressed rage. Some people starve themselves, notably, infants who ruminate, i.e., spit up their food, and teenagers with anorexia nervosa, who refuse to eat though their lives are in danger.

Bill, a quiet newcomer to the encounter group, could contain himself no longer. Turning to Steven, he jumped up and shouted: 'I'm fed up. You're a phoney from the word go. I don't believe a thing you've said.'

Steven paled and gripped his stomach. In a few seconds he recovered and said to the group: 'Now I know what's meant by a gut reaction. After Bill said those hostile things to me, I felt a little sick inside. I really felt it in my gut.'

As Steven now had reason to know, the gastrointestinal system can be a barometer of psychological stress. Popular speech abounds with examples of the close connection between feelings and the gut: 'I can't stomach it'. 'I'm fed up'. 'What's eating you?' 'She nauseates me'. 'I can't swallow that story'.

A baby's first emotions are strongly associated with his eating cycle. The child's whole universe is centred on his need for food. He experiences his first relief from physical discomfort when he is held and nursed. Eating becomes almost identical with comfort and security. For the child, to be fed is to be loved. Hunger represents rejection and insecurity.

Another complex of emotions soon becomes associated with alimentary processes: possessiveness (of food, love, things), greed, jealousy, envy. These aggressive emotions are often considered antisocial and are likely to be repressed. Thus blocked from expression, they may create a permanent tension and exert a chronic disturbance in the digestive tract.

A child first learns to express his emotions in connection with eating. As an infant, he gurgles contentedly when he is full, complains angrily when he is hungry. Later in childhood, he is conscious of giving, as well as getting, pleasure when he eats well and moves his bowels to his parents' satisfaction.

As you mature, you find other ways of expressing emotion. 'We all retain the potential for using our stomach and intestines ... in the service of love, hate, dependence, giving, punishing, domination, frustration and other pleasant and unpleasant feelings.'

A person who chronically used digestive ways of expressing his feelings will start showing symptoms in the misused organs. These symptoms then may develop into fully-fledged psychosomatic diseases.

Tom went through a stressful period when he decided to undertake responsibility for the four children of his dead stepdaughter. For some weeks his stomach membrane was engorged and reddened. His acid secretion, significantly higher than normal began to eat away at the stomach lining. Such a situation, if it persists, sets the stage for a peptic ulcer. When his pay at the hospital was increased, his anxiety about providing for the children was relieved, and his stomach condition returned to normal.

Digestive disturbances may be symbolic of the patient's problem. A patient who can't 'swallow the situation', for example, may develop cardiospasm, a swallowing disorder in which the lower end of the oesophagus contracts.

Nausea and vomiting may occur as forms of symbolic rejection. Vomiting is often the response to stressful situations involving guilt about sex. Thirty-year-old Vera became nauseated whenever she attempted to have any social life with men. For twelve years her illness had forced her to abandon almost all social activity, and she had nearly given up all hope of marriage.

Vera was dominated by her ambitious and tyrannical mother. In childhood, Vera attempted repeatedly to gain her mother's favour. The mother resented the fact that her husband favoured Vera, and began openly to reject her. Vera was then even more emotionally dependent on her mother.

Vera inhibited all sexual activity, which she feared might increase her mother's hostility. Since her mother was the person who originally fed her, guilt and fear felt toward her mother led Vera to reject food. At the age of ten she vomited when a boy brought her food at a party.

When she was 25 a man became interested in her, increasing her guilt and anxiety. Her nausea and vomiting increased to such an extent that she lost 28 pounds in a few months. At a diagnostic clinic Vera was advised to lead a 'more active and normal life'. She misinterpreted this to mean sexual indulgence.

With her mother's explicit consent and active cooperation, she arranged an affair with her employer's son. During the seven months it lasted Vera's condition improved, although she found it difficult to eat in the presence of her lover. When he deserted her to get married, her symptoms reappeared and she returned to live with her mother.

In psychoanalysis, Vera, with great difficulty, acquired some insight into her extreme dependence on her mother and her anxiety-ridden attitudes towards food and sex. She now rarely suffers previous symptoms.

Chronic psychogenic constipation is another common gastrointestinal disturbance. Usually it has its antecedents in strained mother–child relationships in early childhood. When the child reaches the bowel-training stage he may react to the power struggle with his mother by become constipated.

For many children the withholding of faeces has the psychological function of expressing feelings of resistance and negativism towards a world which is perceived as hostile and unaffectionate. Obstinate withholding of faeces serves as a symbolic act of defiance and lays the basis for adult constipation problems. What began as partially conscious resistance in childhood later becomes unconscious constipation in adulthood.

The chronic constipation sufferer has a pessimistic, defeatist attitude. He distrusts or lacks confidence in others and feels unloved and rejected. He may have the feeling that he is being persecuted.

The unconscious emotional statement of people with chronic constipation is: 'I cannot expect anything from anybody, and therefore I do not need to give anything. I must hold on to what I have.' This possessive attitude is the outcome of the feelings of rejection and distrust. The excrement is retained as if it were a valuable possession, an attitude young children often have.

Stomach pain is a common reaction to a stressful situation. One boy developed severe abdominal pain every time his mother drove him to boarding school at the start of the school term. But during the summer holidays when he was driven to the school to pick up his bat which had been left behind he had no stomach pain at all.

Sometimes stomach pain is used as an instrument of punishment and control. Ten-year-old Susie unconsciously used abdominal cramps and diarrhoea to rule her parents. When they went out for an evening they invariably got a frantic call from the babysitter to come home immediately.

Once they found Susie doubled over and screaming with pain. Her paediatrician could find no organic reason for her pain. He suggested that her very real stomach pain was one of her most powerful instruments of control. Prescribed treatment included a concerted effort by Susie's parents to help her accept the controls appropriate to the life of a 10-year-old child.

Stomach symptoms can also be triggered by depression. One young man, Paul, complained of pain in the middle of his stomach which he had for more than two months. 'The pain can be sharp, so sharp that I feel nauseated, or it can be grinding and dull, and that has the same effect'. Since the pain began, he had lost about 30 pounds. His father had cancer of the bowel. One of his symptoms was severe abdominal cramps. 'He had terrible pains. He told me that he would not want to go through such pains again. In addition, he lost a considerable amount of weight.' Paul's symptoms were, thus, similar to his father.

The psychiatrist who treated Paul said he was in mourning for his dying father. 'The pain' represents a somatic identification with his sick father and a physical expression of his reaction to the impending loss of this emotionally important figure to him. Mourning may antedate actual death if the fatal illness is chronic and lingering, as it was in this case. Paul's condition improved in the hospital as a result of a bland diet, supportive therapy, and the fact that the hospital stay was a helpful interruption of his burdensome life.

Fear and anger frequently find expression in abdominal cramps and diarrhoea. Twenty-two-year-old Richard was discharged from the army because of recurrent attacks of severe abdominal pain and diarrhoea. He had been the driver for a captain and had never fought or been in any particular danger.

Richard's mother was a passive, complaining sort of woman who had several abdominal operations and frequent attacks of diarrhoea. His father was a dynamic businessman who treated his family like his business, making arbitrary and rapid fire decisions.

Richard could not recall any emotional problems he had at the time of his attacks. To help shake loose the repressed material, the doctors gave him an injection of sodium pentothal. They told him that he was now driving his truck on a particular day when he had an attack of cramps and diarrhoea. Richard then remembered having heard that enemy troops were in the neighbourhood. Suddenly, his truck broke down. He could hear shooting behind a hill. Richard was forced to stay with his truck until help arrived.

Under the influence of the drug, Richard verbalized his intense fears: 'I'm too young to die. I've been a good boy, I've never harmed anyone. What if I'm hurt or killed? Please God, save me'. He perspired and writhed on the bed as he relived this experience. When the pentothal wore off, Richard remembered that he had been scared but had forgotten the reason for his fear.

Peptic Ulcers

'The pain in my stomach is a constant one,' Andy was telling his doctor. 'The pain is vicious, so vicious I want to tear it out. It gets so bad that I feel like hitting my head against the table. When the pain is at its worst, it's like a gnawing, chewing away inside.'

Andy was describing the symptoms of his peptic ulcer. A peptic ulcer is an open sore in the inner wall of the stomach or on the mucous membrane of the duodenum, the part of the small intestine connecting to the stomach. If in the stomach, it is called a gastric ulcer; in the duodenum, a duodenal ulcer.

A peptic ulcer is almost always the result of stress. In Andy's case, from early in his life his stomach had become sensitive to emotional stress. He had always been picky about food. 'I was never a big eater,' he recalls, 'as a result, Mother paid special attention to what I ate.'

After his father died, when Andy was six, his mother had to go to work, and her special attention to his eating abruptly stopped. 'I had to get my own food until she came back in the evening.'

In the hospital Andy underwent surgery for a large duodenal ulcer. His condition has improved. A psychiatrist who interviewed Andy concludes that his ulcer was the result of stress situations which extended over a considerable period, and which included competition, separation from home and mother, maintaining two jobs, and the recent arrival of a baby.

'Long-standing intense dependency has been a striking feature of this patient's emotional life.' The defences against this have been principally in the form of overactivity and denial.

A peptic ulcer forms when acid stomach juices eat into the stomach or duodenal wall. The acid first erodes the inner membrane, forming a lesion called an acute ulcer. This ulcer may heal with proper diet, antacid medication and a decrease in tension.

But, if the acid is chronically overproduced, it eventually eats into the deeper muscle layer forming a chronic ulcer. At last, it may perforate the stomach wall entirely, permitting gastric juices to flow directly into the abdomen. Without prompt surgery, perforation may cause death.

The typical ulcer sufferer has a great deal of initiative and drive. He is a go-getter and is generally successful in his profession. His field is often a demanding one, requiring quick decisions and constant resolving of problems.

Most ulcer sufferers have intense wishes to be dependent. They want to be loved, mothered, cared for. These desires are holdovers from their needs as infants feeding at the breast.

They actually want, as adults, to be dealt with as if they were still being fed at mother's breast. Both psychologically and physiologically, they respond as if they are hungry all the time. Their stomachs are constantly secreting, as if about to receive food.

These infantile longings are often fought against because they tend to produce feelings of guilt and inferiority. The prospective ulcer patient may overcompensate by exaggerated aggressiveness, ambition and independence. He won't accept help from anyone and burdens himself with responsibilities.

Once the digestive tract has started to acquire a sore spot because of the dependency conflict, other emotions can contribute to the progress of the disease. Anger, fear, hostility and resentment are the most common. But any serious emotional shock may stimulate the ulcer process.

Peptic ulcer symptoms of children differ from those of adults. The pain often cannot be precisely located. It is less clearly related to meals and less often relieved by eating. Nausea and vomiting are more common in children. More often than do adult ulcer patients, children with ulcers suffer from loss of appetite, early morning pain and headaches.

Children with ulcers tend to be unassertive and to have a great deal of anxiety about expressing aggression or anger. They are children whose need for a secure love was not met. They react to emotional stress, especially anger and rejections from other people, with gastrointestinal impairment, including over-secretion of gastric acid. If this state of mind persists, it can lead to an ulcer.

John is much like his father. He is excessively compliant, passive yet stubborn in his intention not to go to school. He is bland, like his mother, with effeminate speech and mannerisms.

Psychiatrists found such youngsters were generally

strong-willed infants and retain an infantile stubbornness in the struggle to dominate their mothers. They are anxious, fearful of rejection and hostile. At the same time, they are passive and withdrawn outside the home.

Their mothers are over-protective and set few limits. The fathers hardly exist for the children. While they seem to have received some love from their parents, the youngsters apparently have no experience in tolerating frustration and no coherent view of reality. They retain infantile patterns of behaviour and an abnormal dependence on their mothers.

Ulcerative Colitis

Ulcerative colitis victims burst with unexpressed rage. The summer he was 11, Alex was sexually molested by an older boy in the neighbourhood. He was badly frightened and for a week or more he was exceptionally withdrawn, hardly uttering a word. For months he would not leave the house unless his parents came with him. Alex's father had gone looking for the older boy, threatening to kill him, but he had disappeared.

A year later, the older boy was picked up by the police. Alex refused to testify in court against his attacker. He was mortified at the thought of having to recount the details of the incident. He was particularly embarrassed because of the women present. But his father, the judge, and the policy all exerted strong pressure on Alex to testify. At last he acquiesced.

In court, Alex stuttered through his ordeal. A week later, he was severely constipated. His parents gave Alex repeated laxatives and enemas.

The constipation then became diarrhoea. Alex was having from ten to sixteen watery bowel movements a day. Soon they were mixed with blood and mucous.

Alex rapidly lost more than 20 pounds. His appetite was poor and he was dehydrated and weak. He cried frequently, and, recalls his father, 'would not let anyone touch him'. The family physician diagnosed this condition as ulcerative colitis and recommended various drugs, but Alex's condition grew worse.

The climax of this situation had come in the courtroom. Despite his great reluctance, Alex was coerced into testifying. Even his mother deserted him In knuckling under and testifying, Alex felt totally defeated. He was overwhelmed with shame and despair.

He also felt hostile and defiant, emotions which he repressed. He complied, but his hostility did not vanish. This complex of emotions often sets the stage for ulcerative colitis. For, at one and the same time, the bloody diarrhoea can represent loss of control and hostile defiance.

Ulcerative colitis is an irritation of the colon (the lower part of the large intestine) due to ulceration. It can be fatal if the ulcer perforates the colon.

The most common symptom is frequent bloody bowel movements. These loose discharges consist mostly of blood, pus and mucous with some faecal particles. Victims also commonly have abdominal cramps, sometimes with fever, vomiting, loss of appetite and dramatic weight loss.

The disease usually has many relapses and remissions before it becomes chronic. These remissions may be distinctly correlated with the patient's emotional life.

The colon reacts sharply to emotion. During periods of tranquillity it is pale and quiet, its secretions of enzymes low. During periods of anger and resentment, however, it becomes engorged with blood and very active. Secretions increase. Spots of abnormal tissue may occur.

Ulcerative colitis is thought to develop when a predisposed person fails to express chronic resentment and anger. On an unconscious level, the mucous membrane of the colon does respond to these repressed emotions. The ensuing engorgement and hyperactivity produces bleeding. Enzymes secreted by the intestine further erode the membrane, leaving it open to bacterial invasion.

Ulcerative colitis is often accompanied by severe depression and feelings of hopelessness and despair. The typical victim is immature and dependent, particularly towards his mother. He often is perfectionistic and rigid. He also tends to be wary of other people. Generally, one parent is domineering and threatening; the other, though quiet and seemingly submissive and martyr-like, controls through aloofness and inconsistency.

Symptoms of ulcerative colitis frequently appear when a person is faced with a situation which he feels he cannot deal with.

Colitis patients are often worried about finances and preoccupied with money matters. The disease may occur in response to financial obligations which are beyond a person's means.

Anorexia Nervosa

The people who starve themselves are victims of anorexia nervosa. Some infants spit up everything; some teenagers will not eat anything.

The mothers of babies who ruminate are almost invariably immature and dependent. They are incapable of providing warm, comfortable and intimate physical care for their babies. Often they are severely depressed and spend little time caring for the infant.

It sometimes happens that a physician has patients (they are more apt to be women) whose appearances are truly shocking. Their eyes seem brilliant. Their cheeks are hollow, and their cheekbones seem to protrude through the skin. Their withered breasts hang from the walls of their chests. Every rib stands out. Their shoulder blades appear to be loosened from their frame. Every vertebrae shows through the skin. The abdominal wall sinks in below the floating rib and forms a hollow like a basin. The thighs and calves of their legs are reduced to a skeleton. One would say it was the picture of an immured nun, such as the older masters have portrayed. These women appear to be fifty to sixty years old.

The syndrome is called **anorexia nervosa**, loss of appetite of psychic origin. It is often a misnomer, since many sufferers, called anorectics, are painfully hungry, especially in the beginning. Yet they cannot or will not eat. About 10% of anorectics starve themselves to death. The anorectic is often overactive, 'sustained by some unknown miracle of energy.'

Linked with the anorexia syndrome is apparently a grossly distorted body image. The most striking aspect of the patient was their denial of emaciation. Although most of the patients resemble the starved inmates of a Nazi concentration camp, not one expressed the slightest concern about being thin. On the contrary, many insisted they were too fat.

For many anorectic children, not eating represents a power play. Food provides weaponry in the struggle between the child and his parents. In early childhood food is a battleground for autonomy.

In adolescence, at an impasse between childhood and adulthood, the youngster may crave both independence and dependence. In psychological terms, not eating represents giving up dependence on the mother and can also express hostility toward the mother.

Sometimes, anorexia nervosa seems to grow out of an extremely ambivalent and guilt-provoking relationship with a parent.

Many anorectic youngsters, both boys and girls, stop eating because of fantasies of oral impregnation: they imagine they can become pregnant through the mouth. Some have the impression that obesity and pregnancy are the same thing. Said one: 'I'm scared to eat, because that would make me fat and I would get a baby that way.'

A boy compared conception, pregnancy and delivery with eating and digestion. 'Something goes into your body, it undergoes a process there, and then comes out' he said.

Another boy connected being fat with being feminine. He started dieting when he felt 'flabby and girlish'.

Frequently anorectics go on binges of uncontrolled eating. The condition, known as 'bulimia', often springs from a depressed or violent mood. A bulimic eats voraciously and indiscriminately, sometimes to the point of unconsciousness. Vast quantities of food may be gobbled up, loaves of bread, meats by the pound, whole cheeses. The over-eating is generally a form of aggression. One girl entirely consumed her sister's very large wedding cake on the night before the wedding.

In some extreme cases there can be severe emaciation due to the bizarre syndrome of both bulimia and vomiting.

Muscular Tension

Your emotions may be expressed through muscular disorders, bone deformities, headache, backache, fatigue. Rheumatoid arthritis victims tend to be seeming martyrs who seek to rule their families with an iron hand.

There is a type of personality often revealed by a tight jaw. Mark is such a person. Getting him to talk is like pulling teeth. He hold things in: emotions, ideas, words. He tends to be stingy; he gives little away, either of himself or his possessions.

Mark's physical appearance matches his personality, understandable since the tensions forming both personality and physique are the same. Mark's parents laughed at him when he expressed his feelings or desires. They treated harshly any strong statement he made in his own behalf. Before Mark entered grammar school, he learned that to talk was to risk ridicule and punishment.

Your body is your personality made visible, for your emotions lead you to adopt special body attitudes. Every expression of your body has a meaning and a history.

Muscular tension, however slight, can be measured by electromyogram, or EMG, a machine which records electrical impulses generated along muscle fibre. EMG readings profile the 'uptight response', the typical reaction pattern of chronically tense people. When startled by a sudden sound, both normal and anxious people show a comparable rise in muscle tension for the two-tenths of a second. A normal person's muscle tension drops quickly. But in anxious people, the whole degree of muscle contraction is high to begin with, the tension continues to rise and remains high for a prolonged period.

When tense muscles chronically pull on bone, they can cause the bone to become deformed. There is considerable evidence that muscle tension can stimulate the growth on which the muscle is anchored.

Headaches

Headaches may be caused by tension of the muscles binding the neck and the head. Additional pain may result from the constriction of arteries supplying the scalp and brain, the product of the tightening of muscles surrounding the blood vessels.

While the vast majority of headaches are caused by emotional stress, headache can be a symptom of a serious bodily condition. Among the organic disorders signalled by headache are kidney disease, liver and gall bladder disturbances, hypertension and brain tumour. The fact that constipation and indigestion often are accompanied by a headache has given rise to the folk notion that a good laxative is the best cure for an aching head. That may work for constipation, but not for tension.

Migraine is more than just a bad headache. An attack often begins with spots before the eyes, numbness and speech difficulties. When the headache hits, it always occurs on one side and is frequently accompanied by vomiting, nausea, chills and fatigue. After the attack the sufferer usually enjoys a temporary sensation of well-being.

The pain of migraine results from the abnormal

expansion of arteries to the cranium, the portion of the skull encasing the brain. Migraine afflicts about one in ten people. Common migraine seems especially likely to arise in response to specific events.

Migraine patients come from families which are undemonstrative and who suppress their feelings of aggression and hostility. They enforce rigid norms and place high value on attainment, doing well in school and making a lot of money.

A migraine sufferer is typically a perfectionistic, ambitious, rigid, and orderly. He is excessively competitive and unable to delegate responsibility. Such people often have an attitude of chronic resentment and are frustrated in not being able to live up to their unrealistic ideals. Faced with an insuperable task, they may come down with an attack of migraine. Panic is a frequent precipitant of attacks.

The most common prelude to migraine is repressed rage.

Low Back Pain

In the low back syndrome, the sufferer's back is stiff and he has difficulty bending and moving. His muscles are abnormally contracted and tender. Often there are shooting pains in his buttocks and legs.

Low-back pain is much like headache. It is very common and possible causes include some extremely serious bodily conditions. Cancer, tuberculosis and kidney disorders are among the severe organic problems producing backache.

A high percentage of physiologic low-back pain is associated with the intervertebral discs, the cushions of elastic tissue separating the vertebrae. One frequent cause of back injury is lifting a heavy object with the spine bent instead of straight.

Most back pain, like most headaches, is either emotional in origin, or represents a minor local condition intensified by psychological factors. Emotional conflicts can contract muscles and constrict blood vessels in the back. These tensions and constrictions can mimic the back pain caused by a slipped and degenerated disc.

Backache is often a conversion reaction representing repressed desires to attack. The stiffness and pain are thought to stem from an unconscious blocking of movements expressing impulses towards destruction.

Depression and Physical Symptoms

Backache is often a reaction to depression

Another major source of backache is the post-traumatic neurosis, a common reaction to sudden physical injury, as from an car accident. The sharp impingement of a force threatening to life and limb is likely to cause otherwise normal people to lose the ability to maintain their psychological equilibrium. A major personality upheaval may result immediately after the accident.

Backache is not the only condition masking depression. Impotence, insomnia, numbness, gastrointestinal disorders, heart palpitations, all are often depressive equivalents. About a fifth of all hypochondriacs are thought to be suffering from underlying depressions.

The depressed person tends to have symptoms that are generalized and a bit vague. A depressed person often feels pressure and a diffused, burning pain inside the chest.

Extended Fatigue

Fatigue is another common symptom of the depressed. The sufferer of fatigue may be unable to perform his daily duties. The slightest task may be a heavy burden. Such exhaustion can be perfectly normal after intense or extended stress. A temporary inability to respond to stimuli seems to be one of the body's ways of restoring equilibrium after unusual effort.

But most cases of prolonged fatigue, in which the person

feels excessively tired after only mild exertion, arise from emotional causes.

The person suffering chronic fatigue often cannot make decisions involving the slightest responsibility. When given an assignment, he becomes utterly confused and helpless. Throughout the day he remains drowsy. He takes to his bed as a haven.

His reaction to his inertia is generally acceptance rather than objection or amazement. He dwells on his tiredness and his need to lie down. He is unable to be with other people for any length of time without becoming restless. Other people find it difficult to be with him since he is depressing and uncommunicative. He finds comfort and safety in blanking out, having no feelings or thoughts. In this trance state he has a sense of invulnerability to any demands put upon him.

While such extreme tiredness seems to express a muscular weakness, the immediate physiological cause may be a deficiency in blood sugar. It is believed that fear and anger are not the only emotions which can stimulate the flow of adrenaline and, in consequence, an increase in the blood's sugar content. Enthusiasm, zest, and purposeful striving are also thought to have a tuning-up effect on the adrenal system.

Fatigue often results from a conflict between passive, dependent wishes and active, aggressive ambition. The fatigued person may suffer a lack of hope of achieving some cherished goal, or perhaps a frustrating struggle against insuperable odds. He may also lack a genuine incentive. Routine activities often are carried out primarily under external pressure on account of internal compulsion, but not on the basis of absorbing interest.

Arthritis

There are several kinds of arthritis. The Greek word means 'inflammation of joint'. The arthritis which occurs in many people after the age of fifty is osteoarthritis, a result of ageing, trauma to the joints and normal wear and tear. It is more common than rheumatoid arthritis and as a rule less damaging. The arthritis referred to in this chapter is entirely rheumatoid.

In rheumatoid arthritis there is inflammation of the joints, usually those of the extremities. Damage is often irreversible. Tissue may fill the fluid sacs between the bones, solidifying the joint and leaving the sufferer stiff and crippled.

The rheumatoid arthritic is three times as likely to be a woman as a man. While the disease can begin at any age, it largely starts off in young adults, the average age at onset is about thirty-five. It is one of the five leading causes of disability among workers.

Rheumatoid arthritis is thought to begin with an inherited susceptibility. An indicator of a person's vulnerability to the disease is possibly a blood protein termed the rheumatoid factor.

Emotional stress evidently tips the balance so that the vulnerable person develops actual symptoms. Only those individuals with significant emotional conflict go on to the development of the disease.

The interplay between emotional and hereditary factors is shown in a study of sets of identical twins of whom one has rheumatoid arthritis. The twin who developed rheumatoid arthritis was involved, shortly before his illness, in a demanding and restricting situation.

Rheumatoid arthritics typically have great difficulty in letting out anger. In a study of 16 women with rheumatoid arthritis, only two would admit to even having angry feelings. In a situation where most people would be 'mad as heck', these women would 'feel hurt' or 'get upset'. Almost never would they reveal their anger to their husbands and children.

The feebleness of their anger is shown by one woman who mentioned a 'serious disagreement' with her husband. One night he said to her, 'You are henpecking me'. This caused her to rush to her car, drive some distance, park for a while, and think. This was the total extent of their 'serious disagreement'. She regarded it as an outburst.

Inability to express anger may make some situations more stressful to the arthritic than to most people. It is generally less stressful for a person to discharge his anger at once, releasing it rather than letting it seethe as resentment. The arthritics bottled up hostility thus provides a chronic stress that can promote the formation of this painful disease.

In addition to controlling their emotional expression, rheumatoid arthritics may seek to dominate in their personal relationships. They try to control their environment with an 'iron hand', a symbolic and dramatic depiction of the physical deformities often seen in advanced stages of the disease. Rheumatoid arthritics may sacrifice themselves to rule.

The typical female rheumatoid arthritic falls into a well-defined personality pattern She is generally demanding and exacting towards her children. At the same time, she will worry about them and do a great deal for them.

Her attention to duty is physically rigorous and helps her discharge her pent-up hostility. The self-punishing aspect of her labours for others also serves to relieve her guilt over feeling angry. She sees herself as being dependable, devoted, active and a good hard worker.

She tends to be a perfectionist and compulsive. She often is nervous, although this may not be apparent to others since she is likely to be introverted. Beneath her reserve, she is depressed, moody, and easily upset. She generally has a strong need for security and tends to be conservative and conforming.

Circumstances preceding the onset of symptoms in a group of patients was as follows:

Angela: Death of mother followed by threat of father to re-marry.

Marie: Separation from husband by his entry into military service.

Phyllis: Emotional rejection by husband.

Melvyn: Separation from family during military service.

Anton: Entrance to college.

Fritz: Death of grandmother, separation from fiancée, and loss of security from change in jobs.

The disease may also be precipitated by events which increase hostility. An increase in the burden of guilt may be a last straw, as well. Guilt may spill over when the person's opportunity for sacrifice becomes thwarted.

The disease may afflict women when unconscious rebellion and resentment against men has been increased by vicissitudes of life. For example, when she is abandoned by a man with whom she felt safe. or when a previously compliant man becomes more assertive, these negative emotions may occur and disease may result.

Sylvia developed painful, stiff muscles immediately after she discovered that her husband was having a love affair with another woman. After persistent pain and stiffness for several months, she developed arthritis.

The typical rheumatoid arthritic, then, is a woman who has a physiological predisposition to the disease. She was brought up in a restrictive household. Her rebellion against her restrictions leads to anxiety. She represses her rebellious tendencies, expressing them only in sports and other acceptable physical activities. In marriage, following her mother's footsteps, she seeks to control the home, employing a self-sacrificing need to serve.

Sex Problems

A woman's menstruation, intercourse and childbirth may be obstructed by feelings of guilt and fear. A man's resentment toward women may cause him impotence and sterility.

Flight from womanhood

Although Nancy's menstrual period lasts only one day, her symptoms are so severe she often has to be hospitalized. She has 'awful pains' in her head and a 'black mist' before her eyes. She feels giddy, and her lower back and thighs ache. Sometimes she feels nauseated and vomits. Often her legs give way and she collapses, then suffers from amnesia.

Nancy's distress springs from a fear of sex, observes her psychiatrist. An anxiety-ridden attitude towards sex and bodily functions was instilled in her throughout her childhood by her 'harsh, brutal and narrow-minded mother'.

A negative attitude toward menstruation is reflected and also promoted, by popular terminology: being unwell, sick, having the curse.

Often, too, a girl has been inadequately prepared for her first period. So instead of feeling proud and grown up at this sign of womanhood, she is likely to feel frightened, repelled and guilty. If a young girl has her first period in a setting of insecurity and family strife, she may thereafter be plagued by abnormally painful periods, called dysmenorrhoea.

Women with dysmenorrhoea tend to fall into two personality types. The first type of woman is like Denise. She is timid and shy, with a small childlike face and fragile physique. As a child, Denise was over-protected and spoiled by her parents, possibly because she was sickly. 'I hate to menstruate', says Denise, 'because it is so dirty'.

The other type is like Fran, who resents the female role. She is hard and aggressive, with a masculine voice and manner. As a child, Fran was a tomboy, fond of rough games and excelling in sports. Most of her friends were boys. She resents menstruation because 'it's messy' and because it is an unfair handicap in competition. Dysmenorrhoea may also be a reaction against motherhood. May, a mother of two young children, never had any menstrual difficulties or problems with pregnancy. When her youngest child was a year and a half, she began to have strong hostile feelings towards her children. Her periods became severely painful.

Her doctor concludes that May equated menstruation with abortion and suffered anxiety and guilt because she did not want more children. She also felt anxious and guilty over her hostility toward her children. Anxiety and guilt can cause abnormal muscular contractions and also disturb hormone balance, the two major physiological factors in dysmenorrhoea. Excessive menstrual bleeding is another symptom associated with emotional problems. Twelve women who bled abnormally were treated and none had an organic disorder. Each woman had begun profuse menstrual bleeding at a time of unusual difficulty and distress. Heavy bleeding occurred whenever the woman was in a situation arousing emotional tension. The women, also suffered anxiety, depression, headache and fatigue.

For emotional reasons a woman's period may stop altogether. This condition, known as amenorrhoea, may last from a month to many years. Often it is the result of shock or stress. In London during World War II many women failed to have their periods after heavy bombings. They began menstruating again when they became less tense. Women who have been the victims of rape or attempted rape may develop amenorrhoea, apparently a result of sex-related fright.

Amenorrhoea can be induced by hypnosis. A hypnotist frequently helped dancers and musicians delay or skip their periods so they would not interfere with a performance.

The condition of amenorrhoea may be associated with guilt and fear about sex. A woman may stop menstruating during an extramarital affair, a cruel irony, since she will immediately suspect she is pregnant.

Loss of menstruation may occur when a woman is depressed, particularly about her sex life. Kathy, unmarried at 25, says, 'I am making a mess of my life'. She had been the mistress of three married men and did not know how to break the pattern. Six months ago she stopped menstruating. Assuming that she was pregnant, she left her lover. She, in fact, was not pregnant, but she has not had a period since.

Guilt about incest precipitated amenorrhoea in Ann, a 19-year-old who says she is 'not a normal woman'. She feels she has too much facial hair, and she hasn't menstruated in two years. She is excessively neat and has an agitated manner. With boys, she is tongue-tied. But she has sexual longings and dreams of marriage.

With great embarrassment, Ann told her doctor that at six she indulged in mutual exploration with her seven-year-old brother. She didn't tell anyone, and she began to worry about death and damnation.

At twelve, she says, she yielded to his urgings to have intercourse. Then she was afraid she was pregnant. Her doctor's sympathetic understanding lessened Ann's guilt about her secret and two days later she menstruated.

Guilt and fear about sexual matters can result in a woman suffering from a wide variety of symptoms in the genital area. Andrea, 40 years old, married two years, came to the gynaecologist complaining of incapacitating pelvic pain. Doctors had previously removed her appendix and part of her right ovary, but to no avail. Since her marriage, the pain had become worse and she said she had 'pus and corruption' in her uterus.

Eight years before, she confessed, she had had an illegal abortion which had resulted in a uterine infection. She had never told her husband about it. The doctor saw that she became very agitated when she discussed it and he conjectured that the 'severe guilt complex' with respect to the abortion was the basis of her pain.

In the cases of extreme aversion to sex, a woman involuntarily contracts her vaginal muscles, a reflex much like blinking the eye when an object comes towards it. This contraction, called vaginismus, may painfully grip the penis during intercourse. Indeed, vaginismus may make it impossible for the penis to penetrate the vagina at all. Some couples had not had intercourse in as much as ten years of marriage. Surprisingly, their husbands seemed to agree that the vaginas were 'too small' for intercourse, although in no case was this the fact.

Apparently husband and wife shared their feelings of fear and guilt about sex, which accounted for the amount of time these couples let elapse before seeking help. Perhaps these women unconsciously chose as husbands timid men who would not be sexually aggressive. In many cases the woman's mother had been dominant, her father submissive like her husband.

Often women with vaginismus are ignorant and fearful that intercourse will be painful. Guilt about sex makes them expect punishment. Some of the women thought of sex as violent aggression. They compared their husband's penises to daggers or big snakes. One woman said, 'It's like a large leather mouse'.

Imaginary Pregnancy

Mary was suffering from pseudocyesis, commonly known as false pregnancy. Like Mary, many of the women who suffer from this condition are extremely anxious to become pregnant.

Naomi is a 27-year-old woman whose husband wants children very much. She has been afraid she would disappoint him by not being able to conceive. For a four to five month period her breasts and abdomen steadily grew larger. She gained 25 pounds. She had morning sickness every day, and her hands and feet were swollen. Her menstruation all but ceased. She told her doctor she had begun to feel the foetus moving. She was busy making baby clothes. But she was not pregnant, her condition was entirely psychogenic.

Pseudocyesis also occurs in women who feel the opposite about pregnancy; they fear and loathe the thought of it. Sometimes, too, women may be suffering from a physical condition, such as a uterine tumour which may terminate menstruation. They may, thus, think they are pregnant and begin to show physiological signs.

Conflict over Motherhood

Stress, resulting from conflicts over pregnancy and birth, can cause an interference in the reproductive process in females.

Women who suffer from such complications as toxaemia of pregnancy, excessive nausea and vomiting and abnormal weight gain tend to be more anxious in general than women with normal pregnancies. They are likely to be more concerned with their bodily functions, more withdrawn. They often have negative attitudes towards sex, menstruation and marriage. Typically, they are more dependent, resentful and childish than women who carry to term without complications.

Anxiety about the birth of a child may be responsible for many cases of prolonged and difficult labour and delivery. In one study women who had expressed fears for themselves and their babies had a much higher rate of complicated labours than women who were not particularly fearful.

Other women may unconsciously avoid pregnancy by becoming ill for the few days when conception is possible. Although consciously they ardently desire children, they may develop severe headaches or nausea during ovulation and thus avoid intercourse. Or they may become extremely tired during those days, or may plan a trip away from home.

The typical infertile woman was probably ailing and timid as a child. She was lacking in self-confidence and had difficulty getting along with other children. As an adult, she seems self-centred and cold. Actually she may be simply unable to show affection.

Other women unable to have children may be aggressive and domineering, professionally and personally. They often are excessively orderly and well-organized and may unconsciously feel that a child would disrupt the carefully maintained organization of their lives.

Miscarriages

Unconscious resistance to motherhood can play a significant part in the occurrence of miscarriages. Many women who have a history of miscarriages have difficulty in accepting the role of mother. Although such women may express strong desires to have children, unconsciously they have conflicts which result in miscarriages.

Some investigators suggest that miscarriage may come about when emotional factors precipitate endocrine changes, such as an increase in adrenaline secretion. This can cause premature contractions of the uterus.

Endocrine changes may also bring about a weakness in the musculature of the cervix, the opening between the uterus and the vagina. This might lead to premature expulsion of the foetus.

Women with a history of miscarriage frequently have unstable and unhappy marriages. The wife often has an infantile attachment to her husband together with hostility towards her mother. In an unsatisfactory marriage a woman may feel that the birth of a child may put an end to fighting with her husband and prevent divorce. But on another level she must know that a baby can never save a marriage and may thus miscarry.

Sometimes organic problems combine with an emotional upset to trigger a miscarriage. One overwrought women in her forties was suffering from an abnormality of the uterus. At a family dinner one Wednesday night she had a violent quarrel with her father-in-law and had a miscarriage that night.

Pursuit of Manhood

Resentment towards women can lead to impotence and sterility.

Modern men also suffer from a couvade syndrome, having psychogenic symptoms during their wife's pregnancies. Surveys show that as many as half of all expectant fathers have physiological disorders ordinarily associated with women approaching childbirth.

One man suffered from a large array of problems during each of his wife's six pregnancies, although he was healthy in between. When his wife became pregnant, he lost his appetite and had indigestion. Headaches and insomnia troubled him and he often had morning sickness. Like a pregnant woman, he had to urinate frequently.

During his wife's labour he would have abdominal cramps and chest pain. He could barely concentrate and found himself doing odd things. During one labour he assisted in the hatching of chicken eggs.

Lost Erection/Urinary Difficulties

In the Middle Ages it was believed that impotence was the result of sorcery: a witch tied knots in a cord or strip of leather and hid it. Until the man found the cord and untied the knots, his impotence would persist. Modern man is not much more enlightened. Witness the large number of 'potency formulas' available in any chemist.

At one time or another, every man is impotent. An erection develops when minute reservoirs under the skin of the penis fill with blood. The mechanism controlling the reservoir valves is so delicate that a slight stress will cause them to open, rendering the penis limp.

Anxiety, fatigue, a strange bedroom, coughing children in the next room, any of a hundred other disturbances can make a sexually active man inactive for a night or several weeks. If he begins to brood and worry, or if his partner is taunting or complaining, the condition can become chronic.

The male's non-interest in sex is one of the reasons for a couple's childlessness. The typical such male comes from a household dominated by an aggressive mother. She controlled him by threatening to withdraw her love if he was not a 'good boy'. She conveyed to him that sex was among the bad things in life. An expert in the treatment of infertility said, 'somewhere in his sexual condition, he learned that sexual activity with women was naughty and that erotic behaviour with himself or with a female might lose him his most precious possession, his mother's love.'

Impotence is almost entirely psychogenic and is the most common psychosomatic complaint of men.

Impotence may also be a way of trying to repress sadistic impulses and fantasies. Some men fantasise that 'the penis is a powerful destructive organ which could do irrevocable harm to the loved woman.' This may spring from the man's unconscious anxiety over castration, which some psycho-analysts believe is the basic motivation of sexual inhibition.

Children often have the notion that the sexual act their parents perform has to do with urination, so closely are genitals and urinary functions connected both in the anatomy and in the unconscious. Conflicts about sex often show up in urinary disorders.

Masturbation can unconsciously be equated with urina-tion and lead to urinary retention. As a teenager, Stan had masturbated a great deal. 'Excessively' is the word he used. At 28, he married; but he found himself completely impo-tent. He conjectured that continued masturbation might be the cause of his impotence, and he stopped masturbating.

Still impotent, he found that he could only urinate in certain circumstances. He had to be in a darkened room with his eyes closed and with absolute silence. These were the circumstances under which he used to masturbate.

At 40 years of age Stan was admitted to the hospital because of his chronic urinary retention. Doctors found no organic reason for the trouble but concluded that urinating had become a substitute for masturbation.

Often, men with urinary retention are repressing hostility and murderous rage. At the same time, they may unconsciously believe that, like those repressed emotions, urine is poisonous and defiling.

Doubts and guilt about sexuality may combine with repressed aggression to produce urinary retention. It is possible for emotional trauma to affect not only the retention of urine but the actual production of urine.

Twenty-nine year old Fred had been married for six months. It was a stormy marriage, marked by frequent quarrelling. After one particularly violent fight, Fred found it impossible to urinate because he had no urine. He did not feel like urinating either. But he perspired a great deal and his bowel movement was more fluid than usual. Fred's doctor found his bladder empty, but found signs of illness. During the next few days, his bladder returned to normal. Fred began to notice that after any upset, he would have no urine for from ten to twelve hours.

Sterility

Sterility in males is sometimes the result of a psychogenic problem with sperm. 'There is little doubt', says Dr Palti of Hadassah University Hospital in Jerusalem, 'that sterility in the male due to disturbed spermatogenesis (production of sperm) may result from emotional stress.'

Under conditions of emotional stress some men chronically produce less sperm or none at all. To collect sperm for analysis, men have to masturbate.

In some men this act produces anxiety and guilt, and their semen produced by masturbation may show no live sperm. On the other hand, the semen ejaculated in sexual intercourse will have a normal live sperm count. In some men, such ambivelence about fatherhood can combine with hostility towards the wife and can result in a rare condition called retrograde ejaculation, also known as dry coitus. Instead of being ejaculated out of the penis, the semen is propelled backward into the urinary bladder. This wrong-way run can be caused by organic disorders such as diabetes mellitus and neurological diseases. It sometimes follows the removal of the prostate.

Breath, Skin and the Supernatural

Respiratory infections, tuberculosis and asthma have emotional components, as do many skin conditions, such as itches, eczema and hair loss. Psychosomatic principles may also account for seemingly supernatural phenomena such as voodoo deaths.

Out of breath

'I have so much difficulty breathing,' 18-year-old Katarina told Sigmund Freud. 'Sometimes it catches me so that I believe I am choking. It suddenly comes upon me. There is first a pressure on my eyes. My head becomes so heavy, and it hums so that I can hardly bear it, and then I become so dizzy that I believe I am falling, and then my chest begins to press together so that I cannot get my breath.'

Freud came to the conclusion that her breathing problem was associated with anxiety. She had her first attack after finding her uncle in an act of adultery. The uncle had earlier made attempts to seduce her.

Freud determined that her breathing difficulty was related to traumatic sexual feelings related to this uncle. Indeed, she realized that the frightening face she hallucinated during her choking attacks was the distorted, enraged face of her uncle. She recalled that when he found out that she had told her aunt about the incident with the other woman, he threatened to 'do something to me ... his face became tense with rage.'

Shortness of breath is often a symptom of respiratory or heart disease. In many cases, though, it is purely a reaction to stress. A truck loader named Charles complained of chronic shortness of breath. He often stays home from work two or three days a week. He was concerned about his heart.

Charles' doctors have concluded that he is anxious and depressed. He is excessively preoccupied with his body and inordinately affected by minor upsets. He is particularly concerned about being less and less able to meet his everyday responsibilities.

Many people react to stress by hyperventilating, breathing too deeply or too fast or both. You may notice this in yourself when you are in the grip of strong emotion. Some people hyperventilate briefly in their sleep, reacting to feelings arising from dreams.

Usually hyperventilation passes after a few minutes as you recover your equilibrium. But if it continues, other changes in your body can soon occur. The level of carbon dioxide in the blood is reduced, causing numbness, tingling, and rapid heartbeat. Before long you may feel weak and faint. You may experience abdominal cramps.

The hyperventilator may also feel short of breath and as if he was suffocating. One woman describes it as 'gasping for breath like you're drowning ... swimming as far as you can and then you can't go any farther.'

If a person continues to hyperventilate, he may begin twitching all over and have convulsions. Some feel they are having heart attacks or are losing their minds. Others are certain they are on the verge of death.

Cold Symptoms

Recent studies suggest that psychological factors play an important part in determining who will get cold symptoms and who will not. The symptoms may arise due to emotional bugs as well as microscopic ones. For example, the mucous lining of the nose swells in response to emotional stress as well as to viral attack. After you have cried, you usually find that you have to blow your nose. For a short while afterwards, you may have the typical symptoms of a cold. Psychiatrists sometimes find that chronic cold symptoms are a substitute for suppressed crying. After the person discharges his grief and sorrow, his supposed cold disappears.

Emotional factors may also influence a person's susceptibility to tuberculosis germs. At the beginning of the century, most TB patients lived in dirty, airless, damp and overcrowded rooms. They were usually undernourished. Living in such conditions made people vulnerable to TB germs.

In recent years, however, researchers have noted that TB patients are often well-nourished and have lived in comfort all their lives. Investigators conclude that a person's state of mind can increase his susceptibility to TB and influence the outcome of this treatment.

Susan, for example, developed TB after a long period of emotional turmoil. Ten years before, she had a child by a man who was an alcoholic. She was unable to decide whether or not to marry him. Still indecisive, she had another child with him. They finally married, but soon divorced.

She, then, married a temperamental artist. Dissatisfied with herself, she took it out on one of her sons who was much like her. She had a negative attitude towards men and had great feelings of weakness. After a year of this marriage, she developed tuberculosis.

A psychiatrist found that she had strong suicidal drives. Susan described a dream about drowning and remarked that it was the kind of death she would prefer. The psychiatrist noted the similarity between death by drowning and collapse of the lungs in TB.

Allergies

The young man was allergic to roses. One day, someone handed him a rose. He began sneezing and his eyes began to water. His nose, also, began running. A noteworthy fact; the rose was made out of paper.

A group of hayfever sufferers were sitting in their allergist's waiting room. They noticed that the pollen count on the doctor's chart showed a great deal of pollen in the air. Several of the patients immediately developed severe hayfever symptoms. Actually the pollen count was not nearly as high as the chart showed. The allergist had arbitrarily raised the figure to test his patients' reactions.

These anecdotes illustrate the strong link between allergy and psychological factors. An allergy is a condition of unusual sensitivity which some people may develop to substances harmless to others. Called allergens, these substances include foods, pollens, house dust, cosmetics, animal hair, medicines, and many others.

When an allergen is taken into the body, antibodies are produced. They treat the allergen as if it were a threatening microbe or a dangerous foreign body. After repeated contact with the allergen, the allergic person may show symptoms in such particularly sensitive tissues as the nose, the eyes, the bronchial tubes, and the skin.

Allergic reactions seem to be partly hereditary. People with allergies commonly have a family history of allergy. But a potentially allergic person may never show any symptoms of allergy.

Emotion can cause symptoms to appear in people who have a potential for allergic reactions. A person who has a hereditary predisposition to allergy may have his symptoms triggered by stressful situations. Hayfever victims often have more severe symptoms during periods of emotional turmoil. Conversely, they may display few symptoms during periods of tranquillity, even though the pollen count may be high.

Asthma

Asthma is characterized by obstruction of the small bronchial tubes. The asthma is often precipitated by

306

emotional states. It may be set off and then be continued by emotional causes.

Parents of asthmatic children are often fully aware of the emotional component of the disease. One mother reported that her son could bring on an attack at will.

Researchers note the power of suggestion in bringing on an attack of asthma and remark that an asthma attack resembles the infant's first cry. 'The shrieking, helplessly sprawling newborn child with blood-red, swollen face.'

A number of male asthmatics were frozen into super-masculine roles – cold, tough and unemotional. Their asthma improved when they were able to weep over feelings of loneliness. Some asthmatics learn to avoid attacks by weeping.

The first attack of asthma is sometimes precipitated by a breaking of the dependent bond between mother and child.

Thin Skin

From itching and hair loss to the seemingly supernatural, the skin is a prime target for the allergic response. Hives, eczema and rashes are common skin allergies. Yet these and other skin disorders also occur in people who show no sign of allergy in skin tests.

As you have probably noticed, your skin is extremely responsive to your state of mind. The next time you are feeling a strong emotion, notice what is happening to your skin. If you are feeling embarrassed or conspicuous, are you blushing? If you are afraid, does your skin feel cold? Are you in a sweat about something? Are you hot under the collar with rage? When you are impatient, are you literally itching to do something?

Dermatologists and psychiatrists find that emotions play a large role in disturbances of the skin. Itching, for example, is often associated with inhibited sexual excitement. This is particularly true of itching of the anus or genitals, erogenous zones which give sexual pleasure when they are scratched. At the same time, the pain and rawness which results from scratching is built-in punishment for the sexual feelings.

One woman was treated who had an intense itch on her head, throat and arms. It soon became clear that she experienced this itch whenever she was on the verge of feeling anxious. 'Itching here', said her doctor, 'was a substitute for anxiety'.

He has also found that repressed rage can produce itching. one man had to wait for the doctor much longer than he had expected. Just as the doctor entered the waiting room, the man experienced a frenzy of itching.

Emotional states seem to play an important part in skin diseases such as acne rosacea and eczema.

In a study of infants who developed eczema, it was concluded that they generally have an abnormally great need to be touched and held, their skin surfaces cry out for stimulation and gratification. At the same time, their mothers often do not like to touch and care for them, depriving them of the very contact they crave.

Alopecia

Sudden hair loss, alopecia, is another skin-related condition which seems strongly associated with emotional factors. The victim may lose hair in patches, or he may become as bald as a billiard ball, losing even his eyebrows. A psychiatrist says there is usually a history of sudden nervous shock preceding the occurrence of partial or total hair loss. The common incidents are the sudden loss of a loved one, a car accident, a financial loss, or a broken engagement.

Doctors at Children's Hospital Medical Center in Boston investigated the relationship between traumatic events and hair loss in children. One two-and-a-half year old boy suddenly lost all his hair, including his eyebrows and eyelashes, two weeks after he had been abruptly weaned from his bottle. His hair partially grew back when his mother gave him back his bottle.

Several children seemed to lose hair as a response to feelings of abandonment.

Hair loss was also associated in several cases with the birth of brothers and sisters.

One curious skin condition strongly associated with emotional factors is painful, spontaneous bruising, termed autoerythrocyte sensitization. The condition usually affects women and is characterized by a sudden pain in an area of the body. A lump appears, then discolouration as blood rises to the surface. There is actual bleeding under the skin. The bruises can be very large and nearly incapacitating.

It was discovered that most people with spontaneous bruising had at one time suffered a physical trauma, such as being hit by a car. It was speculated that these patients developed a skin sensitivity to their own red blood cells. People who develop this condition usually exhibit psychological symptoms of emotional origin, such as severe headaches, fainting spells, numbness, or partial paralysis. A doctor observed that the character structure of patients with the conditions 'exhibits strong hysterical and masochistic features'. They have found, too, that episodes of spontaneous bruising are frequently related to emotionally stressful situations.

A combination of spontaneous bruising and psychogenic bleeding may account for the phenomenon of religious stigmata, the wounds of Christ on the cross. Through the centuries more than 300 people, mostly women, have been recorded as afflicted with Christ's injuries. A stigmatic may spontaneously bleed from hands, feet, and sides, or from the shoulder where Christ bore the cross. Some have scalp bleeding as if from a crown of thorns.

Most stigmatics have disturbed personalities and have long shown hysterical symptoms. Theresa, a Bavarian peasant girl was hospitalized with severe hysteria after an accident. For several years she was unable to walk, speak, or hear. But when Saint Theresa of Lisieux was canonized in 1925, the girl's symptoms disappeared.

Another seemingly supernatural phenomenon is the voodoo death.

For hundreds of years the Western world has received reports of mysterious deaths among primitive people. A young African unknowingly eats a taboo wild hen. When he discovers his transgression, he shudders with fear and is dead before the day is out.

In New Zealand, a Maori woman eats some fruit. When told it has been taken from a forbidden grove, she exclaims, 'The sanctity of the chief has been profaned. His spirit will kill me.' Within 24 hours, she is dead.

Among aborigines of Australia, anyone who breaks a tribal taboo or offends an enemy may be cursed by having a bone pointed at him. The man who discovers that he is being boned by an enemy is a pitiable sight. He stands aghast, his cheeks blanch, his eyes become glassy, and his face becomes horribly distorted. He attempts to shriek, but usually the sound chokes in the throat. The man may froth at the mouth. His body begins to tremble and his muscles twitch. He writhes and moans. After a while he crawls home where he sickens and refuses food. Inevitably he dies. But if the medicine man reverses the curse, a near-dead person can be restored to perfect health within hours.

A doctor from Johns Hopkins Medical School suggests that voodoo deaths in man result from over-stimulation of the parasympathetic nervous system, which causes the heart rate and breathing to slow and body temperature to drop. Within fifteen minutes after trimming the whiskers and facial hair of a rat, depriving the animal of possibly its most important means of contact with the outside world, the animal, otherwise unharmed, would be dead.

Death among these rats seems to follow from a strong feeling of hopelessness and isolation. He observes that a recipient of a curse is suddenly thrust into a position of utter isolation. His family and friends cast him into the realm of taboo and withdraw from him. They act towards him only as if they expected him to die. The victim, himself a believer in black magic, becomes what his tribe wills him to be and concurs in committing a kind of suicide.

A doctor at Harvard Medical School suggests that voodoo death may be explained as 'due to shocking emotional stress, to obvious or repressed terror'.

Heart Disease and Cancer

Heartfelt emotions can lead to circulatory diseases, including hypertension and heart attacks. Some forms of cancer evidently occur frequently in certain personalities. Studies link despair and suggestibility to the development of malignant growths.

Every affection of the mind that is attended with either pain or pleasure, hope or fear, is the cause of an agitation whose influence extends to the heart, an anatomist discovered. In modesty, the cheeks are suffused with blushes. In lust, how quickly is the member extended with blood and erected.

Popular expressions also recognize the close link between states of mind and the heart. Someone who suffers a grave disappointment is said to be heartbroken. In great happiness the heart leaps for joy. In fright, the heart is said to stop. After a terrifying crisis, you might hear someone say, 'My heart was in my mouth'. Your heart goes out to someone in sympathy. You give your heart in love.

A series of stressful situations can also, profoundly alter the heartbeat. Eleven year old Don had never had any heart problems. Then one morning he woke up with a rare and often fatal heart abnormality, paroxysmal ventricular tachycardia. His heart was beating excessively fast and irregularly. It was enlarged and his chest was congested. From lack of sufficient oxygen, he was starting to turn blue.

In the preceding few months, Don's life had changed drastically. He had had his own room in the same house and had essentially the same friends and activities for eight years. But recently his family had begun to build a house. The construction took longer and was more expensive than they had anticipated. While the house was under construction, Don's family rented a small house.

Don had to share a room with his two younger brothers. A neat and ordered person, Don found his new living arrangement filthy and chaotic. His father had to work overtime to help meet the unexpected expenses of the new house. the family missed their summer vacation. Meals and bedtimes became irregular.

When the family finally moved to their partially completed house, Don was faced with the additional pressure of going to a new school. It was soon afterwards that his heart problem developed.

For several months after the initial attack, Don continued to have bouts of pounding and erratic heartbeat. When his parents attempted to control his behaviour, he would throw himself on the floor screaming and thrashing. Fearing he would have a fatal heart attack, his parents began catering to Don's every whim so as to avert his temper tantrums. Don would escalate his demands, and his parents would angrily and guiltily accede.

He was eventually referred to a psychiatric clinic. To help illuminate the way in which Don's emotions were affecting his heart, psychiatrists had his parents keep a heart-rate diary. Four times a day, they took Don's pulse and made a note on his general mood and recent events.

Soon a pattern began to emerge. When Don was impatient, frustrated, annoyed, or competitive, his pulse rate was markedly higher. Don's statements in such situations evidenced a wish to speed things up, possibly accounting for his unconsciously speeded-up heart rate.

During states of emotional tension, the circulation of people with both normal and diseased hearts is slow to recover after exercise. Stress is increasingly recognized as a precipitating factor in heart disease, the general term covering a number of illnesses of the circulatory system.

Some studies suggest that the personality of the typical heart patient makes it difficult for him to avoid stress. Indeed, he seems to have built it into the fabric of his life. He is typically a person with great control and persistence, constantly striving for success and accomplishment. He usually works towards long term goals, postponing early gratification. He is aggressive and competitive.

Researchers have found a particularly close association between emotions and hypertension and high blood pressure. In hypertension, the blood pushes with greater force against artery walls. The heart tends to enlarge, often with impairment of its functioning. Hypertension is a major contributor to stroke and often damages the kidneys and adrenal glands.

In a small percentage of cases, chronic high blood pressure can be traced to specific physiological disease: Cushing's syndrome, toxaemia of pregnancy, lead poisoning, ovarian tumour, pyelonephritis and other kidney disorders. For most cases of hypertension, the cause is not organic but psychological.

The stresses of modern life may particularly produce chronic hypertension in people, who by personality, are unable to express their frustration and anger. The typical hypertensive patient is unassertive and over-compliant. He seems a remarkably controlled person. Like other heart patients, he is usually over-conscientious and over-responsible, often taking on the burdens of others. This makes him feel resentful, but the hypertensive person demands control of these hostile feelings.

Hypertension often occurs in a setting in which an individual has a particularly intense need to express his hostility and assert himself, but circumstances will not permit him to do so.

Hypertensive people usually have a disturbed relationship with their parents.

A heart patient lives with the constant threat of a heart attack, i.e. the sudden blocking of one of the arteries that supply the heart muscle with blood. Often anxiety and depression about the possibility of a heart attack can make an invalid of a person without severe heart disease.

Emotional factors can notoriously precipitate a heart attack in heart patients. In a recent study, 23 of 41 patients with heart attacks had experienced severe anxiety just before the attack.

There is some evidence that extreme anxiety, in the form of panic and terror, can be fatal. Eighty-five percent of the people who die from snakebite do not have enough venom in their bloodstream to account for their sudden deaths. Then how do they die? Researchers suggest that the terror felt by a person may cause heart failure.

Depression is another state of mind frequently associated with the occurrence of heart attacks. Most of the victims have been depressed for several years; many had attempted suicide. They were literally 'down-hearted'.

One doctor's patient illustrated the psychosomatic shift which can occur between depression and heart attack. Simon, 47-years-old, had always suffered from a feeling that he did not fulfil his duties to other people. Driven by guilt, he used to burden himself with overwork.

At the age of forty, Simon had suffered a mild depression after a fight with his employer. He had an episode of heart pain and fainting. His despondency worsened when his only son failed in his studies.

He was eventually hospitalized in a state of extreme agitation. At the psychiatric hospital, his physical condition was found to be good. His blood pressure and electrocardiogram were normal. During the next few weeks, he would often say he wished for a heart attack that would occur 'like a supreme act of justice' and decide whether he was going to live or die.

One day, while sitting in a chair, he was struck by the severe pain of an acute heart attack. Immediately the deep depression disappeared and he recovered, returned to work in a good mood which he described as 'equanimity toward the problems of life since I now have this thing'. He pointed to his heart.

The typical heart attack victim will not accept help from others. He likes to dominate in his family, his work, his community. He is extremely loath to reveal his shortcomings and weaknesses.

The attack-prone person does not react with overt anger and aggression. He may instead turn the aggression towards himself.

Conversely, of course, many heart victims die, not of turning their anger in, but of rage.

A cancer personality? Studies link despair and suggestibility with the development of some malignant growths.

One of the most striking cases involved a woman who repeatedly dreamed that she bit her mother in the breast and made lumps. She also began to dream that she made a lump in her own breast. Concerned, she went to the doctor. He found no evidence of a lump, and assumed that she was suffering from cancerphobia, an extreme fear of cancer. But before long she did develop a cancerous growth on her breast.

The evidence linking psychological factors to the development of cancer is still far from conclusive. But it is mounting and it seems to suggest that only certain types of people succumb to cancer.

'It is as if all my life I have been climbing a very steep mountain. It is very hard work. Every now and then there are ledges I can rest on for a little bit, and even enjoy myself a little, but I've got to keep climbing and the mountain has no top.'

Such a view of life, studies have shown, is typical of a lot of cancer prone people. They feel hopeless and inadequate, as if they will never have the courage or the opportunity to do as they would like and be what they want to be.

The hopelessness some cancer victims feel throughout most of their lives can border on despair.

Researchers have observed that cancer can be induced in laboratory animals by injecting hormones into susceptible body tissues, thereby upsetting the animals' endocrine balance. Hormones may play a similar role in the development of cancerous growths in human beings since psychological attitudes can affect the product of hormones.

A thousand patients who came to chest units for diagnosis and treatment, most of them with cancer, had a similar life pattern. Before their fifteenth birthday, the typical patient with lung cancer had some kind of separation from his parents. One parent died or was away from home for prolonged periods of time, or the parents were chronically unhappy and argumentative.

The adverse situations of lung cancer patients, however, are probably no greater than those of the general population. What is significant is the way they deal with these situations.

Dr Greene, from the University of Rochester medical centre, has come up with similar findings in his studies of patients with leukaemia, cancer of the blood.

A large number of patients had suffered significant loss, such as a job, or the death of a spouse or parent. Because a malignancy may develop slowly, or lie dormant for several years before developing, he took into account all losses occurring for four years before the first symptoms. About half of them were losses occurring within the last year.

Seven patients told the researchers that someone had predicted they would develop the disease. Two additional patients had been 'cursed'.

One of the cursed patients was William, an intelligent, 29-year-old with Hodgkin's disease, a cancer of the lymph glands. Ten years before, William had gone to a amusement park with a group of friends. They watched a fortune teller making predictions about people's lives. 'This is all a lot of nonsense', William had said, in a loud voice.

The fortune teller overheard him. 'You come up here' she called to him. When he began to walk away, she called angrily after him, 'Evil will befall you. You will see an illness that will change your ways and your life will be short. It will happen in ten years!'

At the time he laughed it off and soon forgot the incident. Eight years later he discovered a swelling on his neck which was diagnosed as Hodgkin's disease. William's thoughts turned to the fortune teller.

This curse and the other foreshadows may have had no bearing on the development of the diseases. Yet, it has been concluded, there remains the distinct possibility that the emotions associated with such events may trigger a latent vulnerability to cancer.